Capital, Market and the State

Nijhoff Studies in European Union Law

Series Editors

Fabian Amtenbrink (*Erasmus University Rotterdam*)
Ramses A. Wessel (*University of Groningen*)

VOLUME 20

The titles published in this series are listed at *brill.com/seul*

Capital, Market and the State

Reconciling Free Movement of Capital with Public Interest Objectives

By

Ilektra Antonaki

BRILL
NIJHOFF

LEIDEN | BOSTON

Library of Congress Cataloging-in-Publication Data

Names: Antonaki, Ilektra, 1990- author.
Title: Capital, market and the state : reconciling free movement of capital with public interest objectives / by Ilektra Antonaki.
Description: Leiden ; Boston : Brill Nijhoff, [2022] | Series: Nijhoff studies in European Union law, 2210-9765 ; volume 20 | Based on author's thesis (doctoral - Universiteit Leiden, 2019) issued under title: Privatisations and golden shares : bridging the gap between the State and the market in the area of free movement of capital in the EU. | Includes bibliographical references and index. | Summary: "This book explores how the EU free movement of capital provisions can be interpreted in order to allow certain forms of State participation in the market for the purposes of protecting public interest objectives in the context of privatisations and golden shares"– Provided by publisher.
Identifiers: LCCN 2021038802 (print) | LCCN 2021038803 (ebook) | ISBN 9789004471450 (hardback) | ISBN 9789004473034 (ebook)
Subjects: LCSH: Capital movements–Law and legislation–European Union countries. | Subsidies–Law and legislation–European Union countries. | Government ownership–Law and legislation–European Union countries.
Classification: LCC KJE5175 .A96 2022 (print) | LCC KJE5175 (ebook) | DDC 343.24/03–dc23
LC record available at https://lccn.loc.gov/2021038802
LC ebook record available at https://lccn.loc.gov/2021038803

Typeface for the Latin, Greek, and Cyrillic scripts: "Brill". See and download: brill.com/brill-typeface.

ISSN 2210-9765
ISBN 978-90-04-47145-0 (hardback)
ISBN 978-90-04-47303-4 (e-book)

Copyright 2022 by Koninklijke Brill NV, Leiden, The Netherlands.
Koninklijke Brill NV incorporates the imprints Brill, Brill Nijhoff, Brill Hotei, Brill Schöningh, Brill Fink, Brill mentis, Vandenhoeck & Ruprecht, Böhlau Verlag and V&R Unipress.
All rights reserved. No part of this publication may be reproduced, translated, stored in a retrieval system, or transmitted in any form or by any means, electronic, mechanical, photocopying, recording or otherwise, without prior written permission from the publisher. Requests for re-use and/or translations must be addressed to Koninklijke Brill NV via brill.com or copyright.com.

This book is printed on acid-free paper and produced in a sustainable manner.

Contents

Acknowledgments IX

Introduction 1
  I   Bridging the Gap between the State and the Market in the Context of Capital Liberalisation 1
  II   Academic and Societal Relevance 4
  III Structure of the Book 9

1 Capital Liberalisation at the International and the European Level 11
  I   Capital Liberalisation at the International Level 11
      A *The Theoretical Controversy over Capital Liberalisation* 11
      B *The International Legal Framework Governing Capital Liberalisation* 16
  II   Capital Liberalisation at the European Level 18
      A *A Historical Overview* 18
         1 Treaty of Rome: The Early Tentative Steps 19
         2 The Council Directives 21
         3 The Maastricht Treaty 23
      B *The Current Legal Framework* 24
         1 The Scope of Article 63 TFEU 24
            a) Territorial Scope 24
            b) Material Scope 26
               i) Difference between Capital Movements and Payments 26
               ii) Definition of Capital Movements 26
            c) Relationship with the Other Freedoms 28
         2 Direct Effect of Article 63 TFEU 30
         3 Discrimination and Restrictions 31
         4 Derogations 33
            a) Treaty-based Derogations 33
               i) Article 65 TFEU 33
               ii) Derogations Applicable Only to Capital Movements to/from Third Countries 36
            b) Overriding Reasons in the Public Interest 37
         5 Proportionality 40

2 **Free Movement of Capital and Privatisations**   43
  I   The Theoretical Underpinnings of Privatisation   43
      A   *Definition of Privatisation*   43
      B   *The Theoretical Controversy over Privatisation*   47
  II Privatisation and EU law   52
      A   *The Politico-economic Context*   52
      B   *The EU Legal Framework: The Principle of Neutrality under Article 345 TFEU*   57
          1   The Maximalist Shield Interpretation   58
          2   The Reductionist Shield Interpretation   60
          3   The Sword Interpretation   64
          4   Assessment of the Three Interpretations   66

3 **Free Movement of Capital and Golden Shares**   73
  I   Understanding the Theoretical Controversy over Golden Shares   75
      A   *Definition of Golden Shares*   76
      B   *Golden Shares as Control Enhancing Mechanisms*   76
      C   *The Principle of Proportionality between Ownership and Control*   77
      D   *Varieties of Capitalism: Liberal Market Economies v Coordinated Market Economies*   81
      E   *Corporate Governance and EU Law*   84
      F   *The Takeover Directive and the Golden Shares Case Law*   87
  II Legal Issues Arising from the Golden Shares Case Law   91
      A   *The Horizontal Application of Article 63 TFEU in the Golden Shares Case Law*   91
          1   The Concept of 'Horizontality' in Constitutional Law   92
          2   Horizontal Effect in EU Law   97
              a) Defrenne: Horizontal Effect of Equal Pay   98
              b) Walrave & Koch and Bosman: Horizontal Effect of Free Movement of Workers – Federation Exercising Regulatory Powers   99
              c) Angonese: Horizontal Effect of Free Movement of Workers – Discriminatory Private Conduct   101
              d) Viking and Laval: Horizontal Effect of Freedom of Establishment and Services – Trade Unions   102

		e)	Dansk Supermarked, Van de Haar and Fra.bo: Horizontal Effect of Free Movement of Goods 104
		f)	AMS and Egenberger: Horizontal Effect of the Charter 106
	3		Horizontal Effect of Article 63 TFEU 110
		a)	The Case Law Regarding the Horizontal Effect of Article 63 TFEU 111
		b)	Scholarly Opinions on the Horizontal Effect of Article 63 TFEU 115
		c)	Granting Horizontal Effect to Article 63 TFEU 120
B			*Public Interest Objectives as Justification Grounds in the Golden Shares Case Law* 122
	1		The Objective of Safeguarding Energy Supplies in the Event of a Crisis as Covered by Public Security under Article 65 (1) (b) TFEU 123
	2		The Objective of Ensuring Availability of the Telecommunications Network in the Event of a Crisis as Covered by Public Security under Article 65 (1) (b) TFEU 124
	3		The Objective of Guaranteeing a Service of General Interest as an Overriding Reason in the Public Interest 124
	4		Article 106 (2) TFEU 125
	5		Protection of Workers and of Minority Shareholders 126
	6		Economic Rule 126
C			*Proportionality in the Golden Shares Case Law* 127
D			*The Definition of 'Capital Restrictions' in the Golden Shares Case Law* 137
	1		The Concept of 'Restrictions' in the Free Movement of Goods 139
		a)	The Pre-Keck Case Law on MEEQRS 139
		b)	The Keck Ruling and the Introduction of the Concept of 'Selling Arrangements' 140
		c)	The Post-Keck 'Market Access' Test 144
	2		The Application of *Keck* in the Other Freedoms (Workers, Services and Establishment) 146

3 'Selling Arrangements' in the Golden Shares Case Law 149
4 In Search of a Refined Test for 'Capital Restrictions' 154

Conclusion 163

Bibliography 167
Index 218

Acknowledgments

This book is based on my doctoral dissertation "Privatisations and golden shares: Bridging the gap between the State and the Market in the area of free movement of capital in the EU", defended on 3 September 2019 at Leiden University.

I would like to thank my two supervisors Stefaan Van den Bogaert and Moritz Jesse for their immense support, help, wisdom and motivation throughout my research. I would also like to thank Carel Smith and the Meijers Research Institute and Graduate School for offering me a four-year research grant and for providing me with the necessary guidance and support throughout my research. I am grateful to the members of the PhD Committee, Prof. Christa Tobler, Prof. Pieter Van Cleynenbreugel, Prof. Sacha Garben and Prof. Hildegard Schneider, for the time they invested in reviewing my thesis and for their insightful comments. A very special and warm thank you goes to all my colleagues at the Europa Institute of Leiden Law School for creating the best working environment and for making my homesickness more bearable.

Furthermore, I would like to express my deepest respect and gratitude to Hélène Tserepa-Lacombe and Vittorio Di Bucci for their truly inspiring mentorship during my traineeship at the Legal Service of the European Commission, as well as to Judge Tamara Perišin for her trust, encouragement and invaluable support.

I am also grateful to Prof. Fabian Amtenbrink, Prof. Ramses Wessel, Ms. Ingeborg van der Laan and the whole team of Brill publishing house for publishing the present book.

Finally, this book would have never been accomplished without the support of my dearest parents, family and friends to whom I feel eternally grateful. I would like to thank especially the two protagonists of my life, my husband Marios and my daughter Antigoni for giving me hope and making my life beautiful. This book is dedicated to them.

Ilektra Antonaki

Introduction

1 Bridging the Gap between the State and the Market in the Context of Capital Liberalisation*

The role of the State in the functioning of the Market has played a crucial role in the development of the post-war politico-economic reality. It has been the premise upon which economic theories have been developed, Nobel prizes have been awarded, political ideologies have been forged and national and international policies have been adopted and carried out. In the current globalised economy, the State-Market debate unfolds not only at the national level where the political dynamics are more clearly defined, but also at the international level, which is characterised by a multilevel institutional framework that promotes trade and capital liberalisation as the two economic cornerstones intended to boost global economic growth. However, while most economists would agree that trade liberalisation contributes significantly to economic growth, the same cannot be argued (at least not with the same intensity) about capital liberalisation.[1] Although capital liberalisation can contribute to economic efficiency by removing obstacles to international economic transactions and by promoting foreign investment, there is nevertheless a protracted controversy among economists regarding the extent to which capital movements should be liberalised. It is argued that unfettered capital liberalisation bears risks for financial stability and social equality, which can in turn affect profoundly the economic and social fabric of societies.[2] These risks can be prevented by the implementation and enforcement of a transparent legal framework consisting of measures of prudential supervision and regulation aiming at restricting those capital movements which might threaten public interest objectives.

---

* This book is based on the author's doctoral dissertation *"Privatisations and golden shares: Bridging the gap between the State and the Market in the area of free movement of capital in the EU"* (The Meijers Research Institute and Graduate School of the Leiden Law School of Leiden University), written under the supervision of Prof. Stefaan Van den Bogaert and Dr. Moritz Jesse and defended on 3 September 2019 at Leiden University.

1 Joseph Stiglitz and others, *Stability with Growth: Macroeconomics, Liberalization and Development* (Oxford University Press 2006), pp. 167–168.

2 Andrew Charlton, 'Capital Market Liberalization and Poverty' in José Antonio Ocampo and Joseph Stiglitz (eds), *Capital Market Liberalization and Development* (Oxford University Press 2008), pp. 121–138.

The relationship between capital liberalisation and social inequality has been at the heart of the economic and political debate over the role of the State in the organisation and functioning of the market.[3] Joseph Stiglitz argues that due to the high macroeconomic volatility of capital flows, capital liberalisation is associated with economic instability, increased likelihood of financial crises and rising levels of income inequality.[4] This is why government intervention in the form of certain capital restrictions can mitigate the negative effects that unfettered free movement of capital can have on the economy and the society.[5] Similarly, Thomas Piketty argues the private rate of return on capital (r) can be significantly higher for long periods of time than the rate of growth of income and output (g). The inequality r > g implies that wealth accumulated in the past grows more rapidly than output and wages, which is potentially threatening to democratic societies and to the values of social justice on which they are based.[6] Furthermore, in 2016, eminent economists of the IMF argued that the benefits of capital account liberalisation and austerity – two main aspects of neoliberalism – such as foreign direct investment and reduction of public debt, have been somewhat overplayed, whereas the costs in terms of lower output, retrenched welfare, higher unemployment and increasing income inequality have been underplayed.[7] They noted that 'the increase in inequality engendered by financial openness and austerity might itself undercut growth, the very thing that the neoliberal agenda is ostensibly intent on boosting'.[8]

It can be thus argued that, at the international level, there is a new economic thinking which departs from an unconditional adherence to unfettered capital liberalisation and advocates a more restrictive approach regarding international capital flows in order to prevent the risks of financial instability and social inequality. This economic thinking is to some extent embraced also by international economic organisations such as the IMF and the OECD, which, in view of the controversy surrounding the impact of free capital flows on social

---

[3] The historical origins of this debate can be traced back to the works of Karl Marx as well as those of Karl Polanyi: Karl Marx, *Capital: A Critique of Political Economy* (Verlag von Otto Meisner 1867); Karl Polanyi, *The Great Transformation* (Beacon Press 1944, 1957, 2001).

[4] Jospeh Stiglitz, 'Capital Market Liberalization, Economic Growth and Instability' (2000) 28 *World Development* 1075, at p. 1076.

[5] Ibid.

[6] Thomas Piketty, *Capital in the Twenty-First Century* (The Belknap Press of Harvard University Press 2014), p. 571.

[7] Jonathan Ostry, Prakash Loungani and Davide Furceri, 'Neoliberalism: Oversold?' (2016) 53 *Finance & Development* 38, p. 40.

[8] Ibid, p. 40.

inequality as well as the inconclusive economic evidence regarding their contributory effect to economic growth, argue that capital liberalisation improves economic efficiency only if it is complemented by measures of prudential supervision and regulation, sound macroeconomic policies and transparency.

At the European level, despite the historical compromise between, on the one hand, laissez-faire policies and, on the other hand, strategic interventions from the State to protect social objectives upon which the project of European integration was originally constructed, in the post-Maastricht era it seems that economic integration through deregulation has led to the prevalence of the model of liberal market economies, as opposed to coordinated market economies.[9]

Although in the early days of European integration capital movements were not liberalised completely as a result of the international scepticism regarding their possible contributory effect to financial crises and instability, with the entry into force of the Maastricht Treaty and the introduction of the Economic and Monetary Union, it was decided that the EU would follow the model of unrestricted capital liberalisation in order to facilitate the project of financial integration and the adoption of the euro. Furthermore, it was decided that in order to increase the credibility of the euro as a strong currency at the international level and in order to promote foreign direct investment, the free movement of capital would be applicable not only to Member States but also to third countries.

These developments led to the establishment of a legal framework characterised to a large extent by a strong commitment to the principle of unrestricted capital flows as an important feature of the project of economic integration. This is particularly evident in the case law regarding privatisations and golden shares, where the Court of Justice of the European Union (CJEU) has adopted a broad interpretation of capital restrictions under Article 63 TFEU and has treated forms of public ownership and special shareholding of public authorities in privatised undertakings as measures of economic protectionism inherently incompatible with the Internal Market.

---

9 Fritz W. Scharpf, 'The Double Asymmetry of European Integration Or: Why the EU Cannot Be a Social Market Economy' (2010) 8 *Socio-Economic Review* 211, p. 211; Philip Cerny, *Rethinking World Politics: A Theory of Transnational Neopluralism* (Oxford University Press 2010), p. 139; Kathleen McNamara, *The Currency of Ideas: Monetary Politics in the European Union* (Cornell University Press 1998); Bastiaan Van Apeldoorn, 'The Contradictions of 'Embedded Neoliberalism' and Europe's Multi-level Legitimacy Crisis: The European Project and its Limits' in Jan Drahokoupil, Bastiaan Van Apeldoorn and Laura Horn (eds), *Contradictions and Limits of Neoliberal European Governance: From Lisbon to Lisbon* (Palgrave 2009), p. 24.

Drawing from the international controversy surrounding the costs and benefits of unfettered capital liberalisation, the book starts from the premise that a certain degree of regulation in the area of capital movements is necessary in order to prevent the risk of financial instability, reduce income inequality and protect legitimate social objectives. Based on this theoretical claim, it seeks to investigate how the EU free movement of capital provisions can be interpreted in order to allow room for State participation in the market for the purposes of protecting public interest objectives in the context of privatisations and golden shares.

In order to answer this question, the book examines whether the broad interpretation of the free movement of capital in the case law of the CJEU favours a specific model of market economy and attempts to explore the extent to which the existing legal framework set out in the Treaties offers room for reconciling economic integration with societal values. For this purpose, it analyses the privatisations and golden shares case law as two case studies and suggests certain adjudicative methods, which could allow Member States to determine their property ownership and corporate governance systems without imposing protectionist obstacles on foreign investment.

In this respect, it puts forward two main proposals: firstly, the rediscovery of the principle of neutrality under Article 345 TFEU as a legal provision shielding national decisions to maintain public ownership from Internal Market scrutiny and, secondly, the recalibration of the 'capital restrictions' test in the golden shares case law by reference to a *Keck*-inspired notion of 'investment arrangements'. An interpretation of the free movement of capital provisions based on these two proposals would respect the delicate balance of competences between the EU and the Member States and would facilitate a reconciliation of the capital freedom with public interest objectives.

II   Academic and Societal Relevance

Liberalising capital movements is of vital importance, not only for the achievement of the Internal Market, but also for the realisation of the Economic and Monetary Union.[10] Yet, in comparison with the other fundamental freedoms, the free movement of capital followed a slow historical development. The reason of this slow historical development was most probably the international

---

10   Catherine Barnard, *The Substantive Law of the EU: The Four Freedoms* (Oxford University Press 2016), p. 518.

INTRODUCTION

post-war scepticism about free capital flows, which, due to their high volatility, were associated with increased risk of financial instability.

The adoption of the Maastricht Treaty and the recognition of its direct effect by the CJEU[11] accelerated the evolution of the capital freedom and provided new impetus for legal scholarship. The free movement of capital started attracting significant scholarly attention among European academics, practitioners and policy analysts and gradually developed into a fully-fledged freedom of the EU's Internal Market. In the last two decades, the case law on the free movement of capital has increased exponentially and has offered a great opportunity for the academic community to delve into sensitive legal issues touching upon core sovereign competences such as taxation, property ownership and corporate governance, which for a long time had remained beyond the reach of market integration.

The by now profuse case law on the free movement of capital has the unique feature that it covers a wide range of financial instruments and transactions. The literature on the free movement of capital has followed the evolution of the case law. Apart from the literature examining the general legal issues arising from the free movement of capital provisions,[12] there are also scholarly

---

11   Joined cases C-163/94, C-165/94 and C-250/94 *Criminal proceedings against Lucas Emilio Sanz de Lera, Raimundo Díaz Jiménez and Figen Kapanoglu*, ECLI:EU:C:1995:451, para 41.

12   Jonh Usher, 'The Evolution of the Free Movement of Capital' (2007) 31 *Fordhman International Law Journal* 1533; Jukka Snell, 'Free movement of capital: Evolution as a non-linear process' in Paul Craig and Gráinne De Búrca (eds), *The Evolution of EU Law* (Oxford University Press 2011); Arie Landsmeer, 'Movement of Capital and Other Freedoms' (2001) 28 *Legal Issues of Economic Integration* 57; Steve Peers, 'Free Movement of Capital: Learning lessons or slipping on spilt milk?' in Catherine Barnard and Joanne Scott (eds), *The Law of the Single European Market: Unpacking the Premises* (Hart Publishing 2002); Leo Flynn, 'Free movement of capital' in Catherine Barnard and Steve Peers (eds), *European Union Law* (Oxford University Press 2017), p. 447; Leo Flynn, 'Freedom to Fund?: The Effects of the Internal Market Rules, With Particular Emphasis on Free Movement of Capital' in Ulla Neergaard, Erika Szyszczak, Johan Willem van de Gronden and Markus Krajewski (eds), *Social services of general interest in the EU* (Spinger 2013); Leo Flynn, 'Coming of Age: The Free Movement of Capital Case Law 1993–2002' (2002) 39 *Common Market Law Review* 773; Thomas Horsley, 'The Concept of an Obstacle to intra-EU Capital Movements in EU Law' in Niamh Nic Shuibhne and Laurence W. Gormley (eds), *From Single Market to Economic Union: Essays in Memory of John A Usher* (Oxford Univesrity Press 2012); Philippe Vigneron and others, *Libre circulation des personnes et des capitaux. Rapprochement des legislations* (Les éditions de l' Université de Bruxelles 2006), p. 167; Philippe Partsch, 'Articles 56-60 CE' in Isabelle Pingel (ed), *Rome à Lisbonne: Commentaire article par article des traités UE et CE* (Dalloz 2010), p. 492; Olivier Blin, 'Capitaux' in Denys Simon and Sylvaine Poillot Peruzzetto (eds), *Répertoire de Droit Européen* (Dalloz 2016).

contributions focusing, inter alia, on taxation,[13] golden shares[14] and foreign

[13] Steffen Ganghof and Philipp Genschel, 'Taxation and Democracy in the EU' (2008) 15 *Journal of European Public Policy* 58; Steffen Ganghof, *The Politics of Income Taxation* (ECPR Press 2006); Martha O'Brien, 'Taxation and the Third Country Dimension of Free Movement of Capital in EU Law: The ECJ's Rulings and Unresolved Issues' (2008) 6 *British Tax Review* 628; Axel Cordewener, Georg W. Kofler and Clemens Philipp Schindler, 'Free Movement of Capital, Third Country Relationships and National Tax Law: An Emerging Issue before the ECJ' (2007) 47 *European Taxation* 107; Axel Cordewener, Georg W. Kofler and Clemens Philipp Schindler, 'Free Movement of Capital and Third Countries: Exploring the Outer Boundaries with Lasertec, A and B and Holböck' (2007) 47 *European Taxation* 371; Thomas Horsley, 'Death, Taxes, and (Targeted) Judicial Dynamism – The Free Movement of Capital in EU Law' in Antony Arnull and Damian Chalmers (eds), *The Oxford Handbook of European Union Law* (Oxford University Press 2015), pp. 784–808; Werner Haslehner, '"Consistency" and Fundamental Freesoms: The Case of Direct Taxation' (2013) 50 *Common Market Law Review* 737; Jukka Snell, 'Non-Discriminatory Tax Obstacles in Community Law' (2007) 56 *International and Comparative Law Quarterly* 339; Ryan Murphy, 'Why does tax have to be so taxing? The court revisits the Franked Investment Income litigation (Case Comment)' (2013) 38 *European Law Review* 695; Ryan Murphy, 'Why does tax have to be so taxing? The court revisits the Franked Investment Income litigation' (2013) 38 *European Law Review* 695; Brady Gordon, 'Tax competition and harmonisation under EU law: economic realities and legal rules' (2014) 39 *European Law Review* pp. 790; Axel Cordewener, Georg Kofler and Servaas Van Thiel, 'The Clash Between European Freedoms and National Direct Tax Law: Public Interest Defences Available to the Member States' (2009) 46 *Common Market Law Review* 1951.

[14] Jérémie Houet, Les Golden Shares en droit de l'Union Européenne (Larcier 2015); Carsten Gerner-Beuerle, 'Shareholders Between the Market and the State. The VW Law and other Interventions in the Market Economy' (2012) 49 *Common Market Law Review* 97; Stefan Grundmann and Florian Möslein, 'Golden Shares – State Control in Privatised Companies: Comparative Law, European Law and Policy Aspects' (2001–2002) 4 *EUREDIA* 623; Wolf-Georg Ringe, 'Case C-112/05, Commission v. Germany ("vw law"), Judgment of the Grand Chamber of 23 October 2007, nyr'. (2008) 45 Common Market Law Review 37; Wolf-Georg Ringe, 'Company Law and Free Movement of Capital' (2010) 69 *Cambridge Law Journal* 378; Wolf-Georg Ringe, 'Is Volkswagen the New Centros? Free movement of Capital's Impact on Company Law' in Dan Prentice and Arad Reisberg (eds), *Corporate Finance Law in the UK and EU* (Oxford University Press 2011); Peer Zumbansen and Daniel Saam, 'The ECJ, Volkswagen and European Corporate Law: Reshaping the European Varieties of Capitalism' (2007) 8 *German Law Journal*; Florian Sanders, 'Case C-112/05, European Commission v. Federal Rebulic of Germany: The Volkswagen Case and Art. 56 EC – A Proper Result, Yet Also a Missed Opportunity?' (2007–2008) 14 *Columbia Journal of European Law* 359; Gert-Jan Vossestein, 'Volkswagen: the State of Affairs of Golden Shares, General Company Law and European Free Movement of Capital – A discussion of Case C-112/05 Commission v Germany of 23.10.2007' (2008) 5 *European Company and Financial Law Review* 115; Jonathan Rickford, 'Free movement of capital and protectionism after Volkswagen and Viking Line' in Michel Tison and Eddy Wymeersch (eds), *Perspectives in Company Law and Financial Regulation – Essays in Honour of Eddy Wymeersch* (Cambridge University Press 2009); Jonathan Rickford, 'Protectionism, Capital Freedom and the Internal Market' in Ulf Bernitz and Wolf-Georg Ringe (eds), *Company Law and*

direct investment from the perspective of the free movement of capital in the EU.[15]

This book aspires to make a further contribution to the academic literature on the capital freedom and to the broader academic debate regarding the appropriate institutions and legal arrangements that are necessary in order to achieve economic growth and social justice in Europe.[16]

Economic Protectionism – New Challenges to European Integration (Oxford University Press 2010); Florian Möslein, 'Compliance with ECJ judgments vs. compatibility with EU law – Free movement of capital issues unresolved after the second ruling on the Volkswagen law: Commission v. Germany' (2015) 52 *Common Market Law Review* 801; Jonathan Mukwiri, 'Free movement of capital and takeovers: a case-study of the tension between primary and secondary EU legislation' (2013) 38 *European Law Review* 829; Mads Andenas, Tilmann Gütt and Matthias Pannier, "Free Movement of Capital and National Company Law' (2005) 16 *European Business Law Review* 757; Nadia Gaydarska and Stephan Rammeloo, 'The legality of the "golden share" under EC law' (2009) 5 *Maastricht Working Papers Faculty of Law*; Stephan Rammeloo, 'Past, Present (and Future?) of the German Volkswagengesetz under the EC Treaty' (2007) 4 *European Company Law* 118; Victoria Cherevach and Bas Megens, 'Commission of the European Communities v Federal Republic of Germany Case C-112/05 – The VW Law Case; Some Critical Comments' (2009) 16 *Maastricht Journal of European and Comparative Law* 370; Erika Szyszczak, 'Golden Shares and Market Governance' (2002) 29 *Legal Issues of Economic Integration* 255; Jaron Van Bekkum, 'Golden Shares: A New Approach' (2010) 7 *European Company Law* 13; Andrea Biondi, 'When the State is the Owner – Some Further Comments on the Court of Justice 'Golden Shares' Strategy' in Ulf Bernitz and Wolf-Georg Ringe (eds), *Company Law and Economic Protectionism: New Challenges to European Integration* (Oxford University Press 2010); Harm Schepel, 'Of Capitalist Nostalgia and Financialisation: Shareholder Primacy in the Court of Justice' in Christian Joerges and Carola Glinski (eds), *The European Crisis and the Transformation of Transnational Governance* (Hart Publishing 2014); Nicola Ruccia, 'The New and Shy Approach of the Court of Justice Concerning Golden Shares' (2013) 24 *European Business Law Review* 275.

15 Steffen Hindelang, *The Free Movement of Capital and Foreign Direct Investment: The Scope of Protection in EU Law* (Oxford University Press 2009); Frank G. Barry, *The internationalisation of production in Europe: case studies of foreign direct investment in old and new EU member states* (European Investment Bank 2004); Frank S. Benyon, *Direct Investment, National Champions and EU Treaty Freedoms From Maastricht to Lisbon* (Hart Publishing 2010); Angelos Dimopoulos, *EU Foreign Investment Law* (Oxford University Press 2011); Marc Bungenberg and Jörn Griebel, *International investment law and EU law* (Springer 2011); Marise Cremona, 'The External Dimension of the Internal Market' in (eds), (Oxford:)' in Catherine Barnard and Joanne Scott (eds), *The Law of the Single European Market* (Hart Publishing 2002).

16 See, in particular, Fritz W. Scharpf, 'The Double Asymmetry of European Integration Or: Why the EU Cannot Be a Social Market Economy' (2010) 8 *Socio-Economic Review* 211; Fritz W. Scharpf, 'Legitimacy in the Multilevel European Polity' (2009) 1 *European Political Science Review* 173; Martin Höpner and Armin Schäfer, *A New Phase of European Integration: Organized Capitalisms in Post-Ricardian Europe* (Max Planck Institute for the Study of Societies, MPIfG Discussion Paper 07/04, 2007); Martin Höpner and Armin

The protection of public interest objectives in the privatisations and golden shares case law relates to the broader discussion about the so-called 'social deficit' in Europe and the fundamental clash between economic freedoms and social values, which constitutes the overarching theme of this book. In view of the disrupting social and economic effects of the austerity policies adopted as a response to the financial crisis, the efforts aiming at strengthening the social dimension of the European integration project have recently grown and have attracted significant scholarly attention.[17] In the aftermath of the eurocrisis, the need to protect public interest objectives against unfettered market forces has become pressing and has mobilised support for projects aiming at reinforcing the social component of the EU, such as the initiative of the European Commission for a European Pillar of Social Rights.[18] In this

---

Schäfer, 'Embeddedness and Regional Integration. Waiting for Polanyi in a Hayekian Setting' (2012) 66 *International Organization* 429; Paulette Kurzer, *Markets and Moral Regulation: Cultural Changes in the European Union* (Cambridge University Press 2001); Roger Liddle, 'The European Social Model and the ECJ' (2008) 4 *Social Europe Journal* 27; Jonh Monks, 'European Court of Justice (ECJ) and Social Europe: A Divorce Based on Irreconcilable Differences?' (2008) 4 *Social Europe Journal* 22; James A. Caporaso and Sidney Tarrow, 'Polanyi in Brussels: Supranational Institutions and the Transnational Embedding of Markets' (2009) 63 *International Organization* 593; Martin Rhodes, 'Defending the Social Contract: The EU Between Global Constraints and Domestic Imperatives' in David Hine and Hussein Kassim (eds), *Beyond the Market: The EU and National Social Policy* (Routledge 1998), pp. 36–59; Thomas Faist, 'Social Citizenship in the European Union: Nested Membership' (2001) 39 *Journal of Common Market Studies* 37; Maurizio Ferrera, 'European Integration and National Social Citizenship: Changing Boundaries, New Structuring?' (2003) 36 *Comparative Political Studies* 611; Maurizio Ferrera, Anton Hemmerijck and Martin Rhodes, *The Future of Social Europe: Recasting Work and Welfare in the New Economy – Report prepared for the Portuguese Presidency of the EU* (Celta Editoria 2000).

17 Alicia Hinarejos, *The Euro Area Crisis in Constitutional Perspective* (Oxford University Press 2015); Claire Kilpatrick, 'Are the bailout measures immune to EU Social challenge because they are not EU Law?' (2014) 10 *European Constitutional Law Review* 393; Anastasia Poulou, 'Financial assistance conditionality and human rights protection: What is the role of the EU Charter of Fundamental Rights?' (2017) 54 *Common Market Law Review* 991; Bruno De Witte and Claire Kilpatrick, 'A comparative framing of fundamental rights challenges to social crisis measures in the Eurozone' (2014) 1 *European Journal of Social Law* 2; Alicia Hinarejos, 'Changes to Economic and Monetary Union and Their Effects on Social Policy' (2016) 32 *The International Journal of Comparative Labour Law and Industrial Relations* 231.

18 European Commission, *Recommendation on the European Pillar of Social Rights* (C(2017) 2600 final, 2017); European Commission, *Communication of 26 April 2017 establishing a European Pillar of Social Rights* (COM(2017) 250 final, 2017); Sacha Garben, 'The European Pillar of Social Rights: Effectively Addressing Displacement?' (2018) 14 *European Constitutional Law Review* 210.

context, the overarching theme of the present book is the delicate balancing exercise between economic freedoms and social values, especially in times of ideological contestation over the social face of Europe. For this purpose, the book draws from the theoretical underpinning of 'social market economy' enshrined in Article 3 (3) TEU and attempts to provide a normative assessment of the clash between economic and social objectives in the field of free movement of capital.

III   Structure of the Book

Chapter 1 introduces the concept of capital liberalisation, a politically fraught issue, which has attracted significant scholarly attention from a wide spectrum of disciplines, varying from economists and political scientists to historians and lawyers. After examining the ideological controversies surrounding the costs and benefits of capital liberalisation, its contribution to global economic growth as well as its non-linear historical evolution, Chapter 1 examines briefly the current legal framework governing capital liberalisation at the International level, and then focuses on the free movement of capital under Article 63 TFEU, as one of the fundamental freedoms of the EU's Internal Market.

Chapter 2 attempts to explore the role that EU law has played on the advancement of privatisation as a national economic policy. In order to address this question, Chapter 2 first embarks upon a theoretical analysis of the economic, political and social debate about the costs and benefits of privatisation. Secondly, it seeks to investigate the role that EU law plays in the decision of a national government to privatise or nationalise an undertaking. In this respect, firstly, it explores the ideological foundations of the European Economic Constitution, focusing particularly on the German theory of ordoliberalism and the French theory of 'service public'. Secondly, it examines the different interpretations of the principle of neutrality enshrined in Article 345 TFEU and the significant role that this provision can play in safeguarding the discretion of the Member States to determine their property ownership systems.

Chapter 3 addresses the controversial legal issues arising from the golden shares case law. The use of golden shares in strategically sensitive privatised undertakings (in the energy sector, telecommunications, postal services, airports, car industries etc.) has given rise to a long-running litigation between the Commission and the Member States before the Court of Justice of the European Union. The establishment of special shareholding in national privatised champions has been perceived as an expression of economic protectionism and as a threat or a hindrance to the emergence of a fully competitive market for corporate control. The Court has adopted a rigorous application of the free movement of capital, ruling in the majority of the cases that golden shares constitute capital restrictions due to their deterrent effect on foreign investment. Chapter 3 attempts to assess the far-reaching implications of the golden shares case law for the corporate governance systems of the Member States and the overall organisation and development of their industrial policies. In order to do so, it introduces the theoretical controversy surrounding the function of special rights as control enhancing mechanisms derogating from the principle of proportionality between ownership and control and then focuses on the specific legal issues arising from the golden shares case law, i.e. the horizontal direct effect to Article 63 TFEU, the public interest objectives, the proportionality assessment and the broad interpretation of capital restrictions.

CHAPTER 1

Capital Liberalisation at the International and the European Level

1 Capital Liberalisation at the International Level

A *The Theoretical Controversy over Capital Liberalisation*

The term capital liberalisation is used to describe the removal of measures designed to limit capital flows, in other words the abolition of all restrictions on capital inflows and outflows.[1] Capital flows include several categories of financial transactions, such as foreign direct investment, portfolio investment (i.e. bond and equity flows), financial derivatives (i.e. financial contracts used to trade risks in financial markets), bank related flows and trade credit.[2] The concept of capital liberalisation covers both the underlying capital transaction and the related payment and 'it implies unrestricted convertibility of local currency in international financial transactions'.[3]

The question whether international capital mobility is beneficial for the economy does not have a straightforward answer. Although neoclassical economic theory suggests that the free flow of capital across borders can increase economic efficiency, there is a protracted controversy among economists not only as to the actual benefits of capital liberalisation for economic growth but also as to its possible contributory effect to the worryingly rising levels of income inequality.

Capital account liberalisation is a highly controversial subject, which deeply divides the academic community and raises an animated controversy regarding its actual contribution to global economic growth. The consensus in favour of capital liberalisation has always been less clear-cut than that in favour of globalised trade. Indeed, although the majority of the existing literature has found that trade globalisation has a positive effect on economic growth,[4] the

---

1 IMF, *The Liberalization and Management of Capital Flows – An Institutional View* (Staff Paper of the IMF Executive Board, 2012), p. 10.
2 Ibid; Peter Chowla, *Time for a New Consensus: Regulating Financial Flows for Stability and Development* (London: Bretton Woods Project, 2011), p. 4.
3 IMF, *The Liberalization and Management of Capital Flows – An Institutional View* (2012), p. 10.
4 Athanasios Vamvakidis, 'Regional Trade Agreements or Broad Liberalization: Which Path Leads to Faster Growth?' (1999) 46 *International Monetary Fund Staff Papers* 42; Romain Wacziarg, 'Measuring the dynamic gains from trade' (2011) 15 *The World Bank Economic*

same cannot be said unconditionally about financial liberalisation.[5] The reasons for this scepticism towards international capital mobility relate primarily to the lack of scientific evidence proving a correlation between capital liberalisation and economic growth. Thus, over the years, two economic schools of thought have emerged representing two opposing views regarding capital account liberalisation.

In particular, proponents of capital liberalisation argue that in order to achieve higher levels of growth and economic efficiency, countries and international institutions should promote financial globalisation through the abolition of all measures designed to restrict capital movements.[6] The liberalisation of capital markets is believed to allow countries with limited savings to attract foreign financing for productive domestic investment projects, to enable investors to diversify their portfolios and to spread investment risk more broadly.[7] The process of financial integration enables capital flows to be channelled from developed countries, where the abundance of capital usually implies lower profits for investors, to developing countries, where the scarcity of capital entails higher profits for investors.[8] It is also argued that capital market liberalisation can impose macroeconomic discipline, as countries failing to

---

Review 393; Joseph Stiglitz, José Antonio Ocampo, Shari Spiegel, Ricardo Ffrench-Davis and Deepak Nayyar, *Stability with Growth: Macroeconomics, Liberalization and Development* (Oxford University Press 2006), p. 167–168.

[5] Eswar Prasad, Kenneth Rogoff, Shang-Jin Wei and M. Ayhan Kose, *Effects of Financial Globalization on Developing Countries: Some Empirical Evidence* (2003), p. 3.

[6] IMF, *The Liberalization and Management of Capital Flows – An Institutional View* (2012); Jonathan D. Ostry, Atish R. Ghosh and Anton Korinek, *Multilateral Aspects of Managing the Capital Account* (IMF Staff Discussion Note, 2012); OECD, 'International Capital Mobility: Structural Policies to Reduce Financial Fragility?' (2012) No. 13 *OECD Economics Department Policy Notes*; Joshua Aizenman and Vladyslav Sushko, *Capital Flows: Catalyst or Hindrance to Economic Takeoffs?* (National Bureau of Economic Research Working Paper No 17258, 2011); Janet L. Yellen, *Improving the International Monetary and Financial System* (Speech at the Banque de France International Symposium, Paris, 4 March 2011); Hongyi Chen, Lars Jonung and Olaf Unteroberdoerster, *Lessons for China from financial liberalization in Scandinavia* (European Commission, Economic and Financial Affairs, Economic Papers 383, 2009); M. Ayhan Kose and others, 'Financial Globalization: A Reappraisal' (2009) 56 IMF *Staff Papers*; Frederic S. Mishkin, "Why We Shouldn't Turn Our Backs on Financial Globalization' (2009) 56 IMF *Staff Papers* 139; Maurice Obstfeld, 'International Finance and Growth in Developing Countries: What Have We Learned?' (2009) 56 IMF *Staff Papers* 63.

[7] Barry Eichengreen, Michael Mussa, Giovanni Dell'Ariccia, Enrica Detragiache, Gian Maria Milesi-Ferretti and Andrew Tweedie, *Liberalizing Capital Movements: Some Analytical Issues* (1999); Maurice Obstfeld, 'The Global Capital Market: Benefactor or Menace?' (1998) 12 Journal of Economic Perspectives 9.

[8] IMF, *The Liberalization and Management of Capital Flows – An Institutional View* (2012), pp. 10–11; Sergio Schmukler, 'The Benefits and Risks of Financial Globalization' in Ocampo

implement substantive reforms in their economy will not be able to attract foreign funds.[9] Proponents of this theory oppose any type of capital controls and contend that restrictions on the free movement of capital impose constraints on investment projects, reduce macroeconomic discipline, promote risk-seeking behaviour, moral hazard and corruption, repress the financial sector and distort the allocation of capital.[10]

By contrast, opponents of capital liberalisation contests the correlation between capital liberalisation and economic growth and suggest that in some circumstances free capital flows can be detrimental for national economies.[11]

---

and Stiglitz (eds), *Capital Market Liberalization and Development* (Oxford University Press 2008), at p. 57.

[9] IMF, *The Liberalization and Management of Capital Flows – An Institutional View* (2012), p. 10.

[10] IMF, *The Liberalization and Management of Capital Flows – An Institutional View* (2012), p. 10; Joshua Aizenman and Reuven Glick, 'Sterilization, monetary policy, and global financial integration' (2008) 17 *Review of International Economics* 777; Kristin J. Forbes, 'Capital controls: mud in the wheels of market efficiency' (2005) 25 *Cato Journal* 153; Kristin J. Forbes, 'The Microeconomic Evidence on Capital Controls: No Free Lunch' in Edwards (ed), *Capital Controls and Capital Flows in Emerging Economies: Policies, Practices, and Consequences* (University of Chicago Press 2007); Kristin J. Forbes, 'One Cost of the Chilean Capital Controls: Increased Financial Constraints for Smaller Traded Firms' (2007) 71 Journal of International Economics 294; John Greenwood, 'The costs and implications of PBC sterilization' (2008) 28 The Cato Journal 205.

[11] José Antonio Ocampo and Joseph E. Stiglitz, *Capital Market Liberalization and Development* (Oxford University Press 2008); Joseph Stiglitz, José Antonio Ocampo, Shari Spiegel, Ricardo Ffrench-Davis and Deepak Nayyar, *Stability with Growth: Macroeconomics, Liberalization and Development* (Oxford University Press 2006); Joseph Stiglitz, 'Capital-market Liberalization, Globalization, and the IMF' (2004) 20 *Oxford Review of Economic Policy* 57; Eswar Prasad, Kenneth Rogoff, Shang-Jin Wei and M. Ayhan Kose, *Effects of Financial Globalization on Developing Countries: Some Empirical Evidence* (2003); Ajit Singh, *Capital Account Liberalization, Free Long-term Capital Flows, Financial Crises and Economie Development* (University of Cambridge, ESRC Centre for Business Research – Working Papers, No 245, 2002); Jospeh Stiglitz, 'Financial Market Stability and Monetary Policy' (2002) 7 *Pacific Economic Review* 13; Jospeh Stiglitz, 'Capital Market Liberalization, Economic Growth and Instability' (2000) 28 World Development 1075; Dani Rodrik, 'Who Needs Capital-Account Convertibility?' in Stanley Fischer, Richard N. Cooper, Rudiger Dornbusch, Peter M. Garber, Carlos Massad, Jacques J. Polak, Dani Rodrik and Savak S. Tarapore (eds), *Should the IMF Pursue Capital-Account Convertibility?* (*Essays in International Finance No 207, May 1998*) (International Finance Section, Department of Economics, Princeton University 1998); Alberto Alesina, Vittorio Grilli and Gian Maria Milesi-Ferretti, 'The Political Economy of Capital Controls' in Leonardo Leiderman and Assaf Razin (eds), *Capital Mobility: The Impact on Consumption, Investment, and Growth* (Cambridge University Press 1994); Vittorio Grilli and Gian Maria Milesi-Ferretti, 'Economic Effects and Structural Determinants of Capital Controls' (1995) 42 *IMF Staff Papers* 517.

In particular, for the critics of neoclassical economics, the argument that the case for capital liberalisation is the same as the case for trade liberalisation is a fallacy.[12] Capital is fundamentally different from goods or services,[13] as contrary to the latter the primary function of capital is 'information-gathering' in the form of 'assessing which projects and firms are most likely to yield the highest returns'.[14] Despite the fact that there is evidence proving a correlation between trade integration and economic growth, there is no such evidence in relation to financial integration.[15] Furthermore, despite the fact that trade integration is associated with faster increase in life expectancy and faster reduction in infant mortality in developing countries, such a relationship is not confirmed in relation to financial integration.[16]

Critics of capital liberalisation question the presumption upon which the neoclassical model is based, i.e. that capital markets are perfect, with perfect information, perfect competition, perfect employment and perfect rationality, and argue instead that, under the existing imperfect capitalism with asymmetric information, financial liberalisation may lead to economic instability.[17] They argue that empirical data accumulated over the past decades has not provided any consistent evidence that capital liberalisation brings higher levels of growth, especially insofar as short-term capital flows are concerned.[18] Due to

---

12   Jospeh Stiglitz, 'Capital Market Liberalization, Economic Growth and Instability' (2000) 28 World Development 1075, p. 1079.
13   Carlos F. Díaz-Alejandro, 'Goodbye Financial Repression, Hello Financial Crash' (1985) 19 Journal of Development Economics 1; Joseph Stiglitz, José Antonio Ocampo, Shari Spiegel, Ricardo Ffrench-Davis and Deepak Nayyar, *Stability with Growth: Macroeconomics, Liberalization and Development* (Oxford University Press 2006), p. 170.
14   Jospeh Stiglitz, 'Capital Market Liberalization, Economic Growth and Instability' (2000) 28 World Development 1075, p. 1079.
15   Ibid p. 1078.
16   Eswar Prasad, Kenneth Rogoff, Shang-Jin Wei and M. Ayhan Kose, *Effects of Financial Globalization on Developing Countries: Some Empirical Evidence* (2003), p. 19, citing S.J. Wei and Y. Wu, *The Life-and-Death Implications of Globalization* (National Bureau of Economic Research, Inter-American Seminar in Economics, 2002).
17   Joseph Stiglitz, 'Capital-market Liberalization, Globalization, and the IMF' (2004) 20 Oxford Review of Economic Policy 57, pp. 57–71.
18   Peter Chowla, *Time for a New Consensus: Regulating Financial Flows for Stability and Development* (2011); M. Ayhan Kose and others, *Financial Globalization: A Reappraisal* (IMF Staff Papers, Vol 56, No 1 2009); Alexander Cobham, *Capital Account Liberalisation and Poverty in Go with the flow? Capital account liberalisation and poverty* (Bretton Woods Project and Oxfam, 2001); Dani Rodrik, 'Who Needs Capital-Account Convertibility?' in Fischer and others (eds), *Should the IMF Pursue Capital-Account Convertibility?* (*Essays in International Finance No 207, May 1998*) (International Finance Section, Department of Economics, Princeton University 1998); Joseph Stiglitz, 'Capital-market Liberalization, Globalization, and the IMF' (2004) 20 Oxford Review of Economic Policy 57, p. 60.

the high macroeconomic volatility of capital flows, capital account liberalisation is associated with economic instability, increased likelihood of financial crises and a substantial hindrance of national governments' ability to respond to negative macroeconomic shocks, especially in developping countries.[19] Furthermore, there is increasing evidence that capital liberalisation has a negative effect on poverty and income inequality, as it weakens the bargaining position of labour, it affects disproportionately the poor, who are particularly vulnerable to economic volatility and financial crises, and it limits drastically the regulatory autonomy of national governments to implement redistributive and social policies, since any plan of tax increase is likely to lead to a capital flight, which depending on its scale, might lead to a considerable wealth loss and possibly to a severe financial instability.[20] Finally, opponents of the neo-classical theory argue that market discipline lacks democratic legitimacy and undermines the foundations of a democratic society.[21]

Overall, balancing the costs and benefits of capital liberalisation, it is argued that financial integration can be pursued only insofar as it is combined with risk management, transparency and prudential supervision in order to ensure the safety and soundness of financial markets.[22] International organisations such as the IMF and the OECD recognise the inherent risks of unfettered capital flows, especially for economies which have not reached a certain level of financial and institutional development, and support the view that capital liberalisation improves economic efficiency only if it is complemented by

---

19   Joseph Stiglitz, 'Capital-market Liberalization, Globalization, and the IMF' (2004) 20 Oxford Review of Economic Policy 57, p. 59; Jospeh Stiglitz, 'Capital Market Liberalization, Economic Growth and Instability' (2000) 28 World Development 1075, p. 1079; William Easterly, Roumeen Islam and Joseph Stiglitz, 'Volatility and Macroeconomic Paradigms for Rich and Poor' in Jacques Drèze (ed), *Advances in Macroeconomic Theory* (Palgrave Macmillan UK 2001), pp. 352–372; Jospeh Stiglitz, 'Capital Market Liberalization, Economic Growth and Instability' (2000) 28 World Development 1075, p. 1076.

20   Andrew Charlton, 'Capital Market Liberalization and Poverty' in Ocampo and Stiglitz (eds), *Capital Market Liberalization and Development* (Oxford University Press 2008), pp. 121–138; Joseph Stiglitz, José Antonio Ocampo, Shari Spiegel, Ricardo Ffrench-Davis and Deepak Nayyar, *Stability with Growth: Macroeconomics, Liberalization and Development* (Oxford University Press 2006), p. 185.

21   Joseph Stiglitz, José Antonio Ocampo, Shari Spiegel, Ricardo Ffrench-Davis and Deepak Nayyar, *Stability with Growth: Macroeconomics, Liberalization and Development* (Oxford University Press 2006), p. 188; Joseph Stiglitz, 'Capital-market Liberalization, Globalization, and the IMF' (2004) 20 Oxford Review of Economic Policy 57, p. 62.

22   Sergio Schmukler, 'The Benefits and Risks of Financial Globalization' in Ocampo and Stiglitz (eds), *Capital Market Liberalization and Development* (Oxford University Press 2008), p. 66.

measures of prudential supervision and regulation, sound macroeconomic policies and transparency.[23]

B   *The International Legal Framework Governing Capital Liberalisation*

The free movement of capital is embedded in a regime of multilevel regulation, based on the principle of State sovereignty in capital transfer matters.[24] Tendencies to promote the capital liberalisation have not yet found any reflection in general international law.[25] In legal terms, this constitutes a difference between trade and capital: while there is a multilateral legal framework for international trade in goods and services established by the World Trade Organisation (WTO), there is no such legal framework for international capital flows.[26]

The IMF has limited competence in relation to the capital account policies of its Members. Article VI, Section 3 of the IMF Agreement allows national government to adopt capital controls. It provides that "[m]embers may exercise such controls as are necessary to regulate international capital movements, but no member may exercise these controls in a manner which will restrict payments for current transactions or which will unduly delay transfers of funds in settlement of commitments, except as provided in Article VII, Section 3(b) and in Article XIV, Section 2".

Within the WTO framework there is no strong tendency to liberalise capital movements.[27] The General Agreement on Trade in Services (GATS)[28] includes some elements of capital liberalisation, but only insofar as capital movements are needed for the effective delivery of a service.[29] Article XI (1) GATS provides

---

23   IMF, *The Liberalization and Management of Capital Flows – An Institutional View* (2012), p. 13; Jonathan Ostry, Prakash Loungani and Davide Furceri, 'Neoliberalism: Oversold?' (2016) 53 Finance & Development 38; OECD, *The OECD's Approach to Capital Flow Management Measures Used with a Macro-Prudential Intent* (Report to G20 Finance Ministers, 2015); OECD, *Getting the most out of International Capital Flows* (2011).

24   Matthias Ruffert, *Free Flow of Capital* (2013) referring to *Case Concerning the Payment of Various Serbian Loans Issued in France,* Ser A, No 20, 1929 (Permanent Court of International Justice).

25   Matthias Ruffert, *Free Flow of Capital* (2013).

26   Olivier Jeanne, Arvind Subramanian and John Williamson, *Who Needs to Open the Capital Account?* (Peterson Institute for International Economics 2012), p. 3.

27   Ibid.

28   General Agreement on Trade in Services (adopted 15 April 1994, entered into force 1 January 1995) 1869 UNTS 183.

29   OECD, *International capital flows: Structural reforms and experience with the OECD Code of Liberalisation of Capital Movements* (Report from the OECD to the G20 Sub-Group on Capital Flow Management, 2011).

that 'A Member State shall not apply restrictions on international transfers and payments for current transactions relating to its specific commitments'. Therefore, under the WTO regime, payments are liberalised only to the extent that they are necessary for 'current transactions', i.e. payments which are not for the purpose of transferring capital.[30] A more coherent protection regime of capital movements is provided by International Investment law, consisting of Regional Free Trade Agreements and Bilateral Investment Treaties, which promote capital liberalisation through the expansion of foreign direct investment.[31]

At the same time, the OECD Code of Liberalisation of Capital Movements constitutes a comprehensive international legal instrument regulating capital movements at the international level.[32] The Code stipulates progressive, non-discriminatory liberalisation of capital flows and the right of establishment.[33] By adhering to the Code, the OECD Members have undertaken the obligation to remove restrictions on specified lists of capital movements between residents of different Member countries. The OECD Code covers all capital movements, ranging from direct investment, operations in real estate, operations in securities on capital markets, financial credits and loans, operations in foreign exchange, life assurance to personal capital movements (such as loans, gifts and endowments, inheritances and legacies) and physical movement of capital assets.[34] The OECD Code does not prohibit capital controls but neither does it encourage them. The Code allows for derogations from the obligation to liberalise capital movements, but only in so far as the economic and financial situation justifies such derogation and only for as long as it is deemed necessary. In this regard, a 'peer-review' system is established whereby countries introducing capital controls are examined by their peers in order to make sure that measures are implemented in a transparent and fair manner and are not maintained longer than necessary.

---

30 Matthias Ruffert, *Free Flow of Capital* (2013). It should be noted, however, that international investment law promotes capital liberalisation by protecting inward international investment (without however covering capital outflows by residents), see OECD, *International capital flows: Structural reforms and experience with the OECD Code of Liberalisation of Capital Movements* (2011), p. 4.
31 Matthias Ruffert, *Free Flow of Capital* (2013).
32 OECD, Code of Liberalisation of Capital Movements (12 December 1961) OECD/C(61)96.
33 OECD, 'Investment Policy' <http://www.oecd.org/daf/inv/investment-policy/codes.htm> accessed 31-01-2019.
34 OECD, Code of Liberalisation of Capital Movements (12 December 1961) OECD/C(61)96.

II Capital Liberalisation at the European Level

A *A Historical Overview*

While known as one of the four fundamental freedoms of the EU's Internal Market, the free movement of capital is rather special. Liberalising capital movements is of vital importance, not only for the achievement of the Internal Market, but also for the realisation of the Economic and Monetary Union and the protection of monetary stability in Europe.[35] At the same time, the achievement of capital liberalisation is of paramount importance for the establishment of the Capital Markets Union and the Banking Union, the two initiatives of the European Commission aiming at facilitating financial integration in the EU.[36]

However, despite its crucial role in the completion of financial integration in the EU, the free movement of capital has followed a slow historical development when compared to the other freedoms. This was probably due to the post-war scepticism towards free capital flows, which were notorious for causing financial crises and economic instability. Following the institutional approach of the Bretton Woods system, the EU respected the sovereign right of Member States to introduce restrictions on capital movements and the Court of Justice refused to recognise the direct effect of the Treaty provision on free movement of capital. The most important legislative development came in the late 1980s with the adoption of Directive 88/361, which brought about the full liberalisation of capital movements and gave the single market its full financial dimension.

---

[35] Catherine Barnard, *The Substantive Law of the EU: The Four Freedoms* (Oxford University Press 2016), p. 518–519.

[36] European Commission, *Completing the Capital Markets Union by 2019 – time to accelerate delivery, Communication from the Commission* (COM(2018) 114 final, 2018). The bibliography on the Capital Markets Union and the Banking Union is already very rich. To name but a few, see in particular: Danny Busch and Guido Ferrarini (eds), *European Banking Union* (Oxford University Press 2015); Niamh Moloney, 'European Banking Union: assessing its risks and resilience' (2014) 51 *Common Market Law Review* 1609; Stefan Grundmann, 'The Banking Union Translated into (Private Law) Duties: Infrastructure and Rulebook' (2015) 16 *European Business Organization Law Review* 357; Niamh Moloney, 'Capital markets union: "ever closer union" for the EU financial system?' (2016) 41 *European Law Review* 307; Niamh Moloney, ' Institutional governance and capital markets union: incrementalism or a 'big bang'?' (2016) 13 *European Company and Financial Law Review* 376.

1   Treaty of Rome: The Early Tentative Steps

In comparison with the other fundamental freedoms, the free movement of capital followed a slow historical development, which can be explained by the political and economic controversies of the time and the concomitant suspicion and hesitant attitude of the Member States as well as the European Institutions towards unrestricted capital flows. In the light of the politico-economic climate of the post-war period and the explicit choices of the international monetary system in favour of capital controls, the EU followed the international trend towards restricting capital mobility. As a result, the capital freedom did not follow the same liberalisation process as the other freedoms. The 1956 Spaak Report, which laid down the foundations of the EU's Internal Market, made allusion to the gradual liberalisation of capital movements as the last component of the Internal Market and as a corollary to the free movement of labour.[37] Article 67 of the 1957 Treaty establishing the European Economic Community (Treaty of Rome/EEC Treaty) contained a qualified obligation: the abolition of capital restrictions between Member States was to be achieved only to the extent necessary to ensure the proper functioning of the common market. Furthermore, Member States were allowed to introduce safeguard measures and many financial operations were subject to prior authorisation requirements known as 'exchange controls'.

From the perspective of the theoretical accounts of European Integration, the free movement of capital displays features of *liberal intergovermentalism*, which is not the framework the four freedoms have traditionally been associated with.[38] Up until the beginning of the 1990s, the free movement of capital did not follow the same integration process as the other freedoms. The Commission and the Court were reluctant to proceed to full capital liberalisation and to deprive Member States of their sovereign right to impose capital restrictions. This was due to the general post-war climate and the suspicion towards unfettered capital liberalisation, which was viewed as a potential source of crises and a threat to monetary stability. The Commission was not a staunch supporter of the complete abolition of capital restrictions and the

---

37   Paul-Henri Spaak, *The Brussels Report on the General Common Market* (The European Community for Coal and Steel, 1956): 'As for free movement of capital, this was based on the liberalisation of capital transfers relating to commodity or service transactions or to free movement of labour. It also required recognition of the right of nationals of member countries to acquire capital from any of the six member countries and to transfer and use it within the common market'.

38   Jukka Snell, 'Free movement of capital: Evolution as a non-linear process' in Craig and De Búrca (eds), *The Evolution of EU Law* (Oxford University Press 2011).

Court was reluctant to follow the integrationist approach it had developed in the framework of the other freedoms.[39] By contrast, the liberalisation process was left to the Council, which through the adoption of secondary legislation would gradually open up the capital markets of the Member States.

Against this backdrop, the Court in *Casati* initially refused to recognise direct effect of the relevant provision (Article 67 (1) EEC Treaty), fearing that a complete freedom of capital could 'undermine the economic policy of the Member States or create an imbalance of payments, thereby impairing the proper functioning of the common market'.[40] The case concerned an Italian national residing in Germany who was charged with attempting to export from Italy the sum 24000 Deutsche Marks without the authorisation that was prescribed by the pertinent Italian legislation. He had previously imported that money into Italy without declaring it with a view to purchasing equipment for his business in Germany and he claimed that he was obliged to re-export the currency because the factory from which he intended to buy the equipment was closed for holidays.[41] The Court refrained from applying to the free movement of capital the reasoning it had earlier developped in *Dassonville*[42] and *Cassis de Dijon*.[43] To the contrary, it acknowledged that this was a rather special and sensitive case, which the Member States had decided to exclude from complete liberalisation. The Court first noted that the freedom to move certain types of capital was in practice a precondition for the effective exercise of the other freedoms guaranteed by the Treaty, and in particular the freedom of establishment.[44] Secondly, it underlined that '*capital movements are closely connected with the economic and monetary policy of the Member States*' and that '*it cannot be denied that complete freedom of movement of capital may undermine the economic policy of one of the Member States or create an imbalance in its balance of payments, thereby impairing the proper functioning of the Common Market*'.[45] Thirdly, it emphasised that '*Article 67 (1) differs from the provisions on the free movement of goods, persons and services in the sense that there is an obligation to liberalise capital movements only "to the extent necessary*

---

39 Catherine Barnard, *The Substantive Law of the EU: The Four Freedoms* (Oxford University Press 2016), p. 520.
40 Case 203/80 *Criminal Proceedings Against Guerrino Casati*, ECLI:EU:C:1981:261, para 9.
41 Ibid, para 2.
42 Case 8-74 *Procureur du Roi v Benoît and Gustave Dassonville*, ECLI:EU:C:1974:82.
43 Case 120/78 *Rewe-Zentral AG v Bundesmonopolverwaltung für Branntwein* (*Cassis de Dijon*), ECLI:EU:C:1979:42.
44 Case 203/80 *Casati*, para 8.
45 Ibid, para 9.

to ensure the proper functioning of the Common Market".[46] It underlined that the liberalisation of capital movements '*was a matter for the Council*', which in accordance with Article 69 EEC Treaty was responsible for the adoption of secondary legislation for the progressive implementation of Article 67 EEC Treaty.[47] The Council had indeed adopted two directives, which, however, did not require the Member States to adopt any liberalising measures regarding the physical importation and exportation of financial assets (including bank notes).[48] The Court was, therefore, bound to respect the clear legislative choice of the Council according to which '*it [was] unecessary to liberalise the exportation of bank notes*' and concluded that '*there [was] no reason to suppose that, by adopting that position, [the Council had] overstepped the limits of its discretionary power*'.[49]

2 The Council Directives

Under Article 69 EEC, the Council was authorised to adopt directives concerning the progressive liberalisation of capital movements. The First Capital Directive was adopted in 1960[50] and the Second Capital Directive in 1963.[51] They essentially divided capital movements into four annexed lists (A, B, C and D), which would follow a different degree of liberalisation. The movements covered by lists A and B (such as direct investments, investments in real estate, personal capital movements, gifts and endowments, dowries, inheritances and various operations in securities) were subject to unconditional liberalisation;[52] for movements covered by list C (such as the issue and placing of securities of a domestic undertaking on a foreign capital market), Member States could maintain or reintroduce exchange restrictions if free movement of capital was capable of forming an obstacle to the achievement of its economic policy objectives.[53] Finally, with respect to the capital movements referred to in list D (such as loans, credits and the physical importation and exportation of

---

46   Ibid, para 10.
47   Ibid, para 11.
48   Ibid, para 11.
49   Ibid, para 12.
50   'First Council Directive for the implementation of Article 67 of the Treaty' (1960) *OJ 43*, 12.7.1960, p. 921–932.
51   'Second Council 63/21/EEC Directive of 18 December 1962 adding to and amending the First Directive for the implementation of Article 67 of the Treaty' (1963) *OJ 9*, 22.1.1963, p. 62–74.
52   Articles 1 and 2 of the 'First Council Directive for the implementation of Article 67 of the Treaty' (1960) *OJ 43, 12.7.1960, p. 921–932*.
53   Ibid, Article 3.

financial assets), the directives did not require the Member States to adopt any liberalising measures.

Although the first two directives laid the groundwork for the progressive liberalisation of capital movements, the major breakthrough came with the Third Capital Directive, Directive 88/361,[54] which 'brought about the full liberalisation of capital movements'[55] and gave the single market its full financial dimension. This Directive was adopted on the basis of Articles 69 and 70 (1) of the Treaty of Rome, the two old legal basis provisions which allowed the Council to adopt unanimously secondary measures in the field of the free movement of capital.

The adoption of secondary legislation was not a self-evident decision. The Council was well aware of the risks and potential drawbacks of capital liberalisation and this was imprinted in the Preamble to Directive 88/361. In particular, the Preamble warned that free capital movements could seriously disturb the monetary or financial situation of Member States or cause serious stresses on the exchange markets.[56] It even stated that capital liberalisation might prove harmful for the cohesion of the European Monetary System, the smooth operation of the Internal Market and the progressive achievement of the Economic and Monetary Union.[57] It therefore expressed the view that Member States should, if necessary, be able to take measures to restrict temporarily capital movements, which were liable to seriously disrupt the conduct of their monetary and exchange rate policies.[58] It drew special attention to the serious implications that capital liberalisation could have for the market of secondary residences in Member States located in border areas as well as to the risks of tax evasion and tax avoidance resulting from the divergent national systems of taxation.[59] Furthermore, it recognised that capital liberalisation would be particularly detrimental for the Hellenic Republic and Ireland, which were faced, albeit to differing degrees, with difficult balance-of-payments situations and high levels of external indebtedness. It therefore granted to those two Member States further time to comply with the obligations arising from the Directive.[60]

---

54   'Council Directive 88/361/EEC of 24 June 1988 for the implementation of Article 67 of the Treaty' (1988) *OJ* L 178, 8.7.1988, p. 5–18.

55   Joined cases C-358/93 and C-416/93 *Criminal proceedings against Aldo Bordessa and Vicente Marí Mellado and Concepción Barbero Maestre*, ECLI:EU:C:1995:54, para 17.

56   Preamble to 'Council Directive 88/361/EEC of 24 June 1988 for the implementation of Article 67 of the Treaty' (1988) *OJ* L 178, 8.7.1988, p. 5–18.

57   Ibid.

58   Ibid.

59   Ibid.

60   Preamble to 'Council Directive 88/361/EEC of 24 June 1988 for the implementation of Article 67 of the Treaty' (1988) *OJ* L 178, 8.7.1988, p. 5–18.

Despite the initial hesitation and the possible risks associated with capital liberalisation, Article 1 of Directive 88/361 required Member States to abolish all restrictions on movements of capital taking place between persons resident in Member States. Shortly after the adoption of the Directive, the Court, in *Bordessa*, ruled that this prohibition on capital restrictions laid down in Article 1 thereof was directly effective and thus could be relied upon before national courts by individuals.[61]

Another important feature of Directive 88/361 is the non-exhaustive nomenclature of capital movements contained in Annex I, which includes a wide variety of financial transactions such as direct investments, investments in real estate, operations in securities (e.g. shares and bonds), operations in units of collective investment undertakings, operations in securities and other instruments normally dealt in on the capital market, operations in current and deposit accounts with financial institutions, credits related to commercial transactions, financial loans and credits, sureties, other guarantees and rights of pledge, transfers in performance of insurance contracts, personal capital movements (e.g. gifts and endowments, dowries, inheritances and legacies), physical import and export of financial assets and other capital payments. The Court has ruled that:

> even though Directive 88/361 was adopted on the basis of Articles 69 and 70(1) of the EEC Treaty, which was later replaced by Article 73b et seq. of the EC Treaty, the nomenclature in respect of movements of capital still has the same indicative value, for the purposes of defining the notion of capital movements, as it did before the entry into force of Article 73b et seq.[62]

Therefore, in the absence of a definition of the concept of 'movement of capital' within the meaning of Article 63 (1) TFEU, the Court still uses the non-exhaustive list of capital movements annexed to Directive 88/361 when determining whether a specific transaction qualifies as 'capital movement'.

3   The Maastricht Treaty

The free movement of capital developed into a fully-fledged freedom of the EU's Internal Market in 1993 with the entry into force of the Maastricht Treaty

---

61   Joined cases C-358/93 and C-416/93 *Bordessa*, paras 33–35.
62   Case C-222/97 *Manfred Trummer and Peter Mayer*, ECLI:EU:C:1999:143, para 21; Joined cases C-105/12 to C-107/12 *Staat der Nederlanden v Essent NV, Essent Nederland BV, Eneco Holding NV and Delta NV*, ECLI:EU:C:2013:677, para 40.

and the establishment of the Economic and Monetary Union, which is arguably one of the most significant developments in the history of European Integration. After a long period of economic turmoil and persistent political controversies, the entry into force of the Maastricht Treaty marked the transition to the fourth stage of economic integration, which enabled European economies to not only benefit from an Internal Market with free circulation of goods, persons, services and capital, but also to converge on a macro-economic level, to develop common economic and monetary policies and eventually to adopt a common currency.[63] In order to achieve this transition, it was decided that capital movements had to be liberalised not only within the EU but also in relation to third countries. The entry into force of the Maastricht Treaty was therefore a turning point in the history of European financial integration, as it marked the transition from the post-war scepticism regarding unfettered capital flows to a more liberal aproach to capital liberalisation in the EU.

B   *The Current Legal Framework*
1   The Scope of Article 63 TFEU
a)   *Territorial Scope*

Perhaps the most salient feature distinguishing the free movement of capital from the other freedoms is the fact that it applies to not only to Member States but also to third countries (*erga omnes* effect).[64] The extra-EU territorial

---

63   Bela Balassa, *The Theory of Economic Integration* (Irwin Homewood 2011); André Sapir, 'European Integration at the Crossroads: A Review Essay on the 50th Anniversary of Bela Balassa's Theory of Economic Integration' (2011) 49 *Journal of Economic Literature* 1200. More broadly, on the theory of economic integration, see Richard Baldwin and Anthony Venables, 'Regional economic integration' in Gene Grossman and Kenneth Rogoff (eds), *Handbook of International Economics* (Elsevier 1995), pp. 1597–1644; Richard Baldwin and Charles Wyplosz, *The Economics of European Integration* (McGraw-Hill 2012); Richard Baldwin and others, *Market Integration, Regionalism and the Global Economy* (Cambridge University Press 1999).

64   See, in particular, Michael Lang and Pasquale Pistone (eds), *The EU and Third Countries: Direct Taxation* (Kluwer Law International 2008); Alexandre Maitrot de la Motte, 'Les spécificitéé*L'unité des libertés de circulation – In varietate concordia* (Bruylant 2013), pp. 289–329; Axel Cordewener, Georg W. Kofler and Clemens Philipp Schindler, 'Free Movement of Capital and Third Countries: Exploring the Outer Boundaries with Lasertec, A and B and Holböck' (2007) 47 European Taxation 371; Axel Cordewener, Georg W. Kofler and Clemens Philipp Schindler, 'Free Movement of Capital, Third Country Relationships and National Tax Law: An Emerging Issue before the ECJ' (2007) 47 European Taxation 107; Martha O'Brien, 'Taxation and the Third Country Dimension of Free Movement of Capital in EU Law: The ECJ's Rulings and Unresolved Issues' (2008) 6 British Tax Review 628; Philippe Vigneron, 'L'effet erga omnes de la libre circulation des capitaux dans la Constitution européenne: un retour en arrière?' (2004) 23 *Euredia* 369; Christiana Hjipanayi, 'The Fundamental Freedoms and Third Countries: Recent Perspectives' (2008)

dimension of the free movement of capital was recognised by the Court in *Sandoz*, where it was emphasised that Article 73b (1) of the Treaty (today Article 63 TFEU) covered all restrictions on movement of capital between Member States and between Member States and third countries.[65] This unique feature elevates the free movement of capital to a whole different level, rendering it a potential gateway through which extra-EU investors can approach and ultimately access the EU's Internal Market.

Even though the Treaty does not state the reasons why the scope *ratione loci* of the free movement was extended so as to cover also capital movements to/from third counties, it is commonly accepted that this extension was impelled by the EU's monetary policy.[66] Indeed, the external dimension of the free movement of capital may pursue objectives other than that of establishing the internal market, such as, in particular, that of ensuring the credibility of the single currency on the international financial markets and creating and maintaining financial centres with a world-wide dimension within the Member States.[67]

The external dimension of the free movement of capital has been used in order to bring into the scope of the EU's Internal Market investments and financial transactions to and from third countries, which otherwise would be excluded from the benefits of the single market. In particular, the *erga omnes* effect of the free movement of capital has been interpreted so as to cover restrictions on capital movements involving the provision of financial services between Member States and third countries,[68] national measures which restrict payments of dividends deriving from investments to or from third countries[69] and national tax legislation under which the dividends paid by companies established in a Member State to an investment fund established in

---

48 *European Taxation* 571; Cees Peters and Jan Gooijer, 'The free movement of capital and third countries' (2005) 45 *European Taxation* 475; Joanna Mitroyanni, 'Exploring the Scope of the Free Movement of Capital in Direct Taxation' (2005) 8 *EC Tax Journal* 1; Louis Vogel, *Traité de droit économique, Tome 4: Droit européen des affaires* (Bruylant 2015), pp. 300–302.

65 Case C-439/97 *Sandoz GmbH v Finanzlandesdirektion für Wien*, ECLI:EU:C:1999:499, para 18.

66 *Opinion of Advocate General Bot in Case C-101/05 Skatteverket v A*, ECLI:EU:C:2007:493, paras 75-77.

67 Case C-101/05 *Skatteverket v A*, ECLI:EU:C:2007:804, para 31.

68 Case C-560/13 *Finanzamt Ulm v Ingeborg Wagner-Raith*, ECLI:EU:C:2015:347, para 37.

69 Case C-446/04 *Test Claimants in the FII Group Litigation*, ECLI:EU:C:2006:774, para 183.

a non-Member State are not the subject of a tax exemption, while investment funds established in that Member State receive such an exemption.[70]

However, this expansion of the territorial boundaries of the Internal Market carries an element of risk, especially in cases where third-country investors attempt to extend the scope of other freedoms through the backdoor of the free movement of capital. This is the reason why the delineation of the border between the freedom of establishment or services and the free movement of capital is very important. It should be noted, however, that the extended territorial scope of the free movement of capital is counterbalanced by additional justification grounds available to Member States in order to restrict capital flows to/from third countries.

b) *Material Scope*

i) Difference between Capital Movements and Payments

Article 63 (1) TFEU prohibits all restrictions on capital movements, while Article 63 (2) TFEU prohibits all restrictions on payments. The distinction between 'capital movements' and 'payments' was first recognised by the Court in *Luisi and Carbone*.[71] The Court clarified that: *'current payments are transfers of foreign exchange which constitute the consideration within the context of an underlying transaction, whilst movements of capital are financial operations essentially concerned with the investment of the funds in question rather than remuneration for a service'*.[72] Therefore, the physical transfer of bank notes as a means of payment for a transaction involving the movement of goods or services (such as tourism, medical treatment, education or business) was classified as 'current payment' and not as 'capital movement'.[73] These restrictions on current payments relating to the provision of services had to be abolished by the end of the transitional period.[74]

ii) Definition of Capital Movements

Contrary to the freedom to provide services,[75] the Treaty provisions on the free movement of capital do not define the concept of 'capital movements'.

70　Case C-190/12 *Emerging Markets Series of DFA Investment Trust Company*, ECLI:EU:C:2014:249, para 35.
71　Joined cases 286/82 and 26/83 *Graziana Luisi and Giuseppe Carbone v Ministero del Tesoro* ECLI:EU:C:1984:35.
72　Ibid, para 21.
73　Ibid, paras 22-23.
74　Ibid, para 24. See also Case 308/86 *Criminal proceedings against R. Lambert*, ECLI:EU:C:1988:405.
75　Article 57 TFEU provides a broad definition of 'services' within the meaning of the Treaty, stating that they are normally provided for remuneration on a temporary basis and they

In the absence of any definition of capital movements in the Treaty, the Court has held that the non-exhaustive nomenclature in Annex I of Directive 88/361 has indicative value for the purposes of defining capital movements. This list includes a wide variety of capital movements, such as the physical import and export of financial assets and other capital payments,[76] direct investments,[77] investments in real estate,[78] operations in securities (e.g. resale of shares,[79] bonds,[80] receipt of dividends[81]), financial loans and credits,[82] mortgages and other guarantees,[83] gifts and endowments[84] and inheritances.[85]

---

particularly include activities of an industrial or commercial character, activities of craftsmen and various professions.

[76] Joined cases C-163/94, C-165/94 and C-250/94 *Sanz de Lera*, paras 17-18; Joined cases C-358/93 and C-416/93 *Bordessa*, paras 13-15; Case C-190/17 *Lu Zheng v Ministerio de Economía y Competitividad*, ECLI:EU:C:2018:357.

[77] Joined cases C-282/04 and C-283/04 *Commission v The Netherlands (golden shares)*, ECLI:EU:C:2006:608, para 19; Case C-309/99 *J. C. J. Wouters, J. W. Savelbergh en Price Waterhouse Belastingadviseurs BV tegen Algemene Raad van de Nederlandse Orde van Advocaten, in tegenwoordigheid van: Raad van de Balies van de Europese Gemeenschap*, ECLI:EU:C:2002:98, para 38; Case C-174/04 *Commission v Italy (golden shares)*, ECLI:EU:C:2005:350, para 12; Case C-39/11 *VBV – Vorsorgekasse AG v Finanzmarktaufsichtsbehörde (FMA)*, ECLI:EU:C:2012:327, para 21; Case C-483/99 *Commission v France (golden shares – Sociéte Nationale Elf-Aquitaine)*, ECLI:EU:C:2002:327, para 37; Case C-503/99 *Commission v Belgium (golden shares)*, ECLI:EU:C:2002:328, para 38.

[78] Case C-370/05 *Criminal proceedings against Uwe Kay Festersen*, ECLI:EU:C:2007:59, para 23; Case C-452/01 *Margarethe Ospelt and Schlössle Weissenberg Familienstiftung*, ECLI:EU:C:2003:493, para 7; Joined cases C-515/99, C-519/99 to C-524/99 and C-526/99 to C-540/99 *Hans Reisch and Others*, ECLI:EU:C:2002:135, para 29; Case C-446/04 *Test Claimants in the FII Group Litigation*, paras 23-24.

[79] Richard Baldwin and Charles Wyplosz, *The Economics of European Integration* (MacGraw-Hill Education 2006), para 29.

[80] Case C-329/03 *Trapeza tis Ellados AE v Banque Artesia*, ECLI:EU:C:2005:645, para 34.

[81] Case C-35/98 *Staatssecretaris van Financiën v B.G.M. Verkooijen*, ECLI:EU:C:2000:294, paras 28-30.

[82] Case C-452/04 *Fidium Finanz AG v Bundesanstalt für Finanzdienstleistungsaufsicht*, ECLI:EU:C:2006:631, para 42; Case C-282/12 *Itelcar – Automóveis de Aluguer Lda v Fazenda Pública*, ECLI:EU:C:2013:629, para 14; Case C-39/11 *VBV – Vorsorgekasse*, para 36; Case C-478/98 *Commission v Belgium (Eurobond)*, ECLI:EU:C:2000:497, para 17.

[83] Case C-222/97 *Trummer and Mayer*, paras 24, 34; Case C-279/00 *Commission v Italy*, ECLI:EU:C:2002:89, para 37.

[84] Case C-318/07 *Hein Persche v Finanzamt Lüdenscheid*, ECLI:EU:C:2009:33, paras 24,25.

[85] Case C-256/06 *Theodor Jäger v Finanzamt Kusel-Landstuhl*, ECLI:EU:C:2008:20, para 25; Case C-513/03 *Heirs of M. E. A. van Hilten-van der Heijden*, ECLI:EU:C:2006:131, para 42; Case C-364/01 *The heirs of H. Barbier v Inspecteur van de Belastingdienst Particulieren/ Ondernemingen buitenland te Heerlen*, ECLI:EU:C:2003:665, para 58.

c) *Relationship with the Other Freedoms*

Although in principle the aforementioned types of transactions qualify as capital movements, it is sometimes difficult to determine which fundamental freedom is applicable. The most problematic is the relationship between the free movement of capital and the freedom of establishment. In a situation where the contested national legislation is captured by both the freedom of establishment and the free movement of capital, the question arises which of the two takes precedence over the other. As a general rule, the purpose of the national legislation at issue is the main factor determining which fundamental freedom is applicable.[86] The criterion applied by the Court in order to distinguish between freedom of establishment and free movement of capital is the exercise of *definite influence* over the management of the company. On the one hand, provisions of national law which apply to the possession, by nationals of a Member State, of holdings in the capital of a company established in another Member State allowing them to exert a definite influence on the company's decisions and to determine its activities, fall within the ambit *ratione materiae* of Article 49 TFEU.[87] On the other hand, direct investments, i.e. investments of any kind made by natural or legal persons which serve to establish or maintain lasting and direct links between the persons providing the capital and the company to which that capital is made available in order to carry out an economic

---

[86] Case C-157/05 *Winfried L. Holböck v Finanzamt Salzburg-Land*, ECLI:EU:C:2007:297, para 22; Case C-196/04 *Cadbury Schweppes plc*, ECLI:EU:C:2006:544, paras 31-33; Case C-452/04 *Fidium Finanz*, paras 34, 44-49; Case C-374/04 *Test Claimants in Class IV of the ACT Group Litigation*, ECLI:EU:C:2006:773, paras 37 and 38; Case C-446/04 *Test Claimants in the FII Group Litigation*, para 36; Case C-524/04 *Test Claimants in the Thin Cap Group Litigation*, ECLI:EU:C:2007:161, paras 26-34.

[87] Case C-244/11 *Commission v Greece (golden shares)*, para 21; Case C-212/09 *Commission v Portugal (golden shares – GALP Energia SGPS SA)*, ECLI:EU:C:2011:717, paCase C-196/04 *Cadbury Schweppes*ra 42; Case C-326/07 *Commission v Italy (golden shares)*, ECLI:EU:C:2009:193, para 34; Case C-543/08 *Commission v Portugal (golden shares – EDP)*, ECLI:EU:C:2010:669, para 41; Case C-251/98 *Baars*, para 22; Case C-436/00 *X and Y*, ECLI:EU:C:2002:704, paras 37, 66-68. Case C-446/04 *Test Claimants in the FII Group Litigation*, para 37; Case C81/09 *Idryma Typou AE v Ypourgos Typou kai Meson Mazikis Enimerosis*, ECLI:EU:C:2010:622, para 47; Case C-310/09 *Ministre du Budget, des Comptes publics et de la Fonction publique v Accor SA*, ECLI:EU:C:2011:581, para 32; Case C31/11 *Marianne Scheunemann v Finanzamt Bremerhaven*, ECLI:EU:C:2012:481, para 23; and Case C-35/11 *Test Claimants in the FII Group Litigation*, ECLI:EU:C:2012:707, para 91; Case C-196/04 *Cadbury Schweppes*, para 31. As it was acknowledged by Advocate General Kokott, 'the Court has not established a holding threshold of general application which must be reached in order for a determining influence to be presumed' (see *Opinion of Advocate General Kokott in Case C-311/08 Société de Gestion Industrielle*, ECLI:EU:C:2009:545, para 29).

activity, fall within the scope of Article 63 TFEU.[88] National legislation which is not limited to those shareholdings which enable the holder to have a definite influence on a company's decisions and to determine its activities but which applies irrespective of the size of the holding which the shareholder has in a company may fall within the ambit of both Articles 49 and 63 TFEU.[89]

Regarding the relationship between capital and services, a question arising primarily when financial services are at stake, the Court has introduced the *predominant consideration* criterion. According to this criterion, the freedom to provide services is applicable whenever the restrictive effect on the concerned financial transaction is an *unavoidable consequence* of the restriction on the freedom to provide services.[90] In this respect, in *Fidium Finanz*, the Court held that national rules whereby a Member State makes the granting of commercial credit by a non-EU company subject to prior authorisation, and which provide that such authorisation must be refused if that company does not have its central administration or a branch in that territory, affect primarily the exercise of the freedom to provide services.[91] However, the freedom to provide services does not cover the economic activities of third-country companies. Its territorial scope is limited to intra-EU provision of services. Therefore, the Court concluded that the Treaty provisions on services could not be relied on by an undertaking established in a third country and there were no grounds for examining the compatibility of the national rules with the free movement of capital.[92] This case demonstrates the efforts of the Court to prevent the circumvention of the territorial boundaries of the Internal Market by the invocation of the external dimension of the free movement of capital. The 'predominant consideration' criterion was employed by the Court in order to restrict the ambit and the implications of the *erga omnes* effect of Article 63 TFEU and prevent abusive behaviour from non-EU companies.[93]

---

[88] Case C-212/09 *Commission v Portugal (golden shares – GALP Energia SGPS SA)*, para 43; Case C-112/05 *Commission v Germany (golden shares – Volkswagen I)*, ECLI:EU:C:2007:623, para 18; Case C-326/07 *Commission v Italy (golden shares)*, para 35; Case C-543/08 *Commission v Portugal (golden shares – EDP)*, para 42; Case C-446/04 *Test Claimants in the FII Group Litigation*, paras 36-38; Case C-157/05 *Holböck*, paras 23-25.

[89] Case C81/09 *Idryma Typou*, para 49; Case C-326/07 *Commission v Italy (golden shares)*, para 36.

[90] Case C-452/04 *Fidium Finanz*, para 49.

[91] Ibid, paras 47-49.

[92] Ibid, paras 47, 51.

[93] Martha O'Brien, 'Case C-452/04, Fidium Finanz AG v. Bundesanstalt für Finanzdienstleistungsaufsicht, judgment of the Court of Justice (Grand Chamber) of 3 October 2006' (2007) 44 *Common Market Law Review* 1483, at p. 1495. See also Daniel Smit, 'The relationship between the free movement of capital and the other EC Treaty freedoms

2 Direct Effect of Article 63 TFEU

One of the most important factors why the free movement of capital followed a slow historical development compared to the other freedoms was the fact that up until 1995 the Court had not recognised the direct effect of Article 67 EEC Treaty, thus depriving the individuals of the possibility to rely on it. It was only with the Maastricht Treaty and the advent of the EMU that the Court realised that the time was ripe for the free movement of capital to become directly effective. The recognition of the vertical direct effect of the current Article 63 TFEU, first in *Sanz de Lera*[94] and then in *Skatteverket v. A*,[95] accelerated the evolution of the case law and provided a new impetus for legal scholarship.[96] The question of the horizontal applicability of Article 63 TFEU has not been explicitly dealt with by the Court of Justice. This may be explained by the fact that a substantial part of the case law raising questions on the interpretation of the free movement of capital concerns taxation, 'a quintessentially vertical subject

---

in third country relationships in the field of direct taxation: a question of exclusivity, parallelism or causality?' (2007) 16 EC Tax Review 252; Pasquale Pistone, 'Kirchberg 3 October 2006: Three Decisions that Did ... Not Change the Future of European Taxes' (2006) 34 *Intertax* 582; Tatiana Falcao, 'Third-Country Relations with the European Community: A Growing Snowball' (2009) 37 *Intertax* 307; Sergey Bezborodov, 'Freedom of Establishment in the EC Economic Partnership Agreements: in Search of its Direct Effect on Direct Taxation' (2007) 35 *Intertax* 658; Christiana HJI Panayi, 'Thin Capitalization Glo et al. – A Thinly Concealed Agenda?' (2007) 35 *Intertax* 298; Vassilis Hatzopoulos, 'The Court's approach to services (2006–2012): From case law to case load?' (2013) 50 *Common Market Law Review* 459; Sigrid Hemels and others, 'Freedom of establishment or free movement of capital: Is there an order of priority? Conflicting visions of national courts and the ECJ' (2010) 19 EC Tax Review 19; Mathieu Isenbaert, 'The Contemporary Meaning of 'Sovereignty' in the Supranational Context of the EC as Applied to the Income Tax Case Law of the ECJ' (2009) 18 *EC Tax Review* 264; Ryan Murphy, 'Why does tax have to be so taxing? The court revisits the Franked Investment Income litigation (Case Comment)' (2013) 38 European Law Review 695; Stefan Enchelmaier, 'Always at your service (within limits): the ECJ's case law on article 56 TFEU (2006–11)' (2011) 36 *European Law Review* 615.

94   Joined cases C-163/94, C-165/94 and C-250/94 *Sanz de Lera*, para 41.
95   Case C-101/05 *Skatteverket v A*, para 21.
96   Jukka Snell, 'Free movement of capital: Evolution as a non-linear process' in Craig and De Búrca (eds), *The Evolution of EU Law* (Oxford University Press 2011); Jonh Usher, 'The Evolution of the Free Movement of Capital' (2007) 31 Fordhman International Law Journal 1533; Steve Peers, 'Free Movement of Capital: Learning lessons or slipping on spilt milk?' in Barnard and Scott (eds), *The Law of the Single European Market: Unpacking the Premises* (Hart Publishing 2002); Leo Flynn, 'Free movement of capital' in Barnard and Peers (eds), *European Union Law* (Oxford University Press 2017); Arie Landsmeer, 'Movement of Capital and Other Freedoms' (2001) 28 Legal Issues of Economic Integration 57.

matter'.[97] The question of the horizontal direct effect of Article 63 TFEU in the context of the golden shares case law is analysed in chapter 3.

3 Discrimination and Restrictions

Although rare, cases of direct discrimination do exist in the capital case law and they are treated as manifest infringements of Article 63 TFEU. Thus, the Court has disapplied a Portuguese provision which precluded investors from other Member States from acquiring more than a given number of shares in certain Portuguese undertakings,[98] an Austrian provision which exempted only Austrian nationals from having to obtain authorisation before acquiring a plot of land[99] and an Italian provision exempting only Italian nationals from the requirement of obtaining an authorisation to buy a property in certain parts of the national territory.[100]

In relation to indirect discrimination, the Court has found that the Danish legislation on agriculture imposing a residence requirement, which could be waived only with the authorisation of the minister responsible for agriculture, restricted the free movement of capital.[101] Furthermore, the Belgian rules which resulted in an inheritance consisting of immovable property situated in Belgium being subject to transfer duties that were higher than the inheritance duties payable if the person whose estate was being administered had, at the time of death, been residing in that Member State – were found to have the effect of restricting the movement of capital.[102] Recently, the Court explicitly used the term 'indirect discrimination' when scrutinising the Hungarian legislation under which usufruct rights which had previously been created over agricultural land and the holders of which did not have the status of close relation of the owner of that land were extinguished by operation of law and were, consequently, deleted from the property registers.[103] The Court found that the contested legislation was operating to the disadvantage of nationals of other Member States more than Hungarian nationals and was therefore liable to conceal indirect discrimination based on the usufructuary's nationality or the origin of the capital.[104]

---

97 Catherine Barnard, *The Substantive Law of the EU: The Four Freedoms* (Oxford University Press 2016), p. 526.
98 Case C-367/98 *Commission v Portugal (golden shares)*, ECLI:EU:C:2002:326 para 40.
99 Case C-302/97 *Konle*, para 23.
100 Case C-423/98 *Alfredo Albore*, ECLI:EU:C:2000:401, para 16.
101 Case C-370/05 *Festersen*, para 25.
102 Case C-11/07 *Eckelkamp*, paras 45-46.
103 Joined cases C-52/16 and C-113/16 *'SEGRO' Kft. v Vas Megyei Kormányhivatal Sárvári Járási Földhivatala and Günther Horváth v Vas Megyei Kormányhivatal*, ECLI:EU:C:2018:157.
104 Ibid, para 74.

The wording of Article 63 TFEU goes beyond the mere elimination of unequal treatment on grounds of nationality and prohibits all restrictions on the movement of capital between Member States and between Member States and third countries. Examples of restrictions include, inter alia, golden shares,[105] authorisation requirements,[106] qualification requirements,[107] residence requirements for investments in real estate,[108] foreign currency arrangements in mortgages,[109] and other requirements affecting financial credits,[110] receipt of dividends[111] or corporate taxation.[112]

---

[105] Case C-58/99 *Commission v Italy (golden shares – ENI/Telecom Italia)*, ECLI:EU:C:2000:280; Case C-309/99 *Wouters and others*; Case C-483/99 *Commission v France (golden shares – Sociéte Nationale Elf-Aquitaine)*; Case C-503/99 *Commission v Belgium (golden shares)*; Case C-463/00 *Commission v Spain (golden shares)*, ECLI:EU:C:2003:272; Case C-98/01 *Commission v UK (golden shares)*; Case C-174/04 *Commission v Italy (golden shares)*; Joined cases C-282/04 and C-283/04 *Commission v The Netherlands (golden shares)*; Case C-112/05 *Commission v Germany (golden shares – Volkswagen I)*; Joined cases C-463/04 and C-464/04 *Federconsumatori and Others and Associazione Azionariato Diffuso dell'AEM SpA and Others v Comune di Milano (AEM/Edison)*, ECLI:EU:C:2007:752; Case C-274/06 *Commission v Spain (golden shares)*, ECLI:EU:C:2008:86; Case C-207/07 *Commission v Spain (golden shares in the energy sector)*, ECLI:EU:C:2008:428; Case C-326/07 *Commission v Italy (golden shares)*; Case C-543/08 *Commission v Portugal (golden shares – EDP)*; Case C-171/08 *Commission v Portugal (golden shares – Portugal Telecom SGPS SA)*, ECLI:EU:C:2010:412; Case C-212/09 *Commission v Portugal (golden shares – GALP Energia SGPS SA)*; Case C-244/11 *Commission v Greece (golden shares)*; Case C-95/12 *Commission v Germany (golden shares – Volkswagen II)*, ECLI:EU:C:2013:676.

[106] Joined cases C-358/93 and C-416/93 *Bordessa*, para 25; Joined cases C-163/94, C-165/94 and C-250/94 *Sanz de Lera*, para 141; Case C-54/99 *Association Eglise de scientologie de Paris*, ECLI:EU:C:2000:124, para 14; Case C-302/97 *Konle*, para 39; Joined cases C-515/99, C-519/99 to C-524/99 and C-526/99 to C-540/99 *Reisch*, para 32; Case C-567/07 *Minister voor Wonen, Wijken en Integratie v Woningstichting Sint Servatius*, ECLI:EU:C:2009:593, para 22; Case C-197/11 *Eric Libert and Others v Gouvernement flamand and All Projects & Developments NV and Others v Vlaamse Regering*, ECLI:EU:C:2013:288, paras 46-47; Case C-39/11 *VBV – Vorsorgekasse*, paras 22, 27.

[107] Case C-531/06 *Commission v Italy (pharmacies)*, ECLI:EU:C:2009:315, paras 47-48.

[108] Case C-302/97 *Konle*, para 39; Case C-567/07 *Sint Servatius*, para 39; Case C-197/11 *Libert and Others*, paras 46-47; Case C-452/01 *Margarethe Ospelt*, para 34.

[109] Case C-222/97 *Trummer and Mayer*, paras 26-28.

[110] Case C-484/93 *Svensson*, para 10; Case C-439/97 *Sandoz*, para 31.

[111] Case C-35/98 *Verkooijen*, paras 34-36; Case C-194/06 *Staatssecretaris van Financiën v Orange European Smallcap Fund NV*, ECLI:EU:C:2008:289, para 65; Case C-513/04 *Mark Kerckhaert and Bernadette Morres v Belgische Staat*, ECLI:EU:C:2006:713, para 24; Case C-379/05 *Amurta SGPS v Inspecteur van de Belastingdienst/Amsterdam*, ECLI:EU:C:2007:655, paras 15, 25-28; Case C-101/05 *Skatteverket v A*, paras 41-43; Case C-446/04 *Test Claimants in the FII Group Litigation*, para 74.

[112] Case C-182/08 *Glaxo Wellcome*, paras 53-59; Case C-377/07 *STEKO*, paras 25-27.

4 Derogations

a) *Treaty-based Derogations*

The broad interpretation of the notion of capital restrictions is counterbalanced by the wide range of derogations that can be invoked by Member States in order to justify those restrictions. The express derogations laid down in the Treaty provisions are divided between, on the one hand, those that apply to capital movements to/from both Member States and third countries laid down in Article 65 TFEU and, on the other hand, those that apply exclusively to capital movements to/from third countries.

i) Article 65 TFEU

Article 65 TFEU contains two express derogations, one specific in Article 65 (1) (a) TFEU and one general in Article 65 (1) (b) TFEU.

o Article 65 (1) (a) TFEU (specific derogation – tax differentiation)

Article 65 (1) (a) TFEU contains a rather special derogation that allows Member States to apply national legislation which distinguishes between *resident* and *non-residents* taxpayers in relation to matters of taxation. In the absence of fiscal harmonisation at EU level, Member States felt the need to insert into the Maastricht Treaty (then Article 73d (1) (a) of the Treaty) a derogation that would allow for a certain degree of fiscal differentiation of taxpayers according to their place of residence (fiscal non-residents benefit from tax exemptions in most Member States) or the place where the capital is invested (usually, foreign investments will be discriminated against through less favourable tax treatment).[113] Even before the entry into force of the Maastricht Treaty, national tax legislation differentiating between resident and non-resident taxpayers was justified on the condition that it applied to situations which were not objectively comparable or could be justified by overriding reasons in the general interest, in particular in relation to the cohesion of the tax system.[114] This rule was essentially the codification of the *Schumacker* and *Bachmann* case law.[115] The underlying rationale of this permitted discrimination lies in the sensitive notion of fiscal sovereignty and the principle of territoriality. The principle of territoriality is a principle enshrined

---

113 European Commission, *European Economy* (Directorate-General for Economic and Financial Affairs, No 6/2003), p. 321.
114 Case C-35/98 *Verkooijen*, para 43.
115 Case C-279/93 *Finanzamt Köln-Altstadt v Roland Schumacker*, ECLI:EU:C:1995:31; Case C-204/90 *Bachmann*; Case C-300/90 *Commission v Belgium*, ECLI:EU:C:1992:37.

in international tax law and recognised by EU law, according to which each Member State is entitled to tax profits generated in its territory.[116] Independent tax systems coexist without hierarchy between them and in the EU context this entails the need to ensure a balanced allocation of the Member States' powers to impose taxes.[117]

The tax differentiation set out in Article 65 (1) (a) TFEU is a special provision since it allows economic considerations relating to taxation to be regarded as justification grounds for capital restrictions.[118] However, this provision, insofar as it derogates from the fundamental principle of the free movement of capital, must be interpreted narrowly.[119] The Court has ruled that the principle of territoriality must be exercised in accordance with the principles of EU law.[120] Acceptance of the view that a Member State may freely apply a different treatment solely on the basis of the location of the residence would deprive the rules relating to the free movement of capital of all meaning.[121] In *Lenz*,[122] which concerned the Austrian legislation providing for half-rate taxation only in relation to revenue from capital of Austrian origin, the Court highlighted that Article 65 (1) (a) TFEU must be interpreted strictly and does not render automatically any tax legislation making a distinction between taxpayers by reference to the place of residence or place where they invest their capital compatible with the Treaty.[123] The Court added that this derogation should be read in conjunction with Article 65 (3) TFEU (universality clause), according to which the national legislation shall not constitute a means of arbitrary discrimination or a disguised restriction on the free movement of capital.[124] In other words, the derogation provided for in

---

116　Case C-250/08 *Commission v Belgium (purchase of immovable property)*, ECLI:EU:C:2011:793, para 48; Case C-231/05 *Oy AA*, para 47; Case C-35/08 *Grundstücksgemeinschaft Busley and Cibrian Fernandez v Finanzamt Stuttgart-Körperschaften*, ECLI:EU:C:2009:625, paras 29-30.

117　Case C-250/95 *Futura Participations SA and Singer v Administration des contributions*, ECLI:EU:C:1997:239, para 22; Case C-132/10 *Olivier Halley*, para 75; Case C-479/14 *Sabine Hünnebeck v Finanzamt Krefeld*, ECLI:EU:C:2016:412, paras 49, 65; Case C-342/10 *Commission v Finland*, ECLI:EU:C:2012:688, para 45; Case C-471/04 *Finanzamt Offenbach am Main-Land v Keller Holding GmbH*, ECLI:EU:C:2006:143, para 44.

118　Case C-309/99 *Wouters and others*, para 52.

119　Case C-256/06 *Jäger*, para 40.

120　Case C-250/08 *Commission v Belgium (purchase of immovable property)*, para 48.

121　Ibid, para 50.

122　Case C-315/02 *Anneliese Lenz v Finanzlandesdirektion für Tirol*, ECLI:EU:C:2004:446.

123　Ibid, para 26.

124　Ibid.

Article 65 (1) TFEU is itself limited by Article 65(3) TFEU.[125] Therefore, an unequal treatment permitted under Article 65 (1) (a) TFEU must clearly be distinguished from an arbitrary discrimination or a disguised restriction prohibited under Article 65 (3) TFEU.

o   Article 65 (1) (b) TFEU (general derogation)

Article 65 (1) (b) TFEU is the general derogation clause in the field of free movement of capital, similar to the ones contained in Articles 36, 45 (3) and 52 TFEU concerning the other freedoms. This general derogation recognises three legitimate objectives that Member States can invoke in order to justify the imposition of a restriction on capital movements. First, they are allowed to adopt restrictive measures in order to prevent infringements of national law and regulations, in particular in the field of taxation and prudential supervision of financial institutions.[126] Secondly, the Treaty permits procedures for declarations of capital movements for purposes of administrative or statistical information. Finally, reasons related to public policy or public security can be invoked in order to justify capital restrictions. In this respect, the Court has rules that *'while Member States are free to determine the requirements of public policy and public security in the light of their national needs, they must nonetheless be interpreted strictly as derogations from the fundamental freedoms and 'their scope cannot be determined unilaterally by each Member State without any control of the Union institutions'*.[127] Therefore, public policy and public security might be relied on *'only if there is a genuine and sufficiently serious threat to a fundamental interest of society'*.[128] It further stressed that those derogations must not be misapplied so as to serve purely economic ends and that any person affected have access to legal redress.[129] The Court has accepted that safeguarding supplies of petroleum products in the event of a crisis is a matter of public security capable of justifying restrictions on free movement.[130] Furthermore, in *Kadi I*, the General Court established that the concept of public security covers both the

---

125   Case C-45/17 *Frédéric Jahin*, para 33; Case C-322/11 *K*, ECLI:EU:C:2013:716, para 34; Case C-181/12 *Yvon Welte v Finanzamt Velbert*, ECLI:EU:C:2013:662, para 43.
126   Joined cases C-163/94, C-165/94 and C-250/94 *Sanz de Lera*, para 22; Joined cases C-358/93 and C-416/93 *Bordessa*, para 21.
127   Case C-54/99 *Association Eglise de scientologie de Paris*, para 17.
128   Ibid.
129   Ibid.
130   Case C-483/99 *Commission v France (golden shares – Société Nationale Elf-Aquitaine)*, para 28; Case 72/83 *Campus Oil Limited and others v Minister for Industry and Energy and others*, ECLI:EU:C:1984:256, paras 34-35.

State's internal and external security[131] and that therefore the Member States were entitled under Article 65 (1) (b) TFEU to adopt measures imposing the freezing of individuals funds in connection with the fight against international terrorism.[132]

ii) Derogations Applicable Only to Capital Movements to/from Third Countries

Capital movements to/from third countries are subject to further four derogations: Articles 64, 65(4), 66 and 75 TFEU.

The grandfather clause contained in Article 64 (1) TFEU allows Member States to maintain restrictions that existed on 31 December 1993 under national or Union law on capital movements to or from third countries involving direct investment – including in real estate – establishment, the provision of financial services or the admission of securities to capital markets.[133] According to the same article, in respect of restrictions existing under national law in Bulgaria, Estonia and Hungary, the relevant date shall be 31 December 1999. The Court has emphasised that the list of capital movements in Article 65 (1) TFEU is restrictive and therefore it does not cover capital movements which are not mentioned there, such as inheritances.[134]

Article 64 (2) and (3) and Article 65 (4) TFEU grant legislative powers to the Council to adopt secondary measures regarding capital movements with third countries. In more detail, Article 64 (2) TFEU is a legal basis provision which allows the European Parliament and the Council, acting in accordance with the ordinary legislative procedure, to adopt measures regarding the same types of capital movements to and from third countries as the ones referred to in Article 64 (1) TFEU. Furthermore, Article 64 (3) TFEU allows the Council, acting in accordance with a special legislative procedure, to unanimously, and after consulting the European Parliament, adopt measures which constitute a step backwards in Union law as regards the liberalisation of the movement of capital to or from third countries. Article 65 (4) TFEU allows the Council

---

131   This was already held in relation to the free movement of goods in Case C-367/89 *Aimé Richardt and Les Accessoires Scientifiques SNC*, ECLI:EU:C:1991:376, para 22.
132   Case T-315/01 *Yassin Abdullah Kadi v Council and Commission*, ECLI:EU:T:2005:332, para 110.
133   Alexandre Maitrot de la Motte, 'Les exceptions à la liberté européenne de circulation des capitaux: réflexions sur le champ d'application de l'article 64 TFUE' (2011) 24 *Revue de Droit Fiscal* 26.
134   Case C-181/12 *Welte*, paras 28-29.

to pronounce on the legality of restrictive tax measures adopted by Member States concerning third countries. It has been observed that Article 65 (4) TFEU bears a certain resemblance to Article 108 (2) (3) TFEU, which provides that on application of a Member State, the Council may, acting unanimously, declare certain state aids compatible with the internal market if such decision is justified by exceptional circumstances.[135]

Article 66 TFEU allows the Council, on a proposal from the Commission and after consulting the European Central Bank, to take safeguard measures where, in exceptional circumstances, movements of capital to or from third countries cause, or threaten to cause, serious difficulties for the operation of Economic and Monetary Union.[136] However, the safeguard measures must be strictly necessary and temporary, i.e. for a period not exceeding six months.

Fainally, Article 75 TFEU permits the freezing of funds, financial assets or economic gains belonging to, or owned or held by, natural or legal persons, groups or non-State entities in order to prevent and combat terrorism. This provision constitutes the legal basis for financial sanctions directed against individuals or non-State actors, not towards States.[137] Article 75 TFEU allows the European Parliament and the Council, acting by means of regulations in accordance with the ordinary legislative procedure, to define a framework for administrative measures with regard to capital movements and payments, such as the freezing of funds, financial assets or economic gains belonging to, or owned or held by, natural or legal persons, groups or non-State entities in order to prevent and combat terrorism and related activities. Those measures shall include necessary provisions on legal safeguards, which are intended to ensure that the right to an effective judicial protection of the individuals concerned is respected.

b) *Overriding Reasons in the Public Interest*

Apart from the exhaustive list of express derogations provided for in the Treaties, the Court has created a number of public interest requirements or overriding reasons in the public interest that justify restrictions on capital movements.[138] The definition of the overriding reasons in the public interest

---

[135] Jukka Snell, 'Free movement of capital: Evolution as a non-linear process' in Craig and De Búrca (eds), *The Evolution of EU Law* (Oxford University Press 2011), p. 553.

[136] Case C-101/05 *Skatteverket v A*, para 33.

[137] Bart Van Vooren and Ramses A. Wessel, *EU External Relations Law: Text, Cases and Materials* (Cambridge University Press 2014), p. 396.

[138] Case C-271/09 *Commission v Poland (pension funds)*, ECLI:EU:C:2011:855, para 55; Case C-274/06 *Commission v Spain (golden shares)*, para 35; Case C-112/05 *Commission v Germany*

lies in principle with the Member States, which can indeed decide on the degree or protection which they whish to afford to such legitimate interests and on the way which that protection is to be achieved within the limits prescribed by the principle of proportionality.[139] Thus, in relation to taxation, the Court has recognised as legitimate objectives the need to maintain a balanced allocation of the power to impose taxes between the Member States,[140] the objective of combatting tax evasion and avoidance,[141] the effectiveness of fiscal supervision,[142] the need to safeguard the cohesion of the tax system,[143] the need to ensure effective collection of tax[144] as well as the promotion of research and development.[145] In the field of investment in real estate, the case law acknowledges a town and country planning objective, such as maintaining a permanent population and an economic activity independent of the tourist

---

(*golden shares – Volkswagen I*), para 72; Case C-503/99 *Commission v Belgium* (*golden shares*), para 45; Case C-174/04 *Commission v Italy* (*golden shares*), para 35 ; Case C-309/99 *Wouters and others*, para 49 ; Case C-463/00 *Commission v Spain* (*golden shares*), para 68.

139 Joined cases C-282/04 and C-283/04 *Commission v The Netherlands* (*golden shares*), paras 32-33.

140 Case C-182/08 *Glaxo Wellcome*, paras 31 and 88.

141 Case C-282/12 *Itelcar*, paras 12 and 35.

142 Case C-446/04 *Test Claimants in the FII Group Litigation*, para 47; Case C-101/05 *Skatteverket v A*, para 55; Joined cases C-155/08 and C-157/08 *X and E. H. A. Passenheim-van Schoot v Staatssecretaris van Financiën*, ECLI:EU:C:2009:368, para 55; Case C-262/09 *Wienand Meilicke and Others v Finanzamt Bonn-Innenstadt*, ECLI:EU:C:2011:438, para 41; Case C-318/10 *Société d'investissement pour l'agriculture tropicale SA (SIAT) v État belge*, ECLI:EU:C:2012:415, para 36; Case C-326/12 *Rita van Caster and Patrick van Caster v Finanzamt Essen-Süd*, ECLI:EU:C:2014:2269, paras 46-47.

143 Case C-242/03 *Ministre des Finances v Jean-Claude Weidert and Élisabeth Paulus*, ECLI:EU:C:2004:465, paras 10 and 20-22; Case C-204/90 *Bachmann*, para 28; Case C-300/90 *Commission v Belgium*, para 21; Case C-55/98 *Skatteministeriet v Bent Vestergaard*, ECLI:EU:C:1999:533, para 24 ; Case C-436/00 *X and Y*, para 52; Case C-251/98 *Baars*, para 40; Case C-168/01 *Bosal*, ECLI:EU:C:2003:479, para 30; Case C-315/02 *Anneliese Lenz*, para 35. In a nutshell, in this case law, the Court explained that in order to be able to justify their national legislation granting tax relief under certain conditions on the need to safeguard the cohesion of the tax system, Member States must demonstrate that there is a direct link between the grant of a tax advantage and the offsetting of that advantage by a fiscal levy, and that link has to be maintained to preserve the cohesion of the tax system concerned.

144 Case C-318/10 *SIAT*, para 64; Case C-498/10 *X NV v Staatssecretaris van Financiën*, ECLI:EU:C:2012:635, para 39; Joined cases C53/13 and C80/13 *Strojírny Prostějov et ACO Industries Tábor*, ECLI:EU:C:2014:2011, para 46; Case C-326/12 *Rita van Caster*, paras 46-47.

145 Case C-10/10 *Commission v Austria* (*Gifts for Teaching and Research Institutions*), ECLI:EU:C:2011:399, para 37; Case C-39/04 *Laboratoires Fournier*, ECLI:EU:C:2005:161, para 23.

sector in certain regions,[146] the need to preserve the farming of agricultural land by means of owner-occupancy and to ensure that agricultural property be occupied and farmed predominantly by the owners,[147] the need to preserve a permanent agricultural community, to sustain and develop viable agriculture and to encourage a reasonable use of the available land by resisting pressure on land and by preventing natural disasters[148] and the protection of the environment.[149] As regards direct investments, the Court has recognised that the objective of guaranteeing a service of general interest, such as universal postal service[150] or adequate investment in the electricity and gas distribution systems constitute overriding reasons in the public interests.[151] Requirements related to public housing policy in a Member State and to the financing of that policy are also regarded as overriding reasons in the public interest.[152] Finally, in relation to collective investment undertakings, the Court has held that the need to guarantee the stability and security of the assets administered by an undertaking for collective investment created by a severance fund, in particular by the adoption of prudential rules constitutes an imperative reason of public interest capable of justifying capital restrictions.[153]

The list of overriding reasons in the public interests is an open-ended list, which however, in principle does not cover interests of an economic nature. Indeed, according to the traditional internal market approach, grounds of a purely economic nature cannot constitute overriding reasons in the public interest justifying a restriction of a fundamental freedom guaranteed by the Treaties.[154] In the context of the free movement of capital, the Court has explicitly ruled out objectives such as choosing a strategic partner, strengthening the

---

146 Case C-302/97 *Konle*, para 40; Joined cases C-515/99, C-519/99 to C-524/99 and C-526/99 to C-540/99 *Reisch*, para 34.
147 Case C-370/05 *Festersen*, paras 27-28; The Court observed that these objectives are also consistent with those of the common agricultural policy.
148 Case C-452/01 *Margarethe Ospelt*, paras 38-40.
149 Joined cases C-515/99, C-519/99 to C-524/99 and C-526/99 to C-540/99 *Reisch*, para 34.
150 Joined cases C-282/04 and C-283/04 *Commission v The Netherlands (golden shares)*, para 38.
151 Joined cases C-105/12 to C-107/12 *Essent NV*, para 59; Case 72/83 *Campus Oil*, paras 34-35; Case Case C-503/99 *Commission v Belgium (golden shares)*, para 46; Case C-174/04 *Commission v Italy (golden shares)*, para 40.
152 Case C-567/07 *Sint Servatius*.
153 Case C-39/11 *VBV – Vorsorgekasse*, paras 18 and 31. By analogy the same applies to pension funds, see Case C-271/09 *Commission v Poland (pension funds)*, para 57.
154 Joined cases C-105/12 to C-107/12 *Essent NV*, para 51; Case C-388/01 *Commission v Italy (golden shares)*, ECLI:EU:C:2003:30, para 22; Case C-109/04 *Karl Robert Kranemann v Land Nordrhein-Westfalen*, ECLI:EU:C:2005:187, para 34; Case C-35/98 *Verkooijen*,

competitive structure of the market or modernising and increasing the efficiency of means of the production.[155] However, in recent case law, it seems that the Court is attempting to introduce certain nuances as to the economic nature of some interests. In particular, in *Essent*, it reasoned that national legislation might constitute a justified restriction on a fundamental freedom when it is dictated by reasons of an economic nature *in the pursuit of an objective in the public interest*.[156] This reasoning led to the conclusion that the objectives of combatting cross-subsidisation in order to achieve transparency in the electricity and gas markets and to prevent distortions of competition could constitute overriding reasons in the public interest capable of justifying restrictions on free movement of capital.[157] By the same token, the reasons underlying the choice of the rules of property ownership adopted by the national legislation within the scope of Article 345 TFEU were regarded as factors, which might be taken into consideration as circumstances capable of justifying restrictions on the free movement of capital.[158]

5   Proportionality

The proportionality assessment consists of a tripartite test: firstly, the suitability test, which examines whether the measure is suitable/appropriate to achieve the objective pursued; secondly, the necessity test, which examines whether the measure is necessary in order to achieve the objective pursued, namely whether there are other less restrictive measures capable of producing the same result; and thirdly, the *proportionality stricto sensu*, which examines whether, in case there are no less restrictive means, the measure does not have an excessive effect on the applicant's interests.[159] However, in internal market case law, the third step is often subsumed within the second step and the Court

---

para 48; Case C-120/95 *Nicolas Decker v Caisse de maladie des employés privés*, ECLI:EU:C:1998:167, para 39; Case C-158/96 *Raymond Kohll v Union des caisses de maladie*, ECLI:EU:C:1998:171, para 41; Case C-398/95 *Syndesmos ton en Elladi Touristikon kai Taxidiotikon Grafeion v Ypourgos Ergasias*, ECLI:EU:C:1997:282, para 23; Case C-288/89 *Gouda and Others*, ECLI:EU:C:1991:323, para 11; Case 352/85 *Bond van Adverteerders and others v The Netherlands State*, ECLI:EU:C:1988:196, para 34; Case 7-61 *Commission v Italy*, ECLI:EU:C:1961:31. See also Peter Oliver, 'When, if ever, can restrictions on free movement be justified on economic grounds' (2016) 41 *European Law Review* 147.

155   Case C-309/99 *Wouters and others*, para 52.
156   Joined cases C-105/12 to C-107/12 *Essent NV*, para 52.
157   Ibid, para 56 et seq.
158   Ibid, para 55.
159   Takis Tridimas, 'The principle of proportionality' in Robert Schütze and Takis Tridimas (eds), *Oxford principles of European Union law Volume 1, The European Union legal order* (Oxford University Press 2018), pp. 243–264, at p. 247; Takis Tridimas, *The General*

employs in essence a two-stage test consisting of the suitability and the necessity assessment.[160]

In the area of the free movement of capital, the principle of legal certainty appears sometimes as a third requirement in the proportionality assessment, in addition to the suitability and necessity tests. Legal certainty is a fundamental principle of EU law which requires that rules should be clear and precise so that individuals may ascertain unequivocally what their rights and obligations are and may take steps accordingly.[161] An illustration of the application of the principle of legal certainty is provided in *Eglise de Scientologie*,[162] where the Court held that the French system of prior authorisation for certain categories of direct foreign investments was not consistent with the principle of legal certainty and as such it constituted an infringement of the free movement of capital. Although the system was justifiable on public-policy and public-security grounds, it was deemed to be incompatible with the free movement of capital, as the investors concerned were given no indication as to the specific circumstances in which prior authorisation was required.[163] Such lack of precision did not enable individuals to be apprised of the extent of their rights and obligations deriving from Article 63 TFEU and, therefore, it was contrary to the principle of legal certainty.[164] Systems of prior authorisation are usually regarded to be disproportionate when they lack precision or when a system of declaration could have achieved the same objective.[165] Unlike a system of

---

Principles of EU law (Oxford University Press 2006), p. 139; Paul Craig, *EU Administrative Law* (Oxford University Press 2012), p. 592.

160 Vasiliki Kosta, 'The principle of proportionality in EU law: an interest-based taxonomy' in Joana Mendes (ed), *EU Executive Discretion and the Limits of Law* (Oxford University Press 2019), pp. 198–219.

161 Case 169/80 *Administration des douanes v Société anonyme Gondrand Frères and Société anonyme Garancini*, ECLI:EU:C:1981:171, para 17; Case C-143/93 *Gebroeders van Es Douane Agenten BV v Inspecteur der Invoerrechten en Accijnzen*, ECLI:EU:C:1996:45, para 27; Case C-110/03 *Belgium v Commission*, ECLI:EU:C:2005:223, para 30; Case C-158/06 *Stichting ROM-projecten v Staatssecretaris van Economische Zaken*, ECLI:EU:C:2007:370, para 25; Case C-308/06 *The Queen, on the application of International Association of Independent Tanker Owners (Intertanko) and Others v Secretary of State for Transport*, ECLI:EU:C:2008:312, para 69; Case C-201/08 *Plantanol GmbH & Co KG v Hauptzollamt Darmstadt*, ECLI:EU:C:2009:539, para 46; Case C-344/04 *The Queen, on the application of International Air Transport Association and European Low Fares Airline Association v Department for Transport*, ECLI:EU:C:2006:10, para 68.

162 Case C-54/99 *Association Eglise de scientologie de Paris*.

163 Ibid, para 21.

164 Ibid, para 22.

165 Joined cases C-163/94, C-165/94 and C-250/94 *Sanz de Lera*, paras 20-27. The same reasoning was also followed in Joined cases C-358/93 and C-416/93 *Bordessa*, paras 25-27; Joined cases 286/82 and 26/83 *Luisi and Carbone*, para 34; and Case C-302/97 *Konle*, para 44.

prior authorisation, a system of declarations *'would not suspend the operation concerned but would nevertheless enable the national authorities to carry out, in order to uphold public policy, effective supervision to prevent infringements of national law and regulations'.*[166]

---

[166] C-416/93 *Bordessa*, para 27.

CHAPTER 2

Free Movement of Capital and Privatisations

1   The Theoretical Underpinnings of Privatisation*

A   *Definition of Privatisation*
Privatisation is a particularly complex economic policy issue which involves different stakeholders and conflicting economic and societal interests that need to be reconciled. Some argue that privatisation should be a priority for national governments, as it brings significant efficiency gains and reduces the level of public debt, while some others believe that privatisation is not always desirable especially when it comes to public utilities that are essential for the society as a whole and network industries where it is difficult or even impossible to achieve well-functioning competitive markets. In light of the inconclusive economic evidence, the consensus position among OECD countries is that a government should not privatise a State-owned enterprise before an appropriate and trasperent regulatory framework has been established.[1]

The question to privatise or not to privatise has always been at the centre of public discourse on State intervention in the market, raising crucial economic, political, social and legal issues. Historically associated with Ronald Reagan and Margaret Thatcher, privatisation has been championed by proponents of laissez-faire capitalism as an economic policy leading to increased economic efficiency[2] and to a significant alleviation of public finances through the use of

---

*   This chapter expands on ideas previously discussed in earlier publications: Ilektra Antonaki, 'Free movement of Capital and Privatisation of Public Utilities' in Despina Anagnostopoulou, Lina Papadopoulou, Ioannis Papadopoulos (eds.), *The EU at a Crossroads: Challenges and Perspectives* (Cambridge Scholars Publishing 2016), pp. 73-95; Ilektra Antonaki, 'Free movement of capital and protection of social objectives in the EU: Critical reflections on the case law regarding golden shares and privatisations' in Sacha Garben & Inge Govaere, *The Internal Market 2.0.* (Oxford: Hart Publishing, 2020), pp. 161-184.
1   OECD, *Privatisation in the 21st Century: Recent Experiences of OECD Countries* (2009), p. 13.
2   Ann P. Bartel and Ann E. Harrison, 'Ownership versus Environment: Disentangling the Sources of Public-Sector Inefficiency' (2005) 87 *The Review of Economics and Statistics* 135; Madanmohan Ghosh and John Whalley, 'State Owned Enterprises, Shirking and Trade Liberalization' (2008) 25 *Economic Modelling* 1206; William L. Megginson and Jeffry M. Netter, 'From State to Market: A Survey of Empirical Studies on Privatization' (2001) 39 *Journal of Economic Literature* 321; Muiris MacCarthaigh, 'Managing state-owned enterprises in an age of crisis: an analysis of Irish experience' (2011) 32 *Policy Studies* 215; Kathryn L. Dewenter and Paul H. Malatesta, 'State-owned and privately-owned firms: an empirical analysis of profitability, leverage, and labor intensity' (2001) 91 *American Economic Review* 320.

cash revenues for the purposes of redeeming public debt.[3] Although the rapid public sector expansion that took place in the 1960s and 1970s was regarded as a major contributor not only to economic growth but also to social and political stability, the general perception of the State's intervention in the market was seriously questioned in the mid-1970s as a result of the oil crises.[4] The inability of economies to adjust to external prices shocks led to a significant deterioration in macroeconomic performances and part of the blame was laid on the inflexible large public sectors.[5] In Europe, the *first* and most prominent privatisation wave started in the UK in the 1980s as part of the economic policy followed by Margaret Thatcher.[6] This privatisation wave marked the beginning of a new era of economic policy and political ideology, commonly referred to as 'neoliberalism'.[7] A conventional wisdom was developed that private management and ownership was better than public ownership, as it would bring economic efficiency and it would reduce corruption rates.[8] The ideological doctrine of unfettered free market, deregulation, liberalisation and privatisation became the orthodox economic thinking and the drive to cut State intervention soon spread to the rest of Europe at a remarkable rate.[9] After the fall of the Berlin Wall and the subsequent decline of Communism in Europe, Central and Eastern European countries experienced the *second* privatisation wave in the form of large privatisation schemes aiming at reducing the large public

---

3   Bernardo Bortolotti, Marcella Fantini and Domenico Siniscalco, 'Privatization around the world: evidence from panel data' (2004) 88 *Journal of Public Economics Journal of Public Economics* 305.
4   Richard Hemming and Ali M. Mansoor, *Privatization and Public Enterprises* (IMF, Occasional Paper No 56, 1988), p. 1.
5   Ibid.
6   William Keegan, *Mrs. Thatcher's Economic Experiment* (Penguin 1984); Leaders, 'Privatisation – The $9 trillion sale' *The Economist* (11 January 2014); Tony Prosser and Michael Moran, 'Privatization and Regulatory Change: The Case of Great Britain' in Michael Moran and Tony Prosser (eds), *Privatization and Regulatory Change in Europe* (Open University Press 1994), pp. 35–49.
7   See Kean Birch and Vlad Mykhnenko, 'Varieties of neoliberalism? Restructuring in large industrially dependent regions across Western and Eastern Europe' (2009) 9 *Journal of Economic Geography* 355, at p. 356 referring to Colin Hay, 'The normalizing role of rationalist assumptions in the institutional embedding of neoliberalism' (2004) 33 *Economy and Society* 500 and Wendy Larner, 'Neo-liberalism: policy, ideology, governmentality' (2000) 63 *Studies in Political Economy* 5.
8   Joseph Stiglitz, 'Foreword' in Gérard Roland (ed), *Privatization: Successes and Failures* (Columbia University Press 2008), p. IX.
9   Elke Loeffler, Dominik Sobczak and Frankie Hine-Hughes, *Liberalisation and privatisation in the EU – Services of general interest and the roles of the public sector* (Multi-Science Publishing, European Union 2012).

sectors associated with the former communist regimes and at increasing public revenues.[10] Finally, as a result of the eurocrisis, European states with a high public debt are experiencing the *third* privatisation wave: they have committed to implement an extensive privatisation programme of state-owned assets in a number of key sectors, such as energy, ports, airports, motorways, railways, mining, water supply, waste management, defence industries and real estate assets with a view to reduce the level of public debt and improve public finances.[11]

According to the IMF, privatisation is defined as a *transfer of ownership and control* from the public to the private sector, with particular reference to asset sales.[12] It is therefore equated to total or partial denationalisation and it is the opposite of nationalisation.[13] Similarly, according to the definition given by the OECD, privatisation is any material transaction by which the State's ultimate *ownership* of corporate entities is reduced.[14] This includes direct divestment by the State, divestment of corporate assets by government-controlled investment vehicles as well as the dilution of state positions in State-owned enterprises by secondary share offerings to the non-state shareholders.[15] It may also include some instances of divestment of subsidiaries by State-owned enterprises, when this is a result of government decisions rather than reflecting purely commercial considerations.[16] The definition of privatisation suggested by the OECD does not encompass the transfer of certain commercial activities from State-owned enterprises to private operators through different forms of public-private partnership such as through concessions, delegated management contracts or leasing.[17] By the same token, the dilution of government control over incorporated entities through cancellation of golden shares, share class unifications or changes to the articles of association are excluded from

---

10 Briefing, 'State-owned assets – Setting out the store' *The Economist* (11 January 2014).
11 Eurosummit, *Euro Summit Statement, Brussels, 12 July 2015* (SN 4070/15, 2015).
12 Richard Hemming and Ali M. Mansoor, *Privatization and Public Enterprises* (1988), p. 1. In this paper, it is stated that the words 'privatise' and 'privatisation' appeared for the first time in the 1983 edition of the Webster's Ninth New Collegiate Dictionary, where their earliest recorded use is given as being in 1948. However, S.H. Hanke claims responsibility for popularising these words while serving on the U.S. President's Council of Economic Advisers in 1982 and 1982 (*Washington Post*, January 13, 1986).
13 Ibid.
14 OECD, *Privatisation in the 21st Century: Recent Experiences of OECD Countries* (Report on Good Practices, 2009).
15 Ibid.
16 Ibid.
17 Ibid.

the definition of privatisation.[18] Therefore, the crucial element is the *transfer of corporate assets* from the State to private actors, not the mere transfer of commercial activities.[19]

The method through which privatisation is usually organised depends on the country's characteristics in terms of capital market development and legal infrastructure, the size and nature of the enterprise concerned and the objectives the privatisation seeks to achieve.[20] The most common methods of privatisation include initial public offerings in the capital markets, trade sales to strategic investors, management/employee buy-outs and asset sales, often following the liquidation of the State-owned enterprise concerned.[21]

The term *privatisation* should be distinguished from that of *liberalisation*. While privatisation refers to the transfer of ownership from the public to the private sector, liberalisation refers to the opening up of a specific market sector to competition. It represents essentially a programme of regulatory changes in the direction of moving towards a free-market economy.[22] It is true that more often than not market liberalisation goes hand in hand with the privatisation of public assets, as evidenced in Europe in the early 1990s.[23] However, this does not mean that the one presupposes the other. In fact, the liberalisation of an economic sector can be effected without prior privatisation. In such a scenario, the public enterprise will continue to exist after the liberalisation, but it will no longer enjoy a monopolistic position in the market. It will have to compete with the new private entrants that will emerge as a result of the introduction of competition to the previously closed market. Conversely, a public monopoly can be privatised without a parallel liberalisation of the relevant market. In that case, the public monopoly is transformed into a private monopoly, which, in the absence of competition, will continue to act under the same monopolistic market conditions. Economic studies suggest that efficiency gains are most likely to result from the privatisation of public monopolies only if this

---

18   Ibid.
19   Ibid.
20   Stilpon Nestor and Ladan Mahboodi, 'Privatisation of public utilities: the OECD experience' in OECD (ed), *Privatisation, competition and regulation* (OECD 2000), p. 13.
21   Ibid, p. 13.
22   John Black, Nigar Hashimzade and Gareth Myles, *A Dictionary of Economics*, (Oxford University Press 2009).
23   Erika Szyszczak, *The Regulation of the State in Competitive Markets in the EU* (Hart Publishing 2007), p. 3; Niamh Dunne, *Competition Law and Economic Regulation – Making and Managing Markets* (Cambridge University Press 2015), p. 149; Bertrand Badie, Dirk Berg-Schlosser and Leonardo Morlino, *International Encyclopedia of Political Science* (SAGE Publications 2011).

is combined with the liberalisation of the relevant market.[24] The transfer of a public monopoly to the private sector, with its monopoly power left intact, may not achieve increased productive or allocative efficiency.[25] More importantly, evidence has shown that the privatisation of a previously public monopoly of a network industry, such as the railway system in the UK, may even threaten safety standards through the cutting of resources devoted to the maintenance of such safety standards.[26] It is for this reason that the economists of the IMF support the view that economic efficiency and respect for fundamental public interest considerations can only be achieved if privatisation is combined with liberalisation, in order to foster competition, and by regulation in order to prevent anticompetitive practices and socially disruptive results.[27] In the same vein, economists of the OECD underline that privatisation and competition need to be pursued *in tandem*.[28] In fact, the consensus position among OECD countries is that a government should not privatise an State owned enterprise before an appropriate regulatory framework has been established.[29] This appropriate regulatory framework consists of the introduction of a general and a sectorial anti-trust and enforcement mechanism and the creation of independent regulatory agencies.[30]

B   *The Theoretical Controversy about Privatisation*

The extensive privatisation schemes that were adopted during the previous decades led to a significant expansion of the scholarly research on the economic and social consequences of privatisation.[31] Today, the existing literature

---

[24]   Richard Hemming and Ali M. Mansoor, *Privatization and Public Enterprises* (1988), p. 2.
[25]   Ibid, p. 2. See also Tony Prosser, *The limits of competition law: markets and public services* (Oxford University Press 2005), p. 19; Richard Posner, *Antitrust Law* (The University of Chicago Press 2001) and Robert Bork, *Antitrust Paradox* (Simon & Schuster 1993).
[26]   Tony Prosser, *The limits of competition law: markets and public services* (Oxford University Press 2005), p. 22.
[27]   Richard Hemming and Ali M. Mansoor, *Privatization and Public Enterprises* (1988), p. 2.
[28]   Stilpon Nestor and Ladan Mahboobi, 'Privatisation of public utilities: the OECD experience' in OECD (ed), *Privatisation, competition and regulation* (OECD 2000), p. 18.
[29]   OECD, *Privatisation in the 21st Century: Recent Experiences of OECD Countries* (2009), p. 13.
[30]   Ibid, p. 13.
[31]   Gérard Roland (ed), *Privatization: Successes and Failures* (Columbia University Press 2008); John Vickers and Vincent Wright (eds), *The Politics of Privatisation in Western Europe* (Routledge 2005); Michael Moran and Tony Prosser (eds), *Privatization and Regulatory Change in Europe* (Open University Press 1994); Joseph Stiglitz, *The Economic Role of the State* (Blackwell 1989); Stilpon Nestor and Ladan Mahboobi, 'Privatisation of public utilities: the OECD experience' in OECD (ed), *Privatisation, competition and regulation* (OECD 2000); Raj Chari, *Life After Privatization* (Oxford University Press 2015).

largely confirms that the process of privatisation can generate economic efficiency gains for the previously State-owned enterprises. Privatisation is regarded as a necessary dimension to the internationalisation of the economy.[32] The ideological embracement of privatisation is premised exactly on the economic objectives that are being achieved through the process of privatisation. From the standpoint of economic analysis, privatisation is primarily regarded as a means of improving the economic efficiency of enterprises.[33] In particular, privatisation limits the scope for corruption, clientelism and political interference in decision making,[34] increases managerial incentives by making managers responsible to shareholders who will monitor their performance better than governments and impose the financial discipline of private capital markets.[35] This combination of factors can lead to increased economic efficiency of previously State-owned enterprises. An example of a successful privatisation scheme was the one undertaken in the telecommunications sector in the EU. The privatisation of national telecommunications organisations together with the liberalisation of this market and establishment of a robust regulatory framework led to increased economic efficiency of the undertakings concerned, enhanced competition, lower prices for consumers and better customer services.[36]

The second argument in favour of privatisation relates to its impact on government finances. More precisely, privatisation may lead to a reduction of public deficit, especially if it concerns loss-making enterprises.[37] In fact, in cases of governments facing serious liquidity constraints, the financing of fiscal deficits with the privatisation proceeds is perhaps the most obvious objective of privatisation schemes.[38] In the same vein, governments facing long-lasting debt may use privatisation proceeds in order to reduce public debt.[39] A reduction in

---

32 Erika Szyszczak, 'Golden Shares and Market Governance' (2002) 29 Legal Issues of Economic Integration 255, p. 258.
33 Richard Hemming and Ali M. Mansoor, *Privatization and Public Enterprises* (1988), p. 6; Olivier Bouin, *The Privatisation in Developing Countries: Reflections on a Panacea* (OECD 1992).
34 Joseph Stiglitz, 'Foreword' in Roland (ed), *Privatization: Successes and Failures* (Columbia University Press 2008), p. x.
35 Richard Hemming and Ali M. Mansoor, *Privatization and Public Enterprises* (1988), p. 6.
36 Viktor Mayer-Schonberger and Mathias Strasser, 'Closer look at telecom deregulation: The european advantage' (1998) 12 *Harvard Journal of Law and Technology* 561.
37 Richard Hemming and Ali M. Mansoor, *Privatization and Public Enterprises* (1988), p. 6.
38 Stilpon Nestor and Ladan Mahboodi, 'Privatisation of public utilities: the OECD experience' in OECD (ed), *Privatisation, competition and regulation* (OECD 2000), p. 11.
39 Yannis Katsoulakos and Elissavet Likoyanni, *Fiscal and Other Macroeconomic Effects of Privatization* (FEEM Working Paper No 1132002, 2002), p. 19.

public debt leads in turn to a reduction in fiscal deficit through a decline in net interest payments.[40] This is particularly important for the Member States participating in the Economic and Monetary Union, which presupposes compliance with strict public debt and public deficit criteria. Research has shown that privatisation policies in southern Europe (Spain, Italy, Portugal and Greece) during the 1990s were used by national governments as a short-term economic policy intended to fulfil the convergence criteria in order to allow participation in monetary integration.[41] It has been argued that privatisation schemes might not have been used in order to serve pure economic purposes (such as the economic restructuring and efficiency of the undertakings concerned), but to pursue wider political objectives.[42]

Furthermore, privatisation has significant benefits for the development of a capital market and a market for corporate control.[43] More specifically, enterprises can gain access to private sector financing through privatisation and can spur the development of domestic capital markets as a means of channelling savings in the economy.[44] The British extensive privatisation programme constitutes one of the most successful examples of how privatisation can contribute to the development of equity markets and to the creation of a wide share owning class.[45] If the public assets in question are attractive also to small investors, this can broaden share ownership (ownership diffusion) and foster popular capitalism.[46]

Finally, privatisation may also benefit enterprises that remain within the public sector after the privatisation process, primarily through improvements to existing incentive and control mechanisms.[47] The remaining public

---

40 Ibid, p. 19.
41 Venilde Jeronimo, José Pagán and Gökçe Soydemir, 'Privatization and European Economic and Monetary Union' (2000) 26 *Eastern Economic Journal* 321.
42 Ibid, p. 325.
43 Yannis Katsoulakos and Elissavet Likoyanni, *Fiscal and Other Macroeconomic Effects of Privatization* (2002), p. 6. See also Charlie Weir, 'The Market for Corporate Control' in Douglas Michael Wright, Donald S. Siegel, Kevin Keasey and Igor Filatotchev (eds), *The Oxford Handbook of Corporate Governance* (Oxford University Press 2013), pp. 329–346.
44 Richard Hemming and Ali M. Mansoor, *Privatization and Public Enterprises* (1988), p. 6.
45 Bernardo Bortolotti and Valentina Milella, 'Privatization in Western Europe: Stylized Facts, Outcomes, and Open Issues' in Gérard Roland (ed), *Privatization: Successes and Failures* (Columbia University Press 2008), p. 50.
46 Richard Hemming and Ali M. Mansoor, *Privatization and Public Enterprises* (1988), p. 6; Bernardo Bortolotti and Valentina Milella, 'Privatization in Western Europe: Stylized Facts, Outcomes, and Open Issues' in Roland (ed), *Privatization: Successes and Failures* (Columbia University Press 2008), p. 60.
47 Richard Hemming and Ali M. Mansoor, *Privatization and Public Enterprises* (1988), p. 6.

enterprises (not programmed for sale) may be subject to increased corporate governance rigour and may be forced to implement reforms and to modernize their production systems so as to better respond to consumers' demands and to remain competitive in liberalised market.[48] Furthermore, governments can transfer certain commercial enterprises to the private sector and can focus better on the performance of public enterprises that pursue certain social objectives.

While privatisation has gained ground as an economic policy that improves economic efficiency of State-owned enterprises, there are still economic and non-economic arguments in favour of public ownership.

First, public ownership is regarded to be conducive to the attainment of social objectives.[49] In particular, through public ownership of certain enterprises the State can achieve distributional objectives, such as public-service delivery and widespread access to essential goods and services at reasonable and affordable prices for the consumers.[50] Additionally, public ownership can be used to create employment or to prevent rising unemployment and to combat social inequalities especially in developing countries.[51] Conversely, private ownership or the privatisation of public assets has been associated with adverse employment consequences, such as collective redundancies or insecure employment relations,[52] cutbacks in redistribution and has stirred popular discontent in many countries because of the corruption and cronyism that have stained the reputation of many privatisation processes.[53] An example of this can be found in the 'voucher privatisation programs' (transfer of public assets for free or nominal cost) undertaken by the former Soviet Union and many Eastern European countries that ultimately led to the creation of oligarch-controlled private monopolies.[54]

---

48 Stilpon Nestor and Ladan Mahboodi, 'Privatisation of public utilities: the OECD experience' in OECD (ed), *Privatisation, competition and regulation* (OECD 2000), p. 19.
49 Richard Hemming and Ali M. Mansoor, *Privatization and Public Enterprises* (1988), p. 3.
50 Ibid, p. 3; OECD, *The Size and Sectoral Distribution of SOEs in OECD and Partner Countries* (OECD Publishing 2014).
51 Richard Hemming and Ali M. Mansoor, *Privatization and Public Enterprises* (1988), p. 4.
52 Ibid, p. 4.
53 Gérard Roland (ed), *Privatization: Successes and Failures* (Columbia University Press 2008), pp. 1–2.
54 Jomo Kwame Sundaram, 'A Critical Review of the Evolving Privatization Debate' in Gérard Roland (ed), *Privatization: Successes and Failures* (Columbia University Press 2008), p. 200; John Nellis, *The World Bank, privatization, and enterprise reform in transition economies: a retrospective analysis* (The World Bank Operations Evaluation Department, 2002).

Furthermore, public ownership can be regarded as a response to the failure of private markets to secure efficient outcomes, particularly in countries with weaker regulatory frameworks or in 'network industries' characterised by natural monopoly, such as electricity and gas distribution, water provision and railways.[55] Natural monopolies have traditionally been perceived as rendering competition undesirable or even unfeasible, as the duplication of the network is economically and environmentally difficult and in some case even impossible.[56] In the absence of competition, a privatisation of a natural monopoly linked to the performance of 'universal service obligations' could lead to abuse and distortion of competition, as private monopolists may produce and price at levels which are not socially optimal.[57] In this respect, the privatisation of British railways is often cited as an example of an unsuccessful privatisation which has led to higher prices for consumers, delays, reduced quality of services as well as lower investment in infrastructure and innovation.[58]

Moreover, the maintenance of State control over sectors considered of 'strategic' national interest, such as oil and gas is considered to be another important reason justifying public ownership.[59] Nationalisation of strategic enterprises can act as a safety net to guarantee that the country will not depend on potentially unreliable external sources of supply.[60]

Finally, public ownership can also be used to foster sectors that might not otherwise be developed through private investment: for instance, private investors might be reluctant to finance research and development if the gains are difficult to capitalise on.[61] Other examples of services, which are usually provided by the public sector, include defence and police, environmental protection and the public provision of medical care.[62] In the same vein, many developing countries can benefit from public production in order to develop

---

55   Przemyslaw Kowalski and others, *State-Owned Enterprises, Trade Effects and Policy Implications* (OECD Trade Policy Papers No 147, 2013).
56   Richard Whish and David Bailey, *Competition Law* (Oxford University Press 2012), p. 10.
57   Przemyslaw Kowalski, Max Büge, Monika Sztajerowska and Matias Egeland, *State-Owned Enterprises, Trade Effects and Policy Implications* (2013).
58   Editorial, 'The Guardian view on rail privatisation: going off the tracks' *The Guardian* (05-12-2017) <https://www.theguardian.com/commentisfree/2017/dec/05/the-guardian-view-on-rail-privatisation-going-off-the-tracks> accessed 31-12-2019.
59   OECD, *The Size and Sectoral Distribution of SOEs in OECD and Partner Countries* (OECD Publishing 2014).
60   Richard Hemming and Ali M. Mansoor, *Privatization and Public Enterprises* (1988), p. 4.
61   Przemyslaw Kowalski, Max Büge, Monika Sztajerowska and Matias Egeland, *State-Owned Enterprises, Trade Effects and Policy Implications* (2013).
62   Richard Hemming and Ali M. Mansoor, *Privatization and Public Enterprises* (1988), p. 3.

their infrastructure and their markets, especially in cases where private returns to investment are not sufficiently attractive to private investors.[63]

These arguments explain why, despite ambitious privatisation programmes undertaken in recent decades, many governments nonetheless maintain public ownership in commercial enterprises in strategically sensitive sectors such as electricity and gas, transportation and finance. More precisely, according to a recent OECD report on State-ownership in 34 countries (of which 31 are OECD members), State-owned enterprises value at over USD 2 trillion and employ about 6 million people.[64] Interestingly, the largest SOE sectors in the OECD are found in four European countries: Norway, France, Slovenia and Finland.[65]

II   Privatisation and EU law

A   *The Politico-economic Context*

The question of State participation in the market has shaped the political and economic debate in Europe. Since its very creation, the European project has been conceived as an arduous endeavour to achieve a political compromise between different national interests and to strike a balance between market-driven integration and social objectives. The dividing line between public and private sphere in the economy is not drawn uniformly across the EU.[66] While privatisation has indeed become a widespread phenomenon in all Member States, resulting in major shifts of resources from the public to the private sector, it nevertheless follows different methods in each Member State and leads to different limitations on State participation in the market.[67]

The degree of State participation in the market within individual Member States has been determined by national economic policy objectives. These objectives have often been translated into politico-economic ideologies and have deeply affected not only the market economy systems of the Member

---

63   Ibid, p. 3.
64   OECD, *The Size and Sectoral Distribution of SOEs in OECD and Partner Countries* (OECD Publishing 2014), p. 7. See also Hans Christiansen, *The Size and Composition of the SOE Sector in OECD Countries* (OECD Corporate Governance Working Papers, No 5, 2011).
65   OECD, *The Size and Sectoral Distribution of SOEs in OECD and Partner Countries* (OECD Publishing 2014).
66   Wolf Sauter and Harm Schepel, *State and Market in European Union Law – The Public and Private Spheres of the Internal Market before the EU Courts* (Cambridge University Press 2009), p. 21.
67   Ibid, pp. 19–21.

States but also the European Economic Constitution.[68] The European Economic Constitution is broadly described as consisting of the constitutional principles of direct effect and primacy and of the substantive rules on the Internal Market and Competition Law, complemented by the rules on the Economic and Monetary Union and the Common Commercial Policy.[69] Its content has been inspired primarily by the German ordoliberal tradition focusing on market liberalisation, private autonomy, economic freedoms, strict adherence to competition rules, fiscal discipline and a diminished public sector.[70] Although over the years ordoliberalism might have become diluted throught the influence of neo-classic mainstream economics and the difference between Anglo-Saxon and ordoliberal traditions might have become practically ever less visible,[71] its historical legacy has at the same time been strengthened.[72] The ordoliberal theory or 'the Freiburg school of law and economics',[73] as described

---

68 Wolf Sauter, 'The Economic Constitution of the European Union' (1998) 4 *Columbia Journal of European Law* 27; Christian Joerges, 'The European Economic Constitution and its Transformation Through the Financial Crisis' in Dennis Patterson and Anna Södersten (eds), *A Companion to European Union law and International Law* (Wiley & Sons 2013); Joseph Weiler, 'The Transformation of Europe' (1991) 100 *The Yale Law Journal* 2403; Martin Shapiro, 'Comparative Law and Comparative Politics' (1980) 53 *California Law Review* 537; Wolf Sauter and Harm Schepel, *State and Market in European Union Law – The Public and Private Spheres of the Internal Market before the EU Courts* (Cambridge University Press 2009), pp. 11–18; Leontin-Jean Constantinesco, 'La constitution économique de la C.E.E' (1977) 13 *Revue Trimestrielle de Droit Européen* 244; Wolf Sauter and Harm Schepel, *State and Market in European Union Law – The Public and Private Spheres of the Internal Market before the EU Courts* (Cambridge University Press 2009), p. 11.

69 Erika Szyszczak, *The Regulation of the State in Competitive Markets in the EU* (Hart Publishing 2007), p. 29.

70 Wolf Sauter, 'The Economic Constitution of the European Union' (1998) 4 Columbia Journal of European Law 27, p. 49.

71 The differences between ordoliberalism and classical liberalism were defined by Michel Foucault in 1970 and with the republication of his lectures they have attracted anew scholarly attention. See Michel Foucault, *The Birth of Biopolitics: Lectures at the Collège de France 1978–1979* (Basingstoke: Palgrave-Macmillan 2008); Josef Hien and Christian Joerges, *Ordoliberalism, Law and the Rule of Economics* (Hart Publishing 2017), p. 2.

72 Josef Hien and Christian Joerges, *Ordoliberalism, Law and the Rule of Economics* (Hart Publishing 2017), p. 2.

73 Friedrich A. von Hayek, *Der Wettbewerb als Entdeckungsverfahren* (Kiel 1968); Josef Hien and Christian Joerges, *Ordoliberalism, Law and the Rule of Economics* (Hart Publishing 2017), p. 3; Manfred Streit, 'Economic Order, Private Law and Public Policy: The Freiburg School of Law and Economics in Perspective' (1992) 148 *Journal of International and Theoretical Economics* 675.

in the Ordo Manifesto of 1936,[74] represents an effort to combine the economic theory of classical liberalism with a strict legal framework which is intended to guarantee and protect the optimal functioning of the market.[75]

In more detail, ordoliberalism opposes any form of State intervention in the economy and considers that the role of the State is limited to safeguarding the economic order through the adoption and strict enforcement of an 'Economic Constitution' (*Wirtschaftsverfassung*).[76] The Economic Constitution contains a strong normative bias in favour of a liberal market economy and provides a coherent legal framework, which is essential for the protection of the fundamental principle of private autonomy and individual economic freedoms.[77] Private law is endowed with normative superiority over public intervention and the private law society is endowed with moral superiority over political decision-making procedures.[78] The role of the Economic Constitution is instrumental in the prevention of concentration of both public and private economic power through the prohibition of monopolies, cartels, State planning, and corporatism.[79] Therefore, its mission is both to shield the economy from abuses of political power and to protect the political system from succumbing to economic interests.[80]

At the same time, however, the project of European integration has been also influenced by the French theory of 'service public', which has contributed significantly to the formation and consolidation of the concept of 'social market economy' as an overarching principle underpinning the European project and reinforcing the social component of market integration.[81] This theory

---

74 Franz Böhm, Walter Eucken and Hans Großmann-Dörth, 'Palgrave Macmillan UK' in Alan Peacock and Hans Willgerodt (eds), *Germany's Social Market Economy: Origins and Evolution* (1989).

75 Wolf Sauter, 'The Economic Constitution of the European Union' (1998) 4 Columbia Journal of European Law 27, p. 47.

76 Ibid, p. 46.

77 Ibid, p. 46.

78 Wolf Sauter and Harm Schepel, *State and Market in European Union Law – The Public and Private Spheres of the Internal Market before the EU Courts* (Cambridge University Press 2009), p. 15.

79 Ibid, p. 14.

80 Ibid, p. 14.

81 Emmanuel Cadeau, Didier Linotte and Raphaël Romi, *Droit du service public* (LexisNexis 2014); Didier Linotte and Raphaël Romi, *Droit public économique* (LexisNexis 2012); Jean-Paul Valette, *Le service public à la française* (Paris: Ellipses 2000); Jacques Chevallier, *Le service public* (Paris: PUF [1987] 2008); Stéphane Braconnier, *Droit des services publics* (Paris: PUF 2007); Claudine Desrieux, 'La gestion contractuelle des services publics: Une critique de l'approche par les droits de propriété' (2007) 59 Revue économique 451 ; Marceau Long, 'Service public et réalités économiques du XIXe siècle au droit communautaire' (2001) Revue française de droit administratif (RFDA) 1161; Didier Linotte and

('*service public à la française*') constitutes the foundation of French administrative law and is widely regarded as 'a defining element of French political philosophy and an icon of national identity'.[82] The emergence of this theory coincides with the progress of political liberalism and the development of solidaristic ideologies.[83] Its origins lie in the works of the eminent French legal scholar Léon Duguit (1859–1928), principal representative of the '*Ecole de Bordeaux*' (or '*Ecole du service public*').[84] According to Duguit, the concept of 'service public' encompasses every activity whose fulfilment must be reassured, regulated and controlled by the government, because the fulfilment of this activity is indispensable to the realisation and development of the social interdependence, and it is of such nature that it can only be realised completely by the intervention of the governing force.[85] The State's *raison d'être* is to perform the tasks necessary for the promotion of 'social interdependence'.[86] This means that governmental power derives from the duty of the State to

---

Raphaël Romi, *Services publics et droit public économique* (LexisNexis 2001); Robert Kovar, 'Droit communautaire et service public' (1996) *Revue trimestrielle de Droit Européen* (RTD Eur) 215 ; Jean-Marie Pontier, 'Sur la conception française du service public' (1996) *Recueil Dalloz Sirey* 9; Marceau Long, 'Service public, services publics: déclin ou renouveau?' (1995) *Revue française de droit administratif* (RFDA) 497; Michel Bazex, 'L'appréhension des services publics par le droit communautaire' (1995) *Revue française de droit administratif* (RFDA) 295 ; Philippe Jourdan, 'La formation du concept de service public' (1987) *Revue du droit public et de la science politique en France et à l'étranger* 99; Nicole Belloubet-Frier, 'Service public et droit communautaire' (1994) *Actualité juridique du droit administratif* (AJDA) 270.

82 Wolf Sauter and Harm Schepel, *State and Market in European Union Law – The Public and Private Spheres of the Internal Market before the EU Courts* (Cambridge University Press 2009), p. 16.

83 Marceau Long, 'Service public, services publics: déclin ou renouveau?' (1995) Revue française de droit administratif (RFDA) 497; Jean-Philippe Colson and Pascale Idoux, *Droit Public Économique* (L.G.D.J. 2008), p. 94. The term 'solidaristic ideologies' refers here to ideologies based on the value of social solidarity as opposed to 'individualistic ideologies' based on the value of individual freedom. For a more comprehensive analysis, see Hartley Dean, *Social Policy* (Polity Press 2012), p. 22.

84 Léon Duguit, *Traité de droit constitutionnel* (Paris: De Boccard [1911] 1930) ; Léon Duguit, *Souveraineté et liberté, Leçons faites à l'Université Columbia (New-York) en 1920–1921* (Librairie F. Alcan 1921); Léon Duguit, 'Des fonctions de l'Etat moderne: étude de sociologie juridique ' (1894) *Revue internationale de sociologie* 161; Léon Duguit, *L'État, le droit objectif et la loi positive* (Paris: Dalloz [1901] 2003); Léon Duguit, *Les transformations du droit public* (Hachette Livre BNF [1913] 2014).

85 Léon Duguit, *Traité de droit constitutionnel* (Paris: De Boccard [1911] 1930), II, p. 55.

86 Wolf Sauter and Harm Schepel, *State and Market in European Union Law – The Public and Private Spheres of the Internal Market before the EU Courts* (Cambridge University Press 2009), p. 16, referring to the writings of Léon Duguit.

provide its citizens with the necessary public services.[87] Accordingly, the idea of 'service public' both legitimises and limits the exercise of public power.[88] '*Le service public est le fondement et la limite du pouvoir gouvernemental*'.[89]

Within the framework of the theory of 'service public', public intervention in order to pursue objectives in the *general interest* (a notion which inextricably linked to the concept of 'service public') is elevated to a higher order compared to private law mechanisms for the protection of individual rights and freedoms. At the same time, the functioning of the 'service public' is governed by the fundamental principles of equality, continuity and adaptability (*égalité, continuité* et *adaptabilité*).[90] These three principles constitute the famous '*lois de Rolland*'[91] and have been recognised by the French *Conseil Constitutionnel* as '*exigences du service public*' or as principles governing '*le bon fonctionnement du service public*'.[92]

Within the category of activities that constitute 'services publics', there is a further distinction between '*services publics constitutionnels*' and '*services publics industriels et commerciaux*'.[93] According to the French *Conseil Constitutionnel*, the '*services publics constitutionnels*' correspond to the functions of sovereignty (such as national defence, police, foreign affairs or justice[94]) and cannot be subject to privatisation.[95] To the contrary, the '*services publics industriels et commerciaux*' can in principle be subject to privatisation.[96] However, there are certain activities falling in the latter category, such as the supply of energy, which could potentially have serious implications for the national security.[97] The privatisation of these activities raises important

---

87   Ibid, p. 16.
88   Ibid, p. 16.
89   Léon Duguit, *Traité de droit constitutionnel* (Paris: De Boccard [1911] 1930), II, p. 62.
90   Jean-Philippe Colson and Pascale Idoux, *Droit Public Économique* (L.G.D.J. 2008), p. 147.
91   Louis Rolland, *Précis de droit administratif* (Dalloz 1933), p. 17.
92   Décision n° 2003-480 DC du 31 juillet 2003 *Loi relative à l'archéologie préventive*, ECLI:FR:CC:2003:2003480DC (Conseil Constitutionnel); Décision n° 2002-460 DC du 22 août 2002 *Loi d'orientation et de programmation pour la sécurité intérieure*, ECLI:FR:CC:2002:2002460DC (Conseil Constitutionnel).
93   Nicole Belloubet-Frier, 'Service public et droit communautaire' (1994) Actualité juridique du droit administratif (AJDA) 270.
94   Nicolas Thirion, 'Existe-t-il des limites juridiques à la privatisation des entreprises publiques?' (2002) XVI *Revue internationale de droit économique* 627, p. 646.
95   Décision n° 86-207 DC du 26 juin 1986 *Loi autorisant le Gouvernement à prendre diverses mesures d'ordre économique et social*, ECLI:FR:CC:1986:86207DC (Conseil Constitutionnel).
96   Nicole Belloubet-Frier, 'Service public et droit communautaire' (1994) Actualité juridique du droit administratif (AJDA) 270.
97   Ibid.

issues relating not only to the economic efficiency of the undertakings concerned, but also to strategic national interests. Therefore, the legality of such privatisation is a multidimensional question, which requires a complex legal analysis of the nature of the activities concerned and the possible reconciliation of the various conflicting interests.

B   *The EU Legal Framework: The Principle of Neutrality under Article 345 TFEU*

The legal framework regarding privatisations in the EU covers two grids of primary law provisions: the Treaty provisions on the fundamental freedoms governing the content of privatisations (especially Article 49, 56 and 63 TFEU) and the Treaty provisions on staid aid governing the procedure of privatisations (Article 107 TFEU).[98] At the same time, this framework is complemented by sector-specific secondary legislation (such as energy, telecommunications, postal services etc.) covering important aspects of the liberalisation process.

The aforementioned legal framework is based on the fundamental provision of Article 345 TFEU, which stipulates that *'The Treaties shall in no way prejudice the rules in Member States governing the system of property ownership'*. This provision establishes the *principle of neutrality* of the Treaties with respect to the property ownership systems of the Member States.[99] The 'agnosticism' in relation to the regime of ownership means that the mere fact that an economic activity is carried out by public or private undertakings is not contrary to the Treaties.[100] Consequently, the Treaties, in principle, do not preclude the nationalisation[101] or privatisation of undertakings.[102] In formal terms, Article 345 TFEU protects the competence of the Member States to choose between public or private ownership systems.[103] This allows Member States to organise

---

[98]   European Commission, *Commission Staff Working Document, Guidance Paper on state-aid-compliant financing, restructuring and privatisation of State-owned enterprises* (Brussels, swd(2012) 14 final, 2012).

[99]   Robert Kovar, 'Nationalisations – privatisations et droit communautaire' in Jürgen Schwarze (ed), *Discretionary Powers of the Member States in the Field of Economic Policies and their Limits under the EEC Treaty: Contributions to an International Colloquium of the European University Institute held in Florence on 14–15 May 1987* (Nomos 1988), p. 97.

[100] Paul Craig and Gráinne De Búrca, *EU Law: Text, Cases and Materials* (Oxford University Press 2011), p. 1073.

[101] Case 6-64 *Flaminio Costa v E.N.E.L.*, ECLI:EU:C:1964:66, p. 598.

[102] Case C-244/11 *Commission v Greece (golden shares)*, para 17.

[103] Pieter Van Cleynenbreugel, 'No privatisation in the service of fair competition? Article 345 TFEU and the EU market-state balance after Essent' (2014) 39 *European Law Review* 264; Bram Akkermans and Eveline Ramaekers, 'Article 345 TFEU (ex Article 295 EC), Its Meanings and Interpretations' (2010) 16 *European Law Journal* 292; Fernando Losada Fraga

independently their national economies, giving thus room for a harmonious coexistence of *varieties of capitalism* in Europe.

The symbolic and perhaps enigmatic nature of this provision has given rise to various interpretations. In his annotation on the *Essent* case,[104] Pieter Van Cleynenbreugel distinguished two interpretations of Article 345 TFEU: (1) the shield interpretation according to which Article 345 TFEU completely shields or exempts property ownership rules from the Court's internal market scrutiny and (2) the sword interpretation according to which Article 345 TFEU does not mean that national property ownership choices are not subject to the fundamental rules of the Treaty.[105] The present section builds on and further develops this distinction. In particular, it is argued here that one could distinguish three different interpretative approaches in relation to this nebulous provision corresponding to three different degrees of State participation in the market: (1) the maximalist shield interpretation; (2) the reductionist shield interpretation and (3) the sword interpretation.

1   The Maximalist Shield Interpretation

The 'maximalist shield' interpretation was expressed by Advocate General Ruiz-Jarabo Colomer in his Opinion in the first generation of golden shares cases.[106] The cases concerned restrictions in the acquisition of shares imposed by legislative provisions that conferred special rights to Portugal, France and Belgium in privatised undertakings active primarily in the energy sector.[107]

---

and others, 'Property and European Integration: Dimensions of Article 345 TFEU' (2012) 148 *Tidskrift utgiven av Juridiska föreningen i Finland* 203; Wouter Devroe, 'Privatizations and Community Law: Neutrality Versus Policy' (1997) 34 *Common Market Law Review* 267; Robert Kovar, 'Nationalisations – privatisations et droit communautaire' in Schwarze (ed), *Discretionary Powers of the Member States in the Field of Economic Policies and their Limits under the EEC Treaty: Contributions to an International Colloquium of the European University Institute held in Florence on 14–15 May 1987* (Nomos 1988); Thomas Papadopoulos, 'Privatized Companies, Golden Shares and Property Ownership in the Euro Crisis Era: A Discussion after Commission v. Greece' (2015) 12 *European Company and Financial Law Review* 1.

104   Joined cases C-105/12 to C-107/12 *Essent NV*.

105   Pieter Van Cleynenbreugel, 'No privatisation in the service of fair competition? Article 345 TFEU and the EU market-state balance after Essent' (2014) 39 European Law Review 264.

106   Case C-309/99 *Wouters and others*; Case C-483/99 *Commission v France (golden shares – Sociéte Nationale Elf-Aquitaine)*; Case C-503/99 *Commission v Belgium (golden shares)*.

107   The Portuguese legislation imposed a cap on foreign investment and an authorisation procedure for the acquisition of a holding in certain Portuguese undertakings in excess of a specified level; similarly the French legislation imposed an authorisation procedure of the acquisition of shares exceeding certain limits as well as an opposition procedure regarding corporate decisions to transfer or use as security the majority of the capital of

In his Opinion, Advocate General Colomer first underlined the historic importance of Article 345 TFEU, noting that it was the only provision of the Treaties to be directly inspired by the Schuman Declaration of 9 May 1950. Its position in Part Seven of the TFEU devoted to 'General and Final Provisions' and its forceful and unconditional expression 'in no way' reinforced its 'specific nature and symbolic importance'.[108] However, exactly due to this symbolic importance, the interpretation of Article 345 TFEU was an intricate legal exercise. The Advocate General suggested that a purely *literal* interpretation would not be appropriate, as its terms were rather imprecise and the expression 'system of property ownership' was not a legal but an economic concept.[109] Because of its programmatic nature, only a *historical* and *teleological* interpretative approach could ensure its effectiveness.

In this regard, the *travaux préparatoires* of the Treaty demonstrated that the aim of Article 345 TFEU was to declare the neutrality of the Treaty with respect to the ownership *of the undertakings* in the economic sense, i.e. *as means of production*. Thus, the expression 'system of property ownership' contained in Article 345 TFEU refers not to the civil rules concerning property relations but to *any* interventionist measure which allows the State to contribute to the organisation of the national economy.[110] This includes not only rules, which determine the public or private ownership status of undertakings, but also rules on special rights ('golden shares') that Member States retain in privatised strategically important undertakings, as public interventionist means of implementing national economic-policy objectives.[111] This reasoning echoed the common-sense maxim invoked by the Spanish Government '*he who is able to do the most, can also do the least*' (*argumentum a maiore ad minus*).[112]

In this way, Advocate General Colomer endorsed a 'maximalist shield' interpretative approach of Article 345 TFEU, which in principle *shields* national measures regarding the property ownership systems of undertakings as means of production from the Treaty provisions on the four freedoms. However, he explained that Article 345 TFEU '*does not detract from application of the*

---

four subsidiaries of Société Nationale Elf-Aquitaine; and finally, the Belgian legislation provided an opposition procedure with respect to certain management decisions regarding the transfer of strategic assets or decisions contrary to the country's energy policy.

108   *Opinion of Advocate General Colomer in Cases C-367/98, C-483/99 and C-503/99 Commission v Belgium, Commission v France and Commission v Portugal*, ECLI:EU:C:2001:369, paras 43-45.
109   Ibid, para 47.
110   Ibid, paras 54-56.
111   Ibid, paras 61 and 91.
112   Ibid, para 66.

fundamental rules of the Treaty', in particular the prohibition of discrimination on grounds of nationality.[113] What Article 345 TFEU implies is that measures regarding the property ownership of undertakings '*are not considered to be per se as incompatible with the Treaty: they are covered by the presumption of validity conferred on them by the legitimacy of Article [345 TFEU]*'.[114] He furthermore emphasised that '*the various ways of organising undertakings that are subject to certain form of public supervision, are not, viewed in the abstract, contrary to the Treaty. Their compliance with the fundamental principles of Community law must be assessed specifically, by means of a case-by-case examination of the nature and mode of the operation of the legal situation at issue [...]*'.[115]

On the basis of the aforementioned considerations, he concluded that '*the special prerogatives of the public authorities with which the present infringement proceedings are concerned constitute rules governing public intervention in the activities of certain undertakings, with the aim of imposing economi-policy objectives, and that they are on the same footing as forms of ownership of the undertakings whose organisation is a matter for the Member States by virtue of Article [345 TFEU]. The existence of such rules is not in itself contrary to the fundamental freedoms established by the Treaty, although the specific manner in which they are applied may indeed be so*'.[116] Therefore, he proposed that the Commission's action should be dismissed.[117]

The 'maximalist shield' interpretation excludes any national measure which affects the property ownership system of undertakings from the scope of the fundamental freedoms as a matter of principle. However, it requires a second assessment of the application of the contested measure in a concrete case, which might then restrict one of the fundamental freedoms. Thus, although the *existence* of a measure might be exempted from the scope of the fundamental freedoms, its *application* must nevertheless be reviewed under the Treaty provisions.

2   The Reductionist Shield Interpretation

Contrary to Advocate General Colomer, the Commission was of the opinion that Article 345 TFEU was not relevant to 'golden shares', since they did not concern the public or private ownership system of a company, but rather certain rights and powers relating to the distribution of property ownership of

---

113   Ibid, para 67.
114   Ibid.
115   Ibid, para 90.
116   Ibid, para 91.
117   Ibid, para 92.

that company between private persons.[118] The rationale behind this argument is that once the Member State has proceeded to privatisation, it must ensure that the privatised undertaking functions in full accordance with the principles of a liberal market economy. Therefore, in the Commission's view, 'golden shares' are not covered by the presumption of validity of Article 345 TFEU.

However, when it comes to *stricto sensu* property ownership rules, the Commission purports to remain reverently neutral: it 'has always scrupulously ensured neutrality in its dealings with different forms of ownership'[119] and 'has nothing to say on whether companies responsible for providing general interest services should be public or private and is therefore not requiring privatisation'.[120]

This view was also defended by Advocate General Jääskinen in the *Essent* case,[121] an important case regarding the relationship between free movement of capital and the principle of neutrality under Article 345 TFEU. Before delving into the interpretation of Article 345 TFEU suggested by Advocate General Jääskinen, it is necessary to provide a brief summary of the factual background of the case.

In the *Essent* case, the Court was called upon to appraise the compatibility of the Dutch legislation concerning ownership unbundling of energy suppliers and distributors with the free movement of capital under Article 63 TFEU. The request for a preliminary ruling was made by the Hoge Raad der Nederlanden in proceedings between the Staat der Nederlanden and four companies active in the generation/production, supply and trade of electricity and gas in the Netherlands (Essent NV, Essent Nederland BV, Eneco Holding NV and Delta NV). The national provisions at issue imposed three prohibitions: first, the '*prohibition of privatisation*' (the prohibition of the sale to private investors of shares held in the electricity and gas distribution system operators active in the Netherlands); second, the '*group prohibition*' (the prohibition of any ownership or control links between, on the one hand, companies which are members of the same group as an operator of such distribution systems and, on the other, companies which are members of the same group as an undertaking which generates/produces, supplies or trades in electricity or gas in the Netherlands); and third, '*the prohibition of unrelated activities*' (the prohibition

---

118 Case C-503/99 *Commission v Belgium (golden shares)*, paras 41-42.
119 European Commission, *Bulletin of the European Commission* (No 7/8, Vol 24, 1991), Section 1.2.75.
120 European Commission, *Services of General Interest in Europe* (OJ C281/3, 1996), p. 5.
121 *Opinion of Advocate General Jääskinen in Joined cases C-105/12 to C-107/12 Staat der Nederlanden v Essent NV*, ECLI:EU:C:2013:242.

of engagement by such an operator and by the group of which it is a member in transactions or activities which may adversely affect the operation of the system concerned).

This legislation was adopted with the view to transpose the Second Energy Package,[122] which imposed the obligation of legal unbundling between on the one hand transmission and distribution networks and on the other hand the commercial activities of electricity and gas companies (production and supply of energy). However, the prohibitions imposed by the Dutch legislation (particularly the group prohibition and the prohibition of unrelated activities) amounted to an ownership unbundling and as such they went beyond what was required under the Second Energy Package in force at that time. The ownership unbundling was only introduced with the Third Energy Package,[123] which was, however, not applicable *ratione temporis*. Nevertheless, the Dutch government decided to impose an ownership unbundling of the distribution networks considering that the form of ownership unbundling was most appropriate to pursue the objective of combating cross-subsidisation in the broad sense, including exchange of strategic information, in order to achieve transparency in the electricity and gas markets and to prevent distortions of competition.[124]

The question of the relationship between the free movement of capital under Article 63 TFEU and the principle of neutrality under Article 345 TFEU arose in relation to the prohibition of privatisation. In particular, the Dutch government argued that the prohibition of privatisation constituted a body

---

[122] 'Directive 2003/54/EC concerning common rules for the internal market in electricity and repealing Directive 96/92/EC' (2003) *OJ L 176, 15/07/2003, pp. 37–56*; 'Directive 2003/55/EC concerning common rules for the internal market in natural gas and repealing Directive 98/30/EC' (2003) *OJ L 176, 15/07/2003, pp. 57–78*; 'Regulation (EC) No 1228/2003 on conditions for access to the network for cross-border exchanges in electricity' (2003) *OJ L 176, 15/07/2003, pp. 1–10*; 'Regulation (EC) No 1775/2005 on conditions for access to the natural gas transmission networks' (2005) *OJ L 289, 03/11/2005, pp. 1–13*.

[123] 'Directive 2009/72/EC concerning common rules for the internal market in electricity and repealing Directive 2003/54/EC' (2009) *OJ L 211, 14/08/2009, pp. 55–93*; 'Directive 2009/73/EC concerning common rules for the internal market in natural gas and repealing Directive 2003/55/EC' (2009) *OJ L 211, 14/08/2009, pp. 94–136*; 'Regulation (EC) No 713/2009 establishing an Agency for the Cooperation of Energy Regulators' (2009) *OJ L 211, 14/08/2009, pp. 1–14*; 'Regulation (EC) No 714/2009 on conditions for access to the network for cross-border exchanges in electricity and repealing Regulation (EC) No 1228/2003' (2009) *OJ L 211, 14/08/2009, pp. 15–35*; 'Regulation (EC) No 715/2009 on conditions for access to the natural gas transmission networks and repealing Regulation (EC) No 1775/2005' (2009) *OJ L 211, 14/08/2009, pp. 36–54*.

[124] Joined cases C-105/12 to C-107/12 *Essent NV*, para 49.

of rules governing the system of property ownership within the meaning of Article 345 TFEU. Therefore, the prohibition of privatisation was excluded from the scope of application of Internal Market rules. In other words, according to the Dutch government, by virtue of the presumption of validity under Article 345 TFEU, the prohibition of privatisation escaped the scrutiny of the rules on free movement of capital.[125]

In his Opinion, Advocate General Jääskinen distinguished the situation at issue from the 'golden shares' case law.[126] More precisely, he explained that 'golden shares' could only exist in *already privatised* companies. Thus, the granting of 'golden shares' to the State *presupposes prior privatisation* of the companies concerned. As the State has already exercised its sovereign right in favour of privatisation, the privileged treatment it retains for itself within an essentially *private* property ownership system is not exempted from the Treaty provisions on fundamental freedoms. However, in the case at hand, the Netherlands had not applied a privatisation policy. To the contrary, the national legislation at issue established a *prohibition of privatisation* of the energy distributor system operators. This prohibition was flowing *ineluctably* from the public ownership of the Dutch energy distribution system and as such it was covered by the presumption of validity of Article 345 TFEU.[127] To the extent that this prohibition constituted an *intrinsic consequence* of the ownership system chosen by the Netherlands, it could not be regarded as an obstacle to the free movement of capital in so far as this system is not discriminatory. On the other hand, any restrictive *indirect consequences* other than those directly and inevitably stemming from the public or private system of ownership were to be subject to the fundamental freedoms of the Treaty.[128] This distinction between, on the one hand, *intrinsic/direct/inevitable* consequences of the property ownership system of a Member State and, on the other hand, *indirect* consequences were instrumental in his interpretative approach. The first were to be covered by the presumption of validity under Article 345 TFEU, whereas the latter were to be subject to the scrutiny of the free movement provisions.

Thus, the Commission together with Advocate General Jääskinen adopted the 'reductionist shield' interpretation of Article 345 TFEU, according to which Article 345 TFEU creates a shield against internal market scrutiny only with respect to measures *intrinsically* connected with the ownership system established in a Member State (such as a prohibition of privatisation), but not with

---

125   Ibid, para 24.
126   *Opinion of AG Jääskinen in Joined cases C-105/12 to C-107/12 Essent*, para 46.
127   Ibid, para 49.
128   Ibid, para 42.

respect to measures that only *indirectly* relate to that ownership system (such as golden shares). This interpretative approach is methodologically consistent, as it protects the fundamental right of Member States to opt for either a private or public ownership status of undertakings whilst at the same time subjecting State privileges (golden shares) to the internal market scrutiny.

3 The Sword Interpretation

However, the 'reductionist shield' interpretation was not accepted by the Court. Contrary to Advocate General Jääskinen and the Commission, the Court adopted the third interpretative approach – the 'sword' interpretation of Article 345 TFEU – which corresponds to the least possible degree of State intervention in the market. In the words of Pieter Van Cleynenbreugel, 'rather than creating a shield against internal market scrutiny, Article 345 TFEU neutrality should be interpreted as providing a sword to establish an even more refined balance between economic freedom and state intervention in the market'.[129] While recognising the competence of the Member States to determine their property ownership systems, the Court subjects the *exercise* of this competence to the rules of the Internal Market. The Court rejects the presumption of validity under Article 345 TFEU in both the golden shares case law and in the *Essent* case on the prohibition of privatisation, ruling that this provision merely signifies that each Member State may organise as it thinks fit the system of ownership of undertakings whilst at the same time respecting the fundamental freedoms enshrined in the Treaty.[130]

In general, Article 345 TFEU has been construed narrowly so as not to prevent the application of fundamental rules of the Treaties. In *Fearon*, the Court ruled that '[...] *although [Article 345 TFEU] does not call in question the Member States' right to establish a system of compulsory acquisition by public bodies, such a system remains subject to the fundamental rule of non-discrimination which underlies the chapter of the Treaty relating to the right of establishment*'.[131] The narrow scope of Article 345 TFEU has also been recognised in the field of intellectual property rights. In particular, it has been established that this provision

---

129   Pieter Van Cleynenbreugel, 'No privatisation in the service of fair competition? Article 345 TFEU and the EU market-state balance after Essent' (2014) 39 European Law Review 264, p. 265.

130   Case C-309/99 *Wouters and others*, para 28; Case C-483/99 *Commission v France (golden shares – Sociéte Nationale Elf-Aquitaine)*, para 23; Case C-503/99 *Commission v Belgium (golden shares)*, para 22.

131   Case 182/83 *Robert Fearon & Company Limited v Irish Land Commission*, ECLI:EU:C:1984:335, para 7.

'does not exclude any influence whatever of Community law on the exercise of national industrial property rights'[132] and 'cannot be interpreted as reserving to the national legislature, in relation to industrial and commercial property, the power to adopt measures which would adversely affect the principle of free movement of goods within the common market as provided for and regulated by the Treaty'.[133] Thus, although the system of property ownership continues to be a national competence under Article 345 TFEU, that provision does not have the effect of exempting such a system from the fundamental rules of the Treaty.[134]

In the same vein, in *Opinion 2/15 on the Singapore Agreement*, the Court rejected the argument of the Council and the Member States that certain provisions of the envisaged agreement fell within the competence of the Member States alone in the field of property law.[135] It held that although Article 345 TFEU expresses the neutrality of the EU in relation to the rules existing in Member States governing the system of property ownership, it does not mean that those rules are not subject to the fundamental rules of the EU.[136] The Court explained that the specific provision of the Singapore Agreement did not contain any commitment relating to the rules in Member States governing the system of property ownership.[137] It sought solely to make any nationalisation or expropriation decisions subject to limits which are intended to guarantee investors that such a decision will be adopted under equitable conditions and in compliance with general principles and fundamental rights, in particular with the principle of non-discrimination.[138] Therefore, it reflected the simple fact that, whilst the Member States remain free to exercise their competences regarding property law and to amend accordingly the rules governing the system of property ownership, they are nonetheless not absolved from compliance with those principles and fundamental rights.[139] In this way, the Court exported the internal market rationale to the field of common commercial policy of the EU.

---

132   Joined cases 56 and 58-64 *Établissements Consten S.à.R.L. and Grundig-Verkaufs-GmbH v Commission*, ECLI:EU:C:1966:41, p. 345.
133   Case C-30/90 *Commission v UK*, ECLI:EU:C:1992:74, para 18.
134   Case C-302/97 *Konle*, para 38; Case C-309/99 *Wouters and others*, para 48; Case C-300/01 *Doris Salzmann*, ECLI:EU:C:2003:283, para 39; Case C-452/01 *Margarethe Ospelt*, para 24.
135   *Opinion 2/15*, para 106.
136   Ibid, para 107.
137   Ibid.
138   Ibid.
139   Ibid.

Similarly, in the *Essent* case, the Court, while recognising that the prohibition of privatisation of distributor system operators fell within the scope of Article 345 TFEU, it nonetheless held that this did not exclude the application of the free movement of capital enshrined in Article 63 TFEU.[140] Such a prohibition constituted an 'impediment' for the purposes of Article 63 TFEU since, first, it was liable to prevent or limit the acquisition of shares in the undertakings concerned or to deter investors of other Member States from investing in their capital[141] and, secondly, it constituted an obstacle to the raising of capital by the undertakings concerned, since the acquisition of shares was being restricted.[142]

4   Assessment of the Three Interpretations

It can be argued that the sword interpretation is liable to render Article 345 TFEU devoid of any meaning whatsoever. Some commentators have argued that the dismissal of Article 345 TFEU as irrelevant 'signifies a bias in favour of Community law competence to assess the compatibility of all Member State action and economic policy against the Community norms'.[143] The presumption of neutrality under Article 345 TFEU has been transformed into 'a presumption of illegality of State intervention in the market'.[144]

However, the fact that Article 345 TFEU is a symbolic provision does not mean that it is deprived of any legal content. Its symbolic importance lies in the fact that it reflects the fundamental compromise between State and market that was achieved in the post-war construction of Europe. To deprive Member States of the possibility to opt for a public ownership system could be regarded as amounting to an overt endorsement of the neoclassical economic model despite the proclaimed principle of neutrality of the Treaties. It could in fact be interpreted as meaning that the mere fact that the State owns shares in a company is a restriction on the free movement of capital.[145]

While it is true that the European Economic Constitution favours economic freedoms, deregulation and trade liberalisation, it nonetheless respects the

---

140   Joined cases C-105/12 to C-107/12 *Essent NV*, para 37.
141   Ibid, para 41.
142   Ibid, para 42.
143   Erika Szyszczak, 'Golden Shares and Market Governance' (2002) 29 Legal Issues of Economic Integration 255, p. 279.
144   Erika Szyszczak, *The Regulation of the State in Competitive Markets in the EU* (Hart Publishing 2007), p. 14.
145   Jukka Snell, 'Economic Justifications and the Role of the State' in Panos Koutrakos, Niamh Nic Shuibhne and Phil Syrpis (eds), *Exceptions from EU Free Movement Law: Derogation, Justification and Proportionality* (Hart Publishing 2016), p. 25.

competence and the discretion of the Member States to choose between public and private property. And as the EU is an international organisation governed by the fundamental principle of conferral of powers,[146] respect for the division of competences between the Member States and the EU is of paramount importance for the harmonious coexistence of various actors with conflicting interests and the smooth and constructive evolution of the European project. The role of the judiciary in this sensitive division of competences is all the more crucial, especially in light of the fact that there is no secondary legislation in relation to privatisations, and therefore the interpretative approach of the Court regarding Article 345 TFEU has far-reaching implications for the economic systems of the Member States.

Consequently, it is suggested here that the most legally consistent interpretation of Article 345 TFEU is the *'reductionist shield' interpretation*. Measures *intrinsically* connected with the ownership system established in a Member State (such as a prohibition of privatisation) should be shielded against internal market scrutiny, whereas measures that only *indirectly* relate to that ownership system (such as golden shares) should in principle be subject to the Treaty provisions on the fundamental freedosm (especially the free movement of capital) if they fulfil the conditions of capital restrictions, which are explained in Chapter 4.

Aware of the sensitive nature of the case and the possible consequences of its judgement, the Court tried to moderate its approach: with an enigmatic and ambiguous language it implicitly accepted that Article 345 TFEU could be used as a *justification* ground for restrictions on capital movements. Even though in earlier case law it had explicitly excluded the possibility of invoking Article 345 TFEU in order to justify a restriction on the free movement of capital,[147] it nonetheless explained that:

> [t]hat does not however mean that the interest underlying the choice of the legislature in relation to the rules on the public or private ownership of the electricity or gas distribution system operator may not be taken into consideration as an overriding reason in the public interest.[148]

The Court emphasised that the *Essent* case should be clearly distinguished from the golden shares case law, as the former related to '*an absolute prohibition of privatisation*', whereas the latter '*concerned restrictions created by*

---

146   Arts. 3 (6), 4 (1), 5 (1)-(2) and 13 (2) TEU.
147   Case C-171/08 *Commission v Portugal (golden shares – Portugal Telecom SGPS SA)*, para 64.
148   Joined cases C-105/12 to C-107/12 *Essent NV*, para 53.

privileges which the Member States attached to their position as a shareholder in a privatised undertaking'.[149] For these reasons, the Court held that:

> the reasons underlying the choice of the rules of property ownership adopted by the national legislation within the scope of Article 345 TFEU constitute factors which may be taken into consideration as circumstances capable of justifying restrictions on the free movement of capital.[150]

It could be argued that this reasoning creates an unnecessary fragmentation in the use of justifications in the free movement case law. The Court does not explain why Article 345 TFEU can be used as a justification in case of a prohibition of privatisation, but cannot be used as such in the golden shares case law. Indeed, one might wonder what is the distinguishing factor that renders possible the use of Article 345 TFEU as a justification in the first scenario, but not in the second. Perhaps the rationale behind this differentiation is the same as the rationale used by the Commission and Advocate General Jääskinen in the 'reductionist shield' interpretation: a prohibition of privatisation amounts to a *direct* and *inevitable* consequence of the choice of property ownership system, whereas golden shares presuppose the privatisation of strategic undertakings, which means that the Member State has already exercised its competence regarding property ownership systems and has opted for a model that favours private ownership. Within the framework of a private ownership model, the State, in its capacity as a shareholder, must reverently respect the rules of the game and must not avail itself of special prerogatives in the management of the company that could deter foreign investors.

However, it should be reminded that this approach focused on a prior step, namely that of whether the national measure *falls within the scope of the free movement of capital*. In that regard, the Commission and Advocate General Jääskinen argued that a prohibition of privatisation benefits from the presumption of validity under Article 345 TFEU and thus escapes Internal Market scrutiny, whereas golden shares remain subject to Internal Market scrutiny.

---

149 Ibid, para 54.
150 Ibid, para 55. It should be noted that with respect to the other two prohibitions, the Court acknowledged that the objectives of combating cross-subsidisation in the broad sense, including exchange of strategic information, in order to achieve transparency in the electricity and gas markets, and to prevent distortions of competition could be regarded as overriding reasons in the public interest justifying restrictions on the free movement of capital.

Nevertheless, despite its appeal, this approach was rejected by the Court in relation to the question of whether the measure falls within the scope of free movement rules, only to be later accepted in relation to the question whether the national measure was justified under Article 345 TFEU. It seems that the Court chose to adopt this reasoning in order to remain loyal to the traditional Internal Market approach that dictates first, that the four freedoms must be interpreted widely, whereas exceptions must be construed narrowly and secondly, that although a measure might fall within the competence of the Member States, the *exercise* of that competence must be in accordance with the free movement provisions (although arguably a prohibition of privatisation such as the one in Essent referes to the *existence* of the national competence to opt for a public ownership system, rather than the *exercise* of that competence). But the fact still remains that retaining golden shares in privatised undertakings can be regarded as equivalent to a reduced form of public ownership. If this view is adopted, then the differentiated approach in the use of Article 345 TFEU as a justification does not seem entirely convincing.

Furthermore, the use of Article 345 TFEU as a justification raises another important issue: it might be regarded as opening the door for the use of *economic considerations* for the purpose of justifying restrictions on the fundamental freedoms. According to settled case law, *purely economic grounds cannot serve as justification for obstacles prohibited by the Treaty*.[151] This 'economic rule' was established as early as in 1961 in *Commission v Italy (pork meat)* concerning an Italian rule suspending imports of certain pork-related products from other Member States, where the Court held that Article 36 TFEU is 'directed to eventualities of a non-economic kind'.[152] The rationale of this rule was that the Internal Market, as the cornerstone of the EU, would be seriously undermined if protectionist measures were allowed.[153] Thus, the original target of the general rule prohibiting economic justifications were protectionist measures.

Since then, the 'economic rule' has evolved and has been somewhat attenuated by subsequent case law, most notably by the *Campus Oil* judgment, in which the Court introduced an important qualification: a restriction on free movement is lawful whenever a measure is based equally on economic grounds and on grounds which are admissible under the Treaty.[154] This is known as the

---

151   Case C-398/95 SETTG, paras 22-23 ; Case C-35/98 *Verkooijen*, para 47-48 ; Case C-309/99 *Wouters and others*, para 52; Case C-201/15 AGET *Iraklis*, para 72.
152   Case 7-61 *Commission v Italy (pork)*, ECLI:EU:C:1961:31 at 329.
153   Peter Oliver, 'When, if ever, can restrictions on free movement be justified on economic grounds' (2016) 41 European Law Review 147.
154   Case 72/83 *Campus Oil*, paras 35-36.

'further purpose' doctrine, under which it is exceptionally possible to justify protectionist measures if, apart from their economic objective, they pursue simultaneously another non-economic objective.[155] Thus, in *Campus Oil*, the Court found that the Irish legislation requiring importers of refined petroleum products to purchase certain products from a state-owned refinery was justified on grounds of public security. It held that:

> petroleum products, because of their exceptional importance as an energy source in the modern economy, are of fundamental importance for a country's existence since not only its economy but above all its institutions, its essential public services and even the survival of its inhabitants depend upon them.[156]

In light of the seriousness of the consequences that an interruption in supplies of petroleum products may have for a country's existence, the aim of ensuring a minimum supply of petroleum products at all times is to be regarded as transcending purely economic considerations and thus as capable of constituting an objective covered by the concept of public security.[157] As long as the measure in question pursues an objective that falls within the ambit of one of the derogation grounds provided for under the Treaty (such as public security), the fact that it might also pursue economic considerations cannot exclude the application of the public interest justification in question.[158]

In recent case law, the Court has further developed the approach followed in *Campus Oil* and has expanded even more the 'further purpose' doctrine so as to cover not only objectives with an economic dimension which fall within the ambit of one of the Treaty derogations, but also objectives with an economic dimension which fall within the ambit of an overriding reason in the public interest. In particular, in *AGET Iraklis*, the Court achknowledged that 'considerations connected with the maintenance of employment may, under certain circumstances and conditions, be acceptable justifications'.[159] These considerations include the 'protection of workers' recognised as an overriding reason in the public interest[160] as well as 'the encouragement of employment

---

155 Sue Arrowsmith, 'Rethinking the approach to economic justifications under the EU's free movement rules' (2015) 68 *Current Legal Problems* 307, p. 320.
156 Case 72/83 *Campus Oil*, para 34.
157 Ibid, para 35.
158 Ibid, para 36.
159 Case C-201/15 *AGET Iraklis*, para 75.
160 Ibid, para 73.

and recruitment which, being designed in particular to reduce unemployment, constitutes a legitimate aim of social policy'.[161] Drawing from this ruling, in a recent case concerning the reprivatisation of the Portuguese airline TAP, Advocate General Campos Sánchez-Bordona explained that the 'economic rule' '*does not mean that the Court of Justice is impervious to Member States' economic interests when these are put forward as grounds for hindering freedom of establishment in pursuit of a legitimate social policy objective*'.[162]

It has been argued that in certain fields, such as the financial balance of social and healthcare systems, higher education, the cohesion of the tax system and social protection, the case law has departed from a strict application of the 'economic rule' and that economic exceptions are even expressly provided for by the Treaty.[163] Article 345 TFEU could be regarded as such a provision. Indeed, the property ownership systems of the Member States necessarily entail economic considerations, which in principle cannot be used as justification grounds according to the 'economic rule'. However, it could be argued that the fact that this is an explicit provision of the Treaty renders the 'economic rule' inapplicable. Therefore, Article 345 TFEU can be used as a justification ground despite the fact that it inevitably serves economic interests. Furthermore, the choice of national property ownership system does not only pursue economic objectives, but also other objectives of a non-economic nature that could perhaps fall within the scope of the Treaty derogations. Accordingly, on the basis of the 'further purpose' doctrine, Article 345 could be used as a justification ground. This was in essence the approach that was implicitly chosen in *Essent*, where the Court ruled that reasons underlying the choice of a public ownership system under Article 345 TFEU could be taken into consideration as circumstances capable of justifying restrictions on the free movement of capital resulting from an absolute prohibition of privatisation.

It should be acknowledged that the approach that was ultimately chosen by the Court in the *Essent* case appears to be an important *compromise* aiming to strike a delicate balance between the fundamental freedoms and the public ownership of undertakings intended to safeguard public interest objectives. The departure from a strict application of the 'economic' rule was perhaps inevitable in light of the fact that there are certain economic objectives which are so inextricably linked with or dictated by social objectives that they

---

[161] Ibid, para 74.
[162] *Opinion of Advocate General Campos Sánchez-Bordona in Case C-563/17 Associação Peço a Palavra*, ECLI:EU:C:2018:937, para 95.
[163] Peter Oliver, 'When, if ever, can restrictions on free movement be justified on economic grounds' (2016) 41 European Law Review 147.

cannot be separated from each other. Thus, the use of Article 345 TFEU as a justification for the restriction imposed on the free movement of capital by the prohibition of privatisation can be regarded as a recognition by the Court of the exceptionally sensitive nature of the political choice between public and private ownership and as an effort to mitigate the profound consequences of a possible deprivation of Article 345 TFEU of any legal meaning.

However, the distinction between the use of Article 345 TFEU as an exemption from the scope of capital restrictions as opposed to the use of Article 345 TFEU as a justification can have significant consequences for the outcome of the case. This is because in the first scenario the national measure is excluded altogether from internal market scrutiny, whereas in the second scenario the measure constitutes a restriction which then needs to be balanced against the conflicting public interest objective subject to a strict proportionality assessment. From a legal consisteny perspective, a measure such as a prohibition of privatisation touches upon the *essence* of the national competence to opt for a public ownership system and, therefore, should be excluded from the scope of the Internal Market provisions according to the reductionist shield interpretation. Furthermore, although in *Essent* the use of Article 345 TFEU as a justification ultimately resulted in a compromise between the fundamental freedoms and the national competence to determine the property ownership system, it remains to be seen whether the same outcome will be reached in future cases.

CHAPTER 3

Free Movement of Capital and Golden Shares

The notion of golden shares refers to the special rights that Member States maintain in strategically sensitive privatised companies (telecommunications, electricity and energy production and distribution, postal services, car industries etc.).[*,1] These special rights allow the State to control changes in ownership and/or veto certain strategic decisions in order to prevent hostile takeovers, to guarantee the provision of services of general interest, to safeguard public security and other public interest objectives.[2] The use of golden shares became a widespread phenomenon in Europe in the 1990s and 2000s. Examples of companies in which Member States established special shareholding (either through national legislation or through the Articles of Association of the companies) included, amongst others, Portugal Telecom, the Italian ENEL, the Spanish Repsol, the French Société Nationale Elf-Aquitaine, the Belgian Société Nationale d'Investissement, the Greek Organisation for Telecommunications, the British Airports Authority, the Dutch KPN and the German Volkswagen.

The Commission regarded the establishment of special holdings in national champions as an expression of national economic protectionism restricting the free movement of capital in the EU.[3] Fearing that this trend could severely

---

[*] This chapter expands on ideas previously discussed in earlier publications: Ilektra Antonaki, 'Keck in Capital? Redefining "Restrictions" in the "Golden Shares" Case Law', Erasmus Law Review (2016), Issue 4, pp. 177-188; Ilektra Antonaki, 'Free movement of capital and protection of social objectives in the EU: Critical reflections on the case law regarding golden shares and privatisations' in Sacha Garben & Inge Govaere, *The Internal Market 2.0.* (Oxford: Hart Publishing, 2020), pp. 161-184.

[1] Oxera, *Special rights of public authorities in privatised EU companies: the microeconomic impact* (Report prepared for the European Commission, 2005); Stefan Grundmann and Florian Möslein, 'Golden Shares – State Control in Privatised Companies: Comparative Law, European Law and Policy Aspects' (2001–2002) 4 EUREDIA 623.

[2] European Commission, *Special rights in privatized companies in the enlarged Union – a decade full of developments* (Commission Staff Working Document, 2005).

[3] Ibid, p. 5. See also Jonathan Rickford, 'Protectionism, Capital Freedom and the Internal Market' in Bernitz and Ringe (eds), *Company Law and Economic Protectionism – New Challenges to European Integration* (Oxford University Press 2010), p. 55; Jonathan Rickford, 'Free movement of capital and protectionism after Volkswagen and Viking Line' in Tison and Wymeersch (eds), *Perspectives in Company Law and Financial Regulation – Essays in Honour of Eddy Wymeersch* (Cambridge University Press 2009), p. 62; Jérémie Houet, *Les Golden Shares en droit de l'Union Européenne* (Larcier 2015), p. 296–297 ; Bernard Carayon, *Patriotisme économique, de la guerre à la paix économique* (Editions du Rocher 2006).

obstruct the functioning of the Internal Market, it initiated a number of infringement proceedings against the Member States with special rights in privatised companies.

The golden shares case law raises important legal, political and economic questions, as it addresses issues that lie at the heart of the fundamental interplay between the State and the Market. The conclusion that can be drawn after more than 20 years of litigation[4] is that golden shares constitute in principle a restriction on the free movement of capital because of their dissuasive effect on investment. However, they may be justified on grounds of legitimate objectives in the public interest if the State provides sufficient evidence that the measures at issue comply with a proportionality test, which, in addition to the suitability and the necessity components, assesses also the compliance with the procedural requirements of the principle legal certainty.[5]

The present chapter seeks to assess the far-reaching implications of the golden shares case law not only for the corporate governance systems of the Member States and the organisation of their industrial policies, but also for the broader discussion about the division of competences between the EU and the Member States. In order to do so, it first examines the theoretical controversy surrounding special rights in privatised companies from a corporate governance perspective and then turns to the specific legal issues arising from the case law of the Court of Justice. It argues that the golden shares case law has been characterised by a rigorous application of the rules on the free movement of capital, which in most cases does not allow Member States to maintain special shareholding over privatised companies. By prioritising the interests of foreign investors, the case law favours the constitutional foundations and

---

4   Case C-58/99 *Commission v Italy (golden shares – ENI/Telecom Italia)*; Case C-309/99 *Wouters and others*; Case C-483/99 *Commission v France (golden shares – Sociéte Nationale Elf-Aquitaine)*; Case C-503/99 *Commission v Belgium (golden shares)*; Case C-463/00 *Commission v Spain (golden shares)*; Case C-98/01 *Commission v UK (golden shares)*; Case C-174/04 *Commission v Italy (golden shares)*; Joined cases C-282/04 and C-283/04 *Commission v The Netherlands (golden shares)*; Case C-112/05 *Commission v Germany (golden shares – Volkswagen I)*; Joined cases C-463/04 and C-464/04 *Federconsumatori (AEM/Edison)*; Case C-274/06 *Commission v Spain (golden shares)*; Case C-207/07 *Commission v Spain (golden shares in the energy sector)*; Case C-326/07 *Commission v Italy (golden shares)*; Case C-543/08 *Commission v Portugal (golden shares – EDP)*; Case C-171/08 *Commission v Portugal (golden shares – Portugal Telecom SGPS SA)*; Case C-212/09 *Commission v Portugal (golden shares – GALP Energia SGPS SA)*; Case C-244/11 *Commission v Greece (golden shares)*; Case C-95/12 *Commission v Germany (golden shares – Volkswagen II)*.

5   So far only on one occasion did the Court find that the contested special rights were justified by public interest requirements and were also consistent with the principles of proportionality and legal certainty and that was in Case C-503/99 *Commission v Belgium (golden shares)*.

institutional arrangements of liberal market economies[6] (as opposed to the ones of coordinated market economies) and promotes a company law regime that endorses the principle of proportionality between ownership and control and the principle of shareholders' primacy.[7] This in turn might lead to an erosion of the varieties of capitalism that exist in Europe and to a judicially driven convergence into a specific model of market economy, which might give rise to concerns regarding the respect of the division of competences between the EU and the Member States. In this context, the chapter attempts to investigate whether the interpretation of Article 63 TFEU in the golden shares case law allows room for State participation in the Market for the purposes of protecting public interest objectives and respects the division of competences between the EU and the Member States in the field of corporate governance, whilst at the same time ensuring that Member States do not impose protectionist measures liable to hinder the market access of foreign investors.

1 Understanding the Theoretical Controversy over Golden Shares

In order to evaluate the interpretation of Article 63 TFEU in the golden shares case law and its implications for the corporate governance regime of the Member States, it is necessary first to introduce and understand the theoretical controversy surrounding golden shares. In this regard, this section introduces the definition of golden shares and explains why golden shares constitute control enhancing mechanisms deviating from the principle of proportionality between ownership and control. Subsequently, it introduces the theory of varieties of capitalims, upon which the distinction between liberal and coordinated market economies is based.

---

6   Fritz W. Scharpf, 'The Double Asymmetry of European Integration Or: Why the EU Cannot Be a Social Market Economy' (2010) 8 Socio-Economic Review 211; Martin Höpner and Armin Schäfer, *Integration among unequals: How the heterogeneity of European varieties of capitalism shapes the social and democratic potential of the EU* (MPIfG Discussion Paper, No 12/5 Cologne, Max Planck Institute for the Study of Societies, 2012); Martin Höpner and Armin Schäfer, *A New Phase of European Integration: Organized Capitalisms in Post-Ricardian Europe* (2007); Martin Höpner and Armin Schäfer, 'Embeddedness and Regional Integration. Waiting for Polanyi in a Hayekian Setting' (2012) 66 International Organization 429.

7   Carsten Gerner-Beuerle, 'Shareholders Between the Market and the State. The vw Law and other Interventions in the Market Economy' (2012) 49 Common Market Law Review 97. See also Martha O'Brien, 'Case C-452/04, Fidium Finanz AG v. Bundesanstalt für Finanzdienstleistungsaufsicht, judgment of the Court of Justice (Grand Chamber) of 3 October 2006' (2007) 44 Common Market Law Review 1483, p. 260.

A Definition of Golden Shares

Golden shares are a variety of *priority shares* in which the beneficiary is a public authority. They are defined as the special rights that governments retain in privatised companies, especially the ones considered 'national champions' ('Crown Jewels'), in order to pursue certain public interests objectives or to determine the industrial policy of the national economy.[8] These special rights usually take the form of: (1) a cap on the level of foreign investment, (2) a cap or a prior authorisation procedure for foreign investment and voting rights above certain thresholds, (3) exclusive veto rights on strategic corporate management decisions (such as the winding-up, merger or de-merger of the undertaking, the disposal of certain assets, significant changes to the constitution or the articles of association of the company etc.) and (4) the power to appoint members of the company's Board of Directors. They are set up by governments regardless of their holdings (they might have minority stake or no participation at all in the company) in order to prevent takeovers primarily from foreign companies or to prevent the management of the company from taking actions that are not in line with the national government policy for the sector in which they operate.[9] These special rights are laid down either in *national legislation* (it can be either a *framework law* accompanied by *decree-laws* adopted for the purposes of large privatisation schemes or an *ad hoc company-specific legislation*) or in private instruments such as the *Articles of Association* of a company.[10]

B Golden Shares as Control Enhancing Mechanisms

According to corporate governance theory, golden shares belong to the broader category of control enhancing mechanisms. These are institutional arrangements introducing a discrepancy in the relation between financial ownership (shareholding) and voting power (voting rights).[11] This means that through these institutional arrangements a shareholder can increase his control over the management of the company without holding a proportional stake of equity.[12] Control enhancing mechanisms include a wide variety of mechanisms such as shares with multiple voting rights, shares with loyalty schemes that may increase their voting rights, non-voting shares (with or without

---

8   European Commission, *Special rights in privatized companies in the enlarged Union – a decade full of developments* (2005).
9   Ibid.
10 Ibid.
11 European Commission, *Impact Assessment on the Proportionality between Capital and Control in Listed Companies* (Commission Staff Working Document, 2007), p. 10.
12 Ibid, p. 10.

preference), participating bonds, voting rights ceilings, priority shares, golden shares,[13] pyramid structures, depository certificates of shares sponsored by the company, supermajority requirements, ownership ceilings, share transfer restrictions, staggered/classified board of directors provisions etc.[14]

A study that was conducted by ISS Europe, Shearman and Sterling and the European Corporate Governance Institute in 2007 at the request of the European Commission (as part of its Action Plan for Modernising Company Law and enhancing Corporate Governance in the European Union[15]) showed that control enhancing mechanisms are relatively common across the EU.[16] Of all the 464 European companies considered, 44% had one or more corporate control enhancing mechanisms (or other alternative mechanisms).[17] The countries with the highest proportion of companies featuring at least one of these mechanisms were France, Sweden, Spain, Hungary and Belgium.[18]

C *The Principle of Proportionality between Ownership and Control*

The reason why control enhancing mechanisms have attracted institutional and scholarly attention is because they constitute an important deviation from *the principle of proportionality between ownership and control*. This principle (often referred to as *'one share-one vote' principle*) implies that any shareholder should own the same fraction of cash flow rights and voting rights.[19] In other words, according to the principle of proportionality between ownership and control, the number of votes should correspond to the number of shares that a shareholder holds in the company's share capital. This principle is said to

---

13 It should be noted that golden shares are regarded as CEMs only when they are created by the company itself (i.e. when they are enshrined in the company's Articles of Association or in a shareholders' agreement).
14 European Commission, *Impact Assessment on the Proportionality between Capital and Control in Listed Companies* (2007), p. 10.
15 European Commission, *Modernising Company Law and Enhancing Corporate Governance in the European Union – A Plan to Move Forward* (Communication from the Commission to the Council and the European Parliament, 2003).
16 European Commission, *Impact Assessment on the Proportionality between Capital and Control in Listed Companies* (2007), p. 4.
17 Ibid, p. 4.
18 Ibid, p. 4.
19 OECD, *Lack of Proportionality Between Ownership and Control: Overview and Issues for Discussion* (OECD Steering Group on Corporate Governance, 2007), p. 6. See also George Psarakis, 'One Share – One Vote and the Case for a Harmonised Capital Structure' (2008) 19 *European Business Law Review* 709; Guido Ferrarini, 'One Share – One Vote: A European Rule?' (2006) 3 *European Company and Financial Law Review* 147.

promote 'shareholder democracy',[20] a somewhat delusive notion referring to the decision-making process in a corporation which is based on the amount of *each shareholder's capital contribution* (not the number of shareholders), as opposed to democracy as a political system, which is based on the premise of free elections in which *every citizen* has one vote, irrespective of his background, income or sex.[21]

The theoretical debate on *the principle of proportionality between ownership and control* centres on the potential problems arising from the separation of ownership and control and the need to prevent a potential abusive extraction of private benefits by executive directors and controlling shareholders (the so-called 'private benefits extraction' problem).[22] This relates to the general 'agency problem', the primary problem that corporate law is intended to address. The 'agency problem' arises whenever the welfare of one party ('the principal') depends upon actions taken by another party ('the agent').[23] The problem lies in motivating the agent to act in the principal's interest rather than simply in the agent's own interest.[24] According to corporate governance theory, three generic 'agency problems' may arise within a corporation: (1) the conflict between the firm's owners/shareholders (viewed as 'the principals') and the hired managers (viewed as 'the agents'); (2) the conflict between the controlling shareholders (viewed as 'the agents') and the non-controlling/minority shareholders (viewed as 'the principals'); and (3) the conflict between the firm itself (viewed as 'the agent') and other parties with whom the firm contracts, such as creditors, employees and consumers (viewed as 'the principals').[25] In the first conflict, the 'agency problem' lies in assuring that the managers are responsive to the shareholders' interests rather than pursuing their

---

20   John Edward Parkinson, *Corporate Power and Responsibility: Issues in the Theory of Company Law* (Oxford University Press 1995), p. 160–199; Steef Bartman, 'Shareholder Democracy à la Dworkin' (2010) 7 *European Company Law* 5; Nicola De Luca, 'Unequal Treatment and Shareholders' Welfare Growth: Fairness v. Precise Equality' (2009) 34 *Delaware Journal of Corporate Law* 853; Mieke Olaerts and C. A. Schwarz, *Shareholder democracy: an analysis of shareholder involvement in corporate policies* (Eleven international publishing 2012). See also Case C-101/08 *Audiolux SA e.a v Groupe Bruxelles Lambert SA (GBL) and Others and Bertelsmann AG and Others,* ECLI:EU:C:2009:626, paras 63-64.
21   Steef Bartman, 'Shareholder Democracy à la Dworkin' (2010) 7 European Company Law 5, p. 5.
22   European Commission, *Impact Assessment on the Proportionality between Capital and Control in Listed Companies* (2007), p. 14.
23   Reinier Kraakman and others, *The Anatomy of Corporate Law – A Comparative and Functional Approach* (Oxford University Press 2009), p. 35.
24   Ibid, p. 35.
25   Ibid, p. 36.

own personal interests.[26] In the second conflict, the 'agency problem' lies in assuring that the non-controlling/minority shareholders are not expropriated by the controlling shareholders.[27] Finally, in the third conflict, the 'agency problem' lies in assuring that the firm does not behave opportunistically towards these various other principals, such as by expropriating creditors, exploiting workers or misleading consumers.[28]

The 'agency problems', especially the conflict between shareholders and managers, were identified as early as in the 18th century by Adam Smith, who in his seminal work *The Wealth of Nations* wrote that 'the directors of such companies [joint stock companies] however being the managers rather of other people's money than of their own, it cannot well be expected that they should watch over it with the same anxious vigilance with which the partners in a private copartnery frequently watch over their own. [...] Negligence and profusion, therefore, must always prevail, more or less, in the management of the affairs of such a company'.[29]

The principle of proportionality between ownership and control relates primarily to the second conflict between controlling and non-controlling shareholders. In particular, shareholders who control a proportion of total voting rights much larger than their ownership (and dividend) rights have an incentive to extract value from the company at the expense of non-controlling shareholders.[30] It is argued that discrepancies between ownership and control can exacerbate the misalignment of the incentives of controlling and non-controlling shareholders and at the same time the separation of voting and cash-flow right may compromise the efficiency of markets for corporate control.[31] However, the empirical studies on this issue, included in the aforementioned Report by ISS Europe, Shearman and Sterling and the European Corporate Governance Institute, do not provide sufficient evidence on the existence and extent of private benefit extraction resulting from lack of proportionality. Nevertheless, the Report notes that investors perceive negatively

---

26 Ibid, p. 36.
27 Ibid, p. 36.
28 Ibid, p. 36.
29 Adam Smith, *The Wealth of Nations* (W. Strahan and T. Cadell, London 1776). See also Christine Mallin, *Corporate Governance* (Oxford University Press 2004), p. 11.
30 European Commission, *Impact Assessment on the Proportionality between Capital and Control in Listed Companies* (2007), p. 14.
31 OECD, *Lack of Proportionality Between Ownership and Control: Overview and Issues for Discussion* (2007), p. 4.

all control enhancing mechanisms, and especially priority shares, golden shares, multiple voting shares and voting right ceilings.[32]

The European Commission took into account this Report and subsequently adopted an Impact Assessment on the Proportionality between Capital and Control in Listed Companies, which, after stressing the lack of conclusive evidence regarding the negative effects of control enhancing mechanisms, concluded that it is inadvisable even to recommend prohibiting the ones separating ownership from control, as this could have undesirable effects in terms of, inter alia, hindering long-term policy of companies, hindering companies' access to the capital markets or increasing the monitoring cost for shareholders.[33] Instead, the most suitable solution would be to increase *transparency* regarding them. The Commission could adopt a Recommendation, which would leave Member States the freedom to evaluate which of the transparency options suit best the respective specificities of each legal and industrial system.[34] In the absence of empirical evidence on the existence and extent of shareholder expropriation, adopting further measures could entail a risk of imposing significant costs to issuers and controlling shareholders without a proportional benefit.[35] Thus, after weighing the arguments advanced, Commissioner McCreevy decided that there was no need for action at the EU level on this issue. Therefore, DG Internal Market and Services terminated their work in this area. This should be regarded as an indication that the political institutions of the Union decided to maintain their neutrality with respect to the principle of proportionality between ownership and control and to respect the Member States' right to organise their corporate governance systems as they deem appropriate for their national economies.

Despite the explicit political decision not to adopt any legislative measures prohibiting control enhancing mechanisms and imposing the principle of proportionality between ownership and control as the dominant corporate governance model in Europe, the Court through its golden shares case law, seems to suggest a different pathway. As will be shown in the following sections, by ruling that golden shares are incompatible with the free movement of capital, the Court has implicitly endorsed the principle of proportionality between ownership and control as the overarching principle governing the European corporate governance regime and has potentially opened the door to claims

---

32 European Commission, *Impact Assessment on the Proportionality between Capital and Control in Listed Companies* (2007), p. 6 and 84.
33 Ibid, p. 5.
34 Ibid, p. 6.
35 Ibid, p. 6.

from *intra* and *extra*-EU investors challenging not only golden shares, but also other control enhancing mechanism that might exist in the corporate governance systems of the Member States. Through negative integration, the Court advances a legal reasoning regarding special holdings in privatised undertakings, which gradually leads to a convergence of the various national models of capitalism into one specific model of market economy, that of a *liberal market economy*.

D Varieties of Capitalism: Liberal Market Economies v Coordinated Market Economies

The theory of varieties of capitalism is a political economy theory, developed by Peter Hall and David Soskice, representing a useful framework for understanding the institutional convergences and divergences among the developed economies.[36] It forms part of the political theory of comparative capitalism, which was developed in the 1990s and sought to identify the differences between distinct forms of developed economies (especially between the two paradigm variants of liberal market economies and coordinated market economies).[37] Its main contribution is that it offers a theoretical counter-argument to the globalisation convergence theory and the neoliberal political paradigm, according to which the forces of globalisation would inevitably lead

---

[36] Peter Hall and David Soskice, *Varieties of Capitalism: The Institutional Foundations of Comparative Advantage* (Oxford University Press 2001); Jukka Snell, 'Varieties of Capitalism and the Limits of European Economic Integration' (2012) 13 *Cambridge Yearbook of European Legal Studies* 415; Peer Zumbansen and Daniel Saam, 'The ECJ, Volkswagen and European Corporate Law: Reshaping the European Varieties of Capitalism' (2007) 8 German Law Journal; Daniel Kinderman, *Challenging Varieties of Capitalism's Account of Business Interests – The New Social Market Initiative and German Employers' Quest for Liberalization, 2000–2014* (Max Planck Institute for the Studies of Societies, Cologne, MPIfG Discussion Paper 14/16, 2014); Matthew Allen, 'The Varieties of Capitalism Paradigm: Not Enough Variety?' (2004) 2 *Socio-economic Review* 87.

[37] Chris Brewster, Marc Goergen and Geoffrey Wood, 'Corporate Governance Systems and Industrial Relations' in Adrian Wilkinson and Keith Townsend (eds), *The Future of Employment Relations: New Paradigms, New Developments* (Palgrave Macmillan 2011); Richard Deeg and Gregory Jackson, 'Comparing Capitalisms: The Implications of National Diversity for the Study of International Business' (2008) 39 *Journal of International Business Studies* 540; Ronald Dore, *British Factory, Japanese Factory: The Origins of National Diversity in Industrial Relations* (University of California Press 1973); Jeffrey Hart, *Rival Capitalists: International Competitiveness in the United States, Japan, and Western Europe* (Cornell University Press 1994); James R. Lincoln and Arne L. Kalleberg, *Culture, Control, and Commitment: A Study of Work Organization in the United States and Japan* (Cambridge University Press 1990); Michael E. Porter, *The Competitive Advantage of Nations* (Free Press, New York 1990).

to a convergence of the various economic models into the neoliberal model characterised by financial liberalisation, labour deregulation and privatisation of public assets.[38] Contrary to the predictions of the globalisation convergence theory, the varieties of capitalism theory is based on the hypothesis that the distinctive features shaping the various capitalist models will persist despite the converging forces of globalisation and that national governments and economic players will continue to support national institutional arrangements and economic structures.[39]

The varieties of capitalism doctrine draws from the theory of comparative capitalism and borrows the distinction between liberal market economies and coordinated market economies, as the two ideal models of advanced economies with distinct features and distinct comparative institutional advantages.[40] This distinction is based primarily on the different ways that companies, regarded as the most crucial actors in a capitalist economy, deal with the various coordination problems that they encounter in the organisation of their corporate life.[41]

On the one hand, liberal market economies (represented primarily by the UK and the US – the 'Anglo-Saxon model') have an institutional advantage in supporting radical innovation, which is primarily needed for fast-moving technology sectors based on pioneering scientific research, such as biotechnology, semiconductors, software development etc.[42] The reason is that the institutional arrangements of liberal market economies allow for (1) deregulated,

---

[38] Christian Schweiger, *The EU and the Global Financial Crisis, New Varieties of Capitalism* (Edward Elgar Publishing 2014), p. 4; Hans-Werner Sinn, 'The Dilemma of Globalisation: A German Perspective' (2004) 4 *Economie Internationale* p. 111; Christel Lane, 'Institutional Transformation and System Change: Changes in Corporate Governance of German Corporations' in Glenn Morgan, Richard Whitley and Eli Moen (eds), *Changing Capitalisms? Internationalization, Institutional Change and Systems of Economic Organisation* (Oxford University Press 2006), pp. 78–109; Robert Keohane, *After Hegemony: Cooperation and Discord in the World Political Economy* (Princeton University Press 1984); Samir Amin and David Luckin, 'The Challenge of Globalization' (1996) 3 *Review of International Political Economy* p. 216.

[39] Peter Hall and David Soskice, *Varieties of Capitalism: The Institutional Foundations of Comparative Advantage* (Oxford University Press 2001), p. 57; Peter Hall and Daniel Gingerich, 'Varieties of Capitalism and Institutional Complementarities in the Political Economy: An Empirical Analysis' in Bob Hancké (ed), *Debating Varieties of Capitalism: A Reader* (Oxford University Press 2009), p. 169; Christian Schweiger, *The EU and the Global Financial Crisis, New Varieties of Capitalism* (Edward Elgar Publishing 2014), p. 17–18.

[40] Peter Hall and David Soskice, *Varieties of Capitalism: The Institutional Foundations of Comparative Advantage* (Oxford University Press 2001), p. 8 and 36.

[41] Ibid, p. 6.

[42] Ibid, p. 39.

flexible and highly mobile labour markets which enable companies to hire highly skilled and specialised workers, knowing that they can fire them if the project proves unprofitable; (2) extensive equity markets with dispersed shareholders and a regulatory framework that is favourable to mergers and acquisitions; and (3) the presence of venture capital (i.e. a form of financing to start-up companies) that allows scientists and engineers to bring their own ideas to the market.[43]

On the other hand, coordinated market economies (represented primarily by Germany – the 'German/Continental European model') have an institutional advantage in supporting *incremental innovation*, which is needed in order to attract consumer loyalty and secure continuous improvements in the production process of goods such as machine tools, factory equipment, consumer durables, engines and transport equipment.[44] The reason is that the institutional arrangements of coordinated market economies allow for a labour law regime that provides workers with secure employment and a corporate law regime that gives them the possibility to participate in the management and the decision-making process of the company.[45] This combination incentivises workers to have a genuine interest in the long-term profitability of the company and to develop high levels of industry-specific technical skills.[46] At the same time, inter-firm coordination and corporate governance rules that insulate firms against hostile takeovers and reduce their exposure to volatile capital flows encourage long-term employment and strategies based on product differentiation rather than intense product competition, thus fostering *incremental* rather than radical innovation.[47] Finally, in coordinated market economies capital is provided by banks and long-term investors aiming at ensuring the long-term economic sustainability of the company and the existence of various associations allows the development of cooperation schemes among companies (not always consistent with the anti-trust regulations of liberal market economies).[48]

---

43 Ibid, p. 40.
44 Ibid, p. 39.
45 Ibid, p. 39.
46 Ibid, p. 39.
47 Ibid, p. 40.
48 Jukka Snell, 'Varieties of Capitalism and the Limits of European Economic Integration' (2012) 13 Cambridge Yearbook of European Legal Studies 415, p. 1.

E *Corporate Governance and EU Law*

Corporate governance is defined as a set of relationships between a company's management, its board, its shareholders and other stakeholders.[49] It provides the structure through which the objectives of the company and the means of attaining them are determined.[50] An effective corporate governance framework is essential for economic efficiency and long-term financial stability, as it promotes competition and economic sustainability of corporations, which are regarded as the backbone of the modern globalised market economy system.[51] This holds true particularly for the EU's Internal Market, which must accommodate divergent national corporate systems and institutional arrangements in order to create the optimal market conditions that will ensure the most effective and competitive operation of undertakings and will promote consumer welfare.

Despite the fact that the functioning of an appropriate and efficient corporate governance system is first and foremost the responsibility of the company concerned, the role of the applicable national legal framework is of paramount importance for the establishment of a sustainable corporate governance system which will ensure that certain rules and codes of behaviour are respected in the course of corporate operations.[52] So far, this legal framework remains to a great extent national. Despite some efforts to establish common international rules on the conduct of corporate entities,[53] corporate law and corporate governance is still regulated primarily at national level. This is the case also in the EU. To borrow the famous *dictum* of the Court of Justice, '*companies are creatures of national law*'.[54] There have been efforts to harmonise the field of company law and corporate governance, but they have proved to be a very difficult endeavour in light of the significant national discrepancies in the institutional structures of national corporate governance regimes and the political

---

49 OECD, *G20/OECD Principles of Corporate Governance* (OECD Publishing 2015).

50 Ibid.

51 European Commission, *Action Plan: European company law and corporate governance – a modern legal framework for more engaged shareholders and sustainable companies* (Communication from the Commission to the European Parliament, the Council, the European Economic and Social Committee and the Committee of the Regions, 2012). See also Ronald J. Gilson, 'From Corporate Law to Corporate Governance' in Jeffrey N. Gordon and Wolf-Georg Ringe (eds), *The Oxford Handbook of Corporate Law and Governance* (Oxford University Press 2018), p. 4–27.

52 European Commission, *Action Plan: European company law and corporate governance – a modern legal framework for more engaged shareholders and sustainable companies* (2012).

53 See primarily the OECD Principles of Corporate Governance, which were adopted in 1999.

54 Case 81/87 *The Queen v H. M. Treasury and Commissioners of Inland Revenue, ex parte Daily Mail and General Trust plc.*, ECLI:EU:C:1988:456, para 20.

controversies arising from the different approaches in national industrial policies. The efforts to establish a common regulatory framework in the EU have thus focused on certain specific issues of company law for which a political compromise was deemed feasible and have avoided the most sensitive legal issues dealing with the core of the different national institutional arrangements in the field of corporate governance and industrial relations. As a result, the harmonisation process in the field of company law has resulted in a rather fragmented legal terrain, which consists of several instruments of secondary law (directives and regulations)[55] covering areas such as the formation of limited liability companies,[56] capital and disclosure requirements,[57] accounting and financial reporting rules,[58] domestic mergers and divisions,[59] cross-border mergers and setting up branches in another EU country,[60] business

---

55   For an overview, see European Commission, 'Company Law and Corporate Governance' <https://ec.europa.eu/info/business-economy-euro/doing-business-eu/company-law-and-corporate-governance_en> accessed 31-01-2019.

56   'Directive 2012/30/EU of the European Parliament and of the Council of 25 October 2012 on coordination of safeguards which, for the protection of the interests of members and others, are required by Member States of companies within the meaning of the second paragraph of Article 54 of the Treaty on the Functioning of the European Union, in respect of the formation of public limited liability companies and the maintenance and alteration of their capital, with a view to making such safeguards equivalent' (2012) *OJ L 315, 14.11.2012, p. 74–97*.

57   'Directive 2009/101/EC of the European Parliament and of the Council of 16 September 2009 on coordination of safeguards which, for the protection of the interests of members and third parties, are required by Member States of companies within the meaning of the second paragraph of Article 48 of the Treaty, with a view to making such safeguards equivalent' (2009) *OJ L 258, 1.10.2009, p. 11–19*.

58   'Directive 2013/34/EU of the European Parliament and of the Council of 26 June 2013 on the annual financial statements, consolidated financial statements and related reports of certain types of undertakings, amending Directive 2006/43/EC of the European Parliament and of the Council and repealing Council Directives 78/660/EEC and 83/349/EEC' (2013) *OJ L 182, 29.6.2013, p. 19–76*; 'Directive 2006/43/EC of the European Parliament and of the Council of 17 May 2006 on statutory audits of annual accounts and consolidated accounts, amending Council Directives 78/660/EEC and 83/349/EEC and repealing Council Directive 84/253/EEC' (2006) *OJ L 157, 9.6.2006, p. 87–107*.

59   'Directive 2011/35/EU of the European Parliament and of the Council of 5 April 2011 concerning mergers of public limited liability companies ' (2011) *OJ L 110, 29.4.2011, p. 1–11*; 'Sixth Council Directive 82/891/EEC of 17 December 1982 based on Article 54 (3) (g) of the Treaty, concerning the division of public limited liability companies' (1982) *OJ L 378, 31.12.1982, p. 47–54*.

60   'Eleventh Council Directive 89/666/EEC of 21 December 1989 concerning disclosure requirements in respect of branches opened in a Member State by certain types of company governed by the law of another State' (1989) *OJ L 395, 30.12.1989, p. 36–39*; 'Directive 2005/56/EC of the European Parliament and of the Council of 26 October 2005 on cross-border mergers of limited liability companies' (2005) *OJ L 310, 25.11.2005, p. 1–9*.

registers,[61] as well as rules on the European Company (SocietasEuropea),[62] the European Cooperative Society[63] and the European Economic Interests Groupings.[64]

In its 2012 Action Plan, the Commission acknowledged that the fragmented legal framework of European Company law makes it difficult for users to have a clear overview of the applicable law and carries the risk of unintended gaps and overlaps.[65] It therefore stressed the need for a codification of the rules applicable in this policy area. After conducting a public consultation, the Commission finally adopted a proposal to codify and merge a number of existing company law Directives,[66] which eventually led to the adoption of Directive 2017/1132 relating to certain aspects of company law.[67] This Directive constitutes an important, albeit partial, codification of six Company Law Directives, which are henceforth repealed.[68] Its objective is to make EU company law more

---

61 'Directive 2012/17/EU of the European Parliament and of the Council of 13 June 2012 amending Council Directive 89/666/EEC and Directives 2005/56/EC and 2009/101/EC of the European Parliament and of the Council as regards the interconnection of central, commercial and companies registers' (2012) *OJ L 156, 16.6.2012, p. 1–9*.

62 'Council Regulation (EC) No 2157/2001 of 8 October 2001 on the Statute for a European company (SE)' (2001) *OJ L 294, 10.11.2001, p. 1–21*.

63 'Council Regulation (EC) No 1435/2003 of 22 July 2003 on the Statute for a European Cooperative Society (SCE)' (2003) *OJ L 207, 18.8.2003, p. 1–24*.

64 'Council Regulation (EEC) No 2137/85 of 25 July 1985 on the European Economic Interest Grouping (EEIG)' (1985) *OJ L 199, 31.7.1985, p. 1–9*.

65 European Commission, *Action Plan: European company law and corporate governance – a modern legal framework for more engaged shareholders and sustainable companies* (2012), p. 15.

66 European Commission, *Proposal for a Directive of the European Parliament and of the Council relating to certain aspects of company law (codification)* (COM(2015) 616 final, 2015/0283 (COD), 2015).

67 'Directive (EU) 2017/1132 of the European Parliament and of the Council of 14 June 2017 relating to certain aspects of company law' (2017) *OJ L 169, 30.6.2017, p. 46–127*.

68 'Sixth Council Directive 82/891/EEC of 17 December 1982 based on Article 54 (3) (g) of the Treaty, concerning the division of public limited liability companies' (1982) *OJ L 378, 31.12.1982, p. 47–54*; 'Eleventh Council Directive 89/666/EEC of 21 December 1989 concerning disclosure requirements in respect of branches opened in a Member State by certain types of company governed by the law of another State' (1989) *OJ L 395, 30.12.1989, p. 36–39*; 'Directive 2005/56/EC of the European Parliament and of the Council of 26 October 2005 on cross-border mergers of limited liability companies' (2005) *OJ L 310, 25.11.2005, p. 1–9*; 'Directive 2009/101/EC of the European Parliament and of the Council of 16 September 2009 on coordination of safeguards which, for the protection of the interests of members and third parties, are required by Member States of companies within the meaning of the second paragraph of Article 48 of the Treaty, with a view to making such safeguards equivalent' (2009) *OJ L 258, 1.10.2009, p. 11–19*; 'Directive 2011/35/EU of the European Parliament and of the Council of 5 April 2011 concerning mergers of public limited

reader-friendly and to reduce the risk of inconsistencies and ambiguities, without however amending the substantive content of the provisions it codifies.[69]

F   The Takeover Directive and the Golden Shares Case Law

Perhaps the most controversial directive that has been adopted in the field of EU company law is the 2004 Takeover Directive.[70] The primary objective of the Takeover Directive is to achieve harmonisation of national rules on takeover bids in order to create a level playing field at the European level in the market for corporate control.[71] A 'takeover bid' under Article 2 of the Directive is a public offer made to the holders of securities of a company to acquire all or some of those securities, whether mandatory or voluntary, which follows or has as its objective the acquisition of control of the offeree company in accordance with national law. Voluntary bids can be either *tender (friendly) offers* or *hostile takeovers*. A tender offer occurs when the incumbent majority shareholder or the management of the company agree on the takeover bid.[72] By contrast, a hostile takeover occurs when a bidder attempts to take over a target company whose management is unwilling to approve it.[73]

Due to the politically sensitive nature of hostile takeover regulation, the Directive largely reflects a political compromise[74] and gives Member States the

---

liability companies' (2011) *OJ L 110, 29.4.2011, p. 1–11*; 'Directive 2012/30/EU of the European Parliament and of the Council of 25 October 2012 on coordination of safeguards which, for the protection of the interests of members and others, are required by Member States of companies within the meaning of the second paragraph of Article 54 of the Treaty on the Functioning of the European Union, in respect of the formation of public limited liability companies and the maintenance and alteration of their capital, with a view to making such safeguards equivalent' (2012) *OJ L 315, 14.11.2012, p. 74–97*.

69   European Commission, *Proposal for a Directive of the European Parliament and of the Council relating to certain aspects of company law (codification)* (2015), p. 3.
70   'Directive 2004/25/EC of the European Parliament and of the Council of 21 april 2004 on takeover bids' (2004) *OJ L 142, 30.4.2004, p. 12–23*.
71   Nicola De Luca, *European Company Law: Text, Cases and Materials* (Cambridge University Press 2017), p. 398.
72   Ibid, p. 402.
73   Ibid, p. 402.
74   Vanessa Edwards, 'The Directive on Takeover Bids – Not Worth the Paper It's Written On?' (2004) 1 *European Company and Financial Law Review* 416; Frank Wooldridge, 'The Recent Directive on Takeover Bids' (2004) 15 *European Business Law Review* 147; Heribert Hirte, 'The Takeover Directive – A Mini-Directive on the Structure of the Corporation: Is it a Trojan Horse?' (2005) 2 *European Company and Financial Law Review* 1; Steef Bartman, 'The EC Directive on Takeover Bids: Opting in as a Token of Good Corporate Governance' in Steef Bartman (ed), *European Company Law In Accelerated Progress* (Kluwer Law International 2006); Thomas Papadopoulos, *EU Law and Harmonization of Takeovers in the Internal Market* (Kluwer Law International 2010); Joseph A. McCahery and Erik P.M.

possibility to 'opt-out' from its two most controversial rules, i.e. the board neutrality rule (Article 9 of the Directive) and the break-through rule (Article 11 of the Directive), which are intended to neutralise *ex-post* and *ex-ante* defensive mechanisms which can be adopted by the target company in order to counteract hostile takeovers.[75]

In particular, the board neutrality/passivity rule requires the target company's board of directors to abstain from taking any *ex-post* defensive measures that could frustrate the bid.[76] In other words, it requires the board of directors to 'stay passive' or 'be neutral' once a takeover bid has been launched, whilst it confers the general meeting of shareholders the authority to decide upon the adoption of frustrating actions.[77] *Ex-post* defensive devices to counteract a hostile takeover include shares' repurchases restricting the number of the free floating shares available, mergers increasing the value and number of shares granting control over the company or capital increases, the sale of company's best assets ('crown jewels') etc.[78]

The break-through rule entails the suspension of *ex-ante* defensive measures, i.e. clauses embedded in the company's instruments of incorporation or statutes deterring potential interested investors from making their bids.[79] The *break-through rule* neutralises shares conferring multiple voting rights, targeting primarily the Nordic multiple voting rights model.[80] It should be

---

Vermeulen, 'The Case Against Reform of the Takeover Bids Directive' (2011) 22 *European Business Law Review* 541; Jonathan Mukwiri, 'Reforming EU Takeover Law Remains on Hold' (2015) 12 *European Company Law* 186; Jeremy Grant, *European Takeovers: The Art of Acquisition* (Euromoney Institutional Investor 2018).

75 Alessandro Spano, 'Free Movement of Capital and Golden Shares: A New Perspective on Corporate Control? (Joined Cases C-463/04 and C-464/04 Federconsumatori and Others v Comune di Milano)' (2010) 13 *International Trade and Business Law Review* 291, p. 300.

76 For an extensive discussion about the significance or the triviality of the board neutrality rule see Carsten Gerner-Beuerle, David Kershaw and Matteo Solinas, 'Is the Board Neutrality Rule Trivial? Amnesia about Corporate Law in European Takeover Regulation' (2011) 22 *European Business Law Review* 559.

77 Nicola De Luca, *European Company Law: Text, Cases and Materials* (Cambridge University Press 2017), p. 423.

78 Ibid, p. 423.

79 Ibid, p. 415.

80 Peter O. Mülbert, 'Make It or Break It: The Break-Through Rule as a Break-Through for the European Takeover Directive?' in Guido Ferrarini, Klaus J. Hopt, Jaap Winter and Eddy Wymeersch (eds), *Reforming Company and Takeover Law in Europe* (Oxford University Press 2004); Ulf Bernitz, 'The Attack on the Nordic Multiple Voting Rights Model: The Legal Limits under EU Law' (2004) 15 *European Business Law Review* 1423; Rolf Skog, 'The Takeover Directive, the "Breakthrough" Rule and the Swedish System of Dual CLass Common Stock' (2004) 15 *European Business Law Review* 1439; Paul Krüger Andersen,

noted that there is an exception to the breakthrough rule in relation to golden shares which are compatible with the Treaty. More precisely, Article 11 (7) of Directive 2204/25 provides that the *break-trhough rule* does not apply either where Member States hold securities in the offeree company which confer special rights on the Member States which are compatible with the Treaty, or to special rights provided for in national law which are compatible with the Treaty or to cooperatives. The first category of special rights refers to golden shares originated in the UK, where the *Articles of Association* of privatised companies used to provide for the issuance of special shareholding on behalf of the government.[81] Conversely, the second category of special rights refers to the privatisation schemes in countries like France and Italy, where it is usually the national legislation that attributes special rights to public authorities.[82]

It should be noted, however, that the official endorsement of the board neutrality and the break-through rule provoked fierce political reaction and, in the end, it was decided that these rules would be included in the Directive but only as optional arrangements, not as mandatory rules. Thus, under Article 12 (1) Directive 2004/25, Member States may 'opt-out' from both the board neutrality and the break-through rule if they consider that the market for corporate control must be restricted in order to achieve other objectives. However, if they 'opt-out', they should allow listed companies established within their territories to voluntarily 'opt-in' (Article 12 (2) Directive 2004/25).

The possibility to 'opt-out' from the board neutrality and the break-through rule admittedly leads to national discrepancies which might give rise to unequal treatment of some companies. In particular, this can occur when a listed company having its registered office in Member State A, where both the board neutrality and the breakthrough rules apply, is the target of a hostile takeover bid by a company having its registered office in Member State B, which has 'opted-out' from the board neutrality and the breakthrough rule.[83] In order to prevent this unequal treatment, Article 12 (3) Directive 2004/25 introduces the principle of reciprocity, which allows Member States to decide whether to apply less stringent measures than those arising from the two rules when the bidding company is not subject to the same restrictions.

'The Takeover Directive and Corporate Governance: The Danish Experience' (2004) 15 *European Business Law Review* 1461.

[81] Guido Ferrarini, 'One Share – One Vote: A European Rule?' (2006) 3 European Company and Financial Law Review 147, p. 168.

[82] Ibid, p. 169.

[83] Nicola De Luca, *European Company Law: Text, Cases and Materials* (Cambridge University Press 2017), p. 430.

It has been argued that through its capital case law, the Court of Justice is in effect trying to achieve what the EU legislator failed to achieve when adopting the Takeover Directive, i.e to abolish all restrictions in the market for corporate control. Some scholars claim that, in the absence of political consensus, the application of the golden shares standards to national company law will undoubtedly advance the harmonisation process in the field of takeover bids.[84] It has actually been suggested that the possibility of a Member State to 'opt-out' from the board neutrality and the break-through rule should be subject to judicial review for conformity with the free movement of capital.[85] This is because, as it is argued, the Takeover Directive is only a minimum harmonisation directive and the stricter rules that can be adopted by the Member States must be compatible with the fundamental freedoms.[86] The case law indeed confirms that the stricter rules adopted within the framework of a minimum harmonisation directive are subject to judicial review in order to ensure their conformity with the fundamental freedoms.[87] However, this approach seems to disregard the decision of the EU legislator to leave discretion to the Member States in relation to some politically sensitive issues.

In the field of corporate governance, if the rationale of the golden shares case law is applied by the Court to all company law arrangements – and especially to the ones relating to takeover regulation – it will inevitably lead to a liberalisation of the market for corporate control through negative integration, despite the explicit decision of the EU legislator to grant discretion to the Member States as to whether they wish to keep in place defensive mechanisms against hostile takeovers. This judicially driven liberalisation of the market for corporate control is open to criticism not only in relation to its political legitimacy but also in relation to its economic justification. It is in fact disputed whether the *principle of proportionality between ownership and control/*

---

84 Alberto Artés, 'Advancing Harmonization: Should the ECJ Apply Golden Shares' Standards to National Company Law?' (2009) 20 *European Business Law Review* 457, p. 481.

85 Mads Andenas, Tilmann Gütt and Matthias Pannier, "Free Movement of Capital and National Company Law' (2005) 16 European Business Law Review 757, p. 785.

86 Ibid.

87 Case C-201/15 *AGET Iraklis*, where the Court held that Directive 98/59 cannot, in principle, be interpreted as precluding a national regime which confers upon a public authority the power to prevent collective redundancies by a reasoned decision adopted after the documents in the file have been examined and predetermined substantive criteria have been taken into account (para 34), but nevertheless examined the compatibility of the national legislation in questions with the freedom of establishment under Article 49 TFEU.

'one share one vote principle' (which constitutes the underlying rationale of the breakthrough rule) is justified by economic efficiency.[88]

In view of the far-reaching implications of the application of the free movement of capital to national takeover regulation for the corporate governance systems of the Member States, it is necessary to develop a concrete and coherent legal test for the determination of what constitutes a capital restriction. As argued in the following sections, company law arrangements and in particular defensive mechanisms against hostile takeovers (even the ones contained in private acts) can in principle be subject to Internal Market scrutiny, but they should not be regarded as capital restrictions if they do not derogate from ordinary company law and they do not grant an undue advantage to the State as opposed to private investors. The analysis that follows focuses on the most controversial legal issues arising from the golden shares case law and explores the legal ramifications of a possible extrapolation of the golden shares rationale to all company law mechanisms.

II Legal Issues Arising from the Golden Shares Case Law

A *The Horizontal Application of Article 63 TFEU in the Golden Shares Case Law*

The question of the horizontal applicability of Article 63 TFEU is relevant in light of the private nature of some instruments granting golden shares to public authorities and its importance becomes even more evident when considering the width of private company law arrangements (Articles of Association, bylaws shareholders' agreements, codes of conduct etc.) that can be challenged through the use of the free movement of capital. So far, the Court has not given any precise answer to the question whether the free movement of capital can be invoked in relations between private parties.

A possible recognition of the horizontal effect of Article 63 TFEU would allow individuals to challenge a wide spectrum of private instruments, thus expanding even more the already broad scope of measures affecting capital movements. For instance, the corporate governance model of the Scandinavian countries (Sweden, Finland and Denmark), which grants multiple voting rights through dual class share structures, might be challenged before the Court of

---

[88] Guido Ferrarini, 'One Share – One Vote: A European Rule?' (2006) 3 European Company and Financial Law Review 147, p. 173–177.

Justice as a restriction on capital movements.[89] This might have an intrusive effect into the sphere of private autonomy. However, as will be shown below, the intrusion into the sphere of private autonomy can be prevented either through a delineation of the scope of 'capital restrictions' or through a balancing exercise between economic freedoms and social values at the justifications/proportionality level.

The present section focuses on the horizontal effect of Article 63 TFEU and aims to explore whether it is *feasible* and *desirable* in view of its broader implications for the principle of private autonomy and the choice of market economy model within the Member States. In order to achieve this, it proceeds in three main steps. The fist part explores the theoretical underpinnings of the concept of horizontality (or 'third-party effect') as a controversial topic in national constitutional law. This is necessary in order to understand the origins and the rationality of horizontality and to illustrate that the reasons justifying the horizontal application of fundamental rights in the context of constitutional and international law apply *mutatis mutandis* in the context of EU law. The second part briefly outlines the jurisprudential developments in EU law in relation to the horizontal direct effect of the free movement of goods, persons, services and certain provisions of the Charter of Fundamental Rights and sketches the academic debate so far. Finally, the third part seeks to expound the possibility of a horizontal application of Article 63 TFEU under the existent golden shares case law and to propose a comprehensive solution that balances all conflicting interests and promotes the effective and uniform application of EU law.

1   The Concept of 'Horizontality' in Constitutional Law

The doctrine of horizontal direct effect of Treaty provisions in EU law originates from the controversial concept of 'horizontality' or 'third-party effect' (*Drittwirkung*) of the fundamental rights enshrined in national constitutions. In particular, in national constitutional law there is a long-standing debate regarding the scope of application of the fundamental rights protected under the constitution. Thus, over the years, two main approaches to human rights

---

89   Institutional Shareholder Services Inc., 'Analysis: Differentiated Voting Rights in Europe' <https://www.issgovernance.com/analysis-differentiated-voting-rights-in-europe/> accessed 31-01-2019; Niclas Hagelina, Martin Holménb and Bengt Pramborgc, 'Family ownership, dual-class shares, and risk management' (2006) 16 *Global Finance Journal* 283; Ben Amoako-Adu, Vishaal Baulkaran and Brian F. Smith, 'Executive compensation in firms with concentrated control: The impact of dual class structure and family management' (2011) 17 *Journal of Corporate Finance* 1580.

protection have been developped. On the one hand, the *vertical* theory holds that fundamental rights can be invoked by individuals only against the State. On the other hand, the *horizontal* theory expands the scope of application of fundamental rights so as to cover relations between private individuals as well.[90] It should be noted that the concept of horizontal effect can take three distinct manifestations: (1) *'direct* horizontal effect', i.e. imposition of direct fundamental rights obligations on private individuals and possibility of bringing direct claims against individuals for breaches of fundamental rights; (2) *'indirect* horizontal effect', i.e. judicial interpretation of the law applicable in a private dispute in the light of and in conformity with fundamental rights provisions; and (3) 'state-mediated effect'/ 'positive obligations', i.e. the obligation imposed on the State to take all necessary measures in order to ensure the effective protection of fundamental rights not only in the public sphere but also in the private sphere.[91]

The theoretical underpinnings of the two theories reflect different political philosophies and different views about the interconnection between the public and the private sphere. In particular, the vertical approach to human rights protection is inspired by the political and economic theory of *classical liberalism*[92] and is premised on a rigid distinction between public and private sphere.[93] Supporters of the vertical theory argue that most human rights

---

90   For an overview of the constitutional debate regarding the dichotomy between vertical and horizontal approach to human rights protection see: Murray Hunt, 'The "horizontal effect" of the Human Rights Act' (1998) *Public Law* 423; Deryck Beyleveld and Shaun D. Pattinson, 'Horizontal applicability and horizontal effect' (2002) 118 *Law Quarterly Review* 623; H.W.R. Wade, 'Horizons of horizontality' (2000) 116 *Law Quarterly Review* 217; Jonathan Morgan, 'Questioning the True Effect of the Human Rights Act' (2002) 22 *Legal Studies* 259; Gavin Phillipson and Alexander Williams, 'Horizontal Effect and the Constitutional Constraint' (2011) 74 *Modern Law Review* 878; Stephen Gardbaum, 'The "Horizontal Effect" of Constitutional Rights' (2003) 102 *Michigan Law Journal* 387.

91   Eleni Frantziou, 'The Horizontal Effect of the Charter of Fundamental Rights of the EU: Rediscovering the Reasons for Horizontality' (2015) 21 *European Law Journal* 657, p. 662.

92   David Dyzenhaus, 'The New Positivists' (1989) 39 *University of Toronto Law Journal* 361.

93   Murray Hunt, 'The "horizontal effect" of the Human Rights Act' (1998) Public Law 423, p. 424; Andrew Clapham, *Human Rights in the Private Sphere* (Clarendon Press, Oxford 1996); William P. Marshall, 'Diluting Constitutional Rights: Rethinking State Action' (1985) 80 *Northwestern University Law Review* 558; Cass R. Sustein, *The Partial Constitution* (Harvard University Press 1998); Erwin Chemerinsky, 'Rethinking State Action' (1985) 80 *Northwestern University Law Review* 503; Brian Slattery, 'Charter of Rights and Freedoms – Does it Bind Private Persons' (1985) 63 *Canadian Bar Review* 148; Andrew S. Butler, 'Constitutional Rights in Private Litigation: A Critique and Comparative Analysis' (1993) 22 *Anglo-American Law Review* 1; Stephen Gardbaum, 'The Place Of Constitutional

instruments 'have been forged in the crucible of flagrant abuses of State power' and that, therefore, the purpose of human rights protection is 'to preserve the integrity of the private sphere against coercive intrusion by the State'.[94] It is not the purpose of human rights law to interfere with legal relations between private individuals. Relations between private individuals must remain outside the reach of human rights protection. The sanctity and maximisation of this shielded private sphere should be the ultimate goal of the society.[95] Liberal autonomy presupposes that private actors are able to operate in a private domain, where their reasons for acting in a certain way or another are free from public scrutiny.[96]

On the other end of the spectrum, advocates of the horizontal approach to human rights protection reject the view that there is a pre-political/natural private sphere that precedes the State as a fallacy of classical liberalism.[97] They show greater commitment to *social democratic norms*, which regard the State as having not only *negative* obligations, which essentially require the State not to interfere with the exercise of individual rights, but also *positive* obligations, which in practice require national authorities to take all necessary measures to safeguard human rights ('bestowing of entitlements from the State').[98] The doctrine of *positive obligations* is linked to the political theory of 'active State', which is the theoretical foundation of both *direct* and *indirect* horizontal effect.[99] An active State is a State which ensures that fundamental rights are fully protected within its jurisdiction not only in State-citizen relations but also in relations between private individuals, either by making sure that the

---

Law in the Legal System' in Michel Rosenfeld and András Sajó (eds), *The Oxford Handbook of Comparative Constitutional Law* (Oxford University Press 2012).

94 Murray Hunt, 'The "horizontal effect" of the Human Rights Act' (1998) Public Law 423.

95 Ibid.

96 Mark Tushnet, 'The issue of state action/horizontal effect in comparative constitutional law' (2003) 1 *International Journal of Constitutional Law* 79, p. 89.

97 Murray Hunt, 'The "horizontal effect" of the Human Rights Act' (1998) Public Law 423.

98 Mark Tushnet, 'The issue of state action/horizontal effect in comparative constitutional law' (2003) 1 International Journal of Constitutional Law 79, p. 90. For the distinction between negative and positive obligations in Human Rights Law see Dinah Shelton and Ariel Gould, 'Positive and Negative Obligations' in Dinah Shelton (ed), *The Oxford Handbook of International Human Rights Law* (Oxford University Press 2013); Jean-François Akandji-Kombe, *Positive obligations under the European Convention on Human Rights – A guide to the implementation of the European Convention on Human Rights* (Human rights handbooks, No 7, Council of Europe, 2007); Hugh Breakey, 'Positive Duties and Human Rights: Challenges, Opportunities and Conceptual Necessities' (2015) 63 *Political Studies* 1198.

99 Mark Tushnet, 'The issue of state action/horizontal effect in comparative constitutional law' (2003) 1 International Journal of Constitutional Law 79, p. 90.

legislature enacts laws protecting human rights and abolishing discrimination or by allowing the judiciary to apply human rights horizontally (directly or indirectly).[100] Adherents of the horizontal approach express their fear that concentration of private power can be as dangerous as coercive State power. In fact, they argue that the power to deprive someone of the opportunity to earn a living sometimes poses as great a threat to liberty as does the exercise of State power to imprison someone.[101] Therefore, in their view, all types of law (both legislation and common law governing relations between private parties) should be subject to judicial review in order to ensure their compatibility with human rights.[102] This, they claim, does not spell the end of private autonomy, as the arrangements chosen by private parties might still pass the justification and proportionality test.[103]

Ultimately, the issue of horizontality boils down to a fundamental question: what is the function of a constitution? Some might reasonably argue that it is merely a law for lawmakers, a Hobbesian social contract between rulers and ruled, whereas some others might convincingly assert that it should be regarded as a normative charter governing the relations between individuals in a society, as a Lockean social contract among equal citizens.[104] Adherents of the vertical approach proclaim values such as private autonomy, privacy and market efficiency.[105] They espouse the view that the most crucial function of a constitution is to provide the law for the lawmaker, not for the citizen.[106] Conversely, supporters of the horizontal approach regard the constitution as expressing a society's most fundamental values and therefore as applicable to all its members.[107] These fundamental values are threatened at least as much by powerful private actors as by governmental institutions, especially in light of the widespread recent privatisation of many governmental activities.[108] At the same time, they question the validity of the argument based on private autonomy, arguing that private actors are in any case regulated by other types

---

100   Ibid.
101   Ibid, p. 91.
102   Murray Hunt, 'The "horizontal effect" of the Human Rights Act' (1998) Public Law 423.
103   Ibid.
104   Stephen Gardbaum, 'The Place Of Constitutional Law in the Legal System' in Rosenfeld and Sajó (eds), *The Oxford Handbook of Comparative Constitutional Law* (Oxford University Press 2012), p. 178.
105   Ibid, p. 177.
106   Ibid, p. 177.
107   Ibid, p. 177.
108   Ibid, p. 177.

of legislation, and therefore it is unclear why private autonomy is 'especially or distinctively threatened by constitutional regulation'.[109]

Although the vertical and the horizontal theory represent two polarised extremes, they mark the outer edges of a wide spectrum of possible scenarios where the application of human rights instruments might be triggered either by the State acting in its private capacity (for instance, as a landlord or an employer) or by private parties exercising collective regulatory powers or being in a dominant position of power (for instance, a sport association, a trade union or a corporation imposing certain terms on consumers or employees). Although not purely vertical, these scenarios contain a *quasi-public* element, which renders them without much hesitation susceptible to judicial review in order to ensure compliance with human rights. The judiciary in charge of adjudicating such a dispute might employ various legal remedies in order to give effect to the rights of individuals, without necessarily recognising the direct horizontal effect of human rights provisions.

This intermediate third position in between the two polarised extremes of vertical and direct horizontal effect is known as the concept of *indirect* horizontal effect. This concept originates from national constitutional judgments establishing the duty of the judiciary to uphold and protect fundamental rights and freedoms also in disputes between individuals. The two most prominent examples are the landmark *Lüth* ruling[110] of the German Federal Constitutional Court which established the German doctrine of '*mittelbare Drittwirkung*' (*in casu* in relation to the freedom of expression),[111] and the *Shelley v Kraemer* ruling[112] of the US Supreme Court, which expanded the scope of the 'state action' doctrine[113] so as to cover not only governmental conduct but also court orders

---

109 Ibid, p. 177.
110 *Lüth*, BVerfGE 7, 198 (1958) (Bundesverfassungsgericht).
111 Greg Taylor, 'The Horizontal Effect of Human Rights Provisions, the German Model and Its Applicability to Common-Law Jurisdictions' (2002) 13 *King's College Law Journal* 187; Basil S. Markesinis, 'Privacy, freedom of expression, and the horizontal effect of the Human Rights Bill: lessons from Germany' (1999) 115 *Law Quarterly Review* 47; Ulrich Preuß, 'The German Drittwirkung Doctrine and Its Socio-Political Background' in András Sajó and Renáta Uitz (eds), *The Constitution in Private Relations: Expanding Constitutionalism* (Eleven International Publishing 2005); Georg Sommeregger, 'The Horizontalization of Equality: The German Attempt to Promote Non-Discrimination in the Private Sphere via Legislation' in András Sajó and Renáta Uitz (eds), *The Constitution in Private Relations: Expanding Constitutionalism* (Eleven International Publishing 2005).
112 *Shelley v. Kraemer,* 334 US 1 (1948) (United States Supreme Court).
113 For the academic debate in the US regarding the state action issue see: Stephen Gardbaum, 'Where the (state) action is' (2006) 4 *International Journal of Constitutional Law* 760; András Sajó and Renáta Uitz (eds), *The Constitution in Private Relations: Expanding Constitutionalism* (Eleven International Publishing 2005); Harold W. Horowitz, 'The

and granted *indirect* horizontal effect to the 'equal protection clause' of the Fourteenth Amendment.[114]

2 Horizontal Effect in EU Law

The question of horizontality in EU law has been adressed in several landmark judgments of the Court of Justice and has sparked an animated debate among scholars. In view of the rich literature on the topic,[115] this section restricts itself

---

Misleading Search for State Action under the Fourteenth Amendment' (1957) 30 *Southern California Law Review* 208; Larry Alexander, 'The Public/Private Distinction and Constitutional Limits on Private Power' (1993) 10 *Constitutional Commentary* 361; Richard S. Kay, 'The State Action Doctrine, the Public-Private Distinction, and the Independence of Constitutional Law' (1993) 10 *Constitutional Commentary* 329; Erwin Chemerinsky, 'Rethinking State Action' (1985) 80 Northwestern University Law Review 503.

[114] Mark Tushnet, 'The issue of state action/horizontal effect in comparative constitutional law' (2003) 1 International Journal of Constitutional Law 79, p. 81.

[115] Stefaan Van den Bogaert, 'Horizontality: The Court Attacks?' in Catherine Barnard and Joanne Scott (eds), *The Law of the Single European Market – Unpacking the Premises* (Hart Publishing 2002); Christoph Krenn, 'A missing piece in the horizontal effect "jigsaw": Horizontal direct effect and the free movement of goods' (2012) 49 *Common Market Law Review* 177; Harm Schepel, 'Constitutionalising the Market, Marketising the Constitution, and to Tell the Difference: On the Horizontal Application of the Free Movement Provisions in EU Law' (2012) 18 *European Law Journal* 177; Miguel Poiares Maduro, 'The Chameleon State – EU Law and the blurring of the private/public distinction in the market' in Rainer Nickel (ed), *Conflict of Laws and Laws of Conflict in Europe and Beyond – Patterns of Supranational and Transnational Juridification* (Intersentia 2010); Kara Preedy, 'Fundamental Rights and Private Acts – Horizontal Direct or Indirect Effect? – A Comment' (2000) 8 *European Review of Private Law* 125; Erica Howard, 'ECJ Advances Equality in Europe by Giving Horizontal Direct Effect to Directives' (2011) 17 *European Public Law* 729; Pedro Cabral and Ricardo Neves, 'General Principles of EU Law and Horizontal Direct Effect' (2011) 17 *European Public Law* 437; Paul Verbruggen, 'The Impact of Primary EU Law on Private Law Relationships: Horizontal Direct Effect under the Free Movement of Goods and Services' (2014) 22 *European Review of Private Law* 201; Eva Julia Lohse, 'Fundamental Freedoms and Private Actors – towards an 'Indirect Horizontal Effect' (2007) 13 *European Public Law* 159; Justin Nogarede, 'Levelling the (Football) Field: Should Individuals Play by Free Movement Rules?' (2012) 39 *Legal Issues of Economic Integration* 381; Vassilios Skouris, 'Effet Utile Versus Legal Certainty: The Case-law of the Court of Justice on the Direct Effect of Directives' (2006) 17 *European Business Law Review* 241; Michael Dougan, 'When worlds collide! Competing visions of the relationship between direct effect and supremacy' (2007) 44 *Common Market Law Review* 931; Filippo Fontanelli, 'General Principles of the EU and a Glimpse of Solidarity in the Aftermath of Mangold and Kücükdeveci' (2011) 17 *European Public Law* 225; Harm Schepel, 'The Enforcement of EC Law in Contractual Relations: Case Studies in How Not to 'Constitutionalize' Private Law' (2004) 12 *European Review of Private Law* 661; Rufat Babayev, 'Contractual Discretion and the Limits of Free Movement Law' (2015) 23 *European Review of Private Law* 875; Alan Dashwood, 'Viking and Laval: Issues of Horizontal Direct Effect' (2007) 10 *Cambridge Yearbook of European Legal Studies* 525;

to a brief overview of the case law and the most prominent scholarly opinions expressed thereon in order to summarise the main controversies surrounding the horizontal application of the fundamental freedoms in the private sphere. This jurisprudential and scholarly background is in turn hoped to shed light on the salient question whether and to what extent the judicial reasoning regarding the horizontal effect of the other freedoms can be extrapolated to the free movement of capital.

a) *Defrenne: Horizontal Effect of Equal Pay*

Most legal analyses of the question of horizontality in EU law starts with *Defrenne*,[116] a landmark judgment concerning the horizontal direct effect of Article 119 EEC Treaty (today Article 157 TFEU) on equal pay between men and women. While *Defrenne* focused on Article 157 TFEU, it nevertheless set the tone for the case law that followed regarding the horizontal application of the fundamental freedoms. The question was whether the principle that men and women should receive equal pay for equal work could be relied on by an air hostess against her employer, a private airline company, before the Cour du travail of Brussels. The Court answered in the affirmative. Rejecting the argument based on a strict textual approach that Article 157 TFEU refers expressly only to 'Member States'. It clarified that the fact that certain Treaty provisions are formally addressed to the Member States does not prevent rights from being conferred at the same time on any individual who has an interest in the performance of the duties thus laid down.[117] Following a reasoning similar to the one adopted by the US supreme Court in *Shelley v Kraemer*, the Court in Luxembourg accepted that the reference to 'Member States' in

---

Peter Oliver and Wulf-Henning Roth, 'The internal market and the four freedoms' (2004) 41 Common Market Law Review 407; Lawrence W. Gormley, 'Private Parties and the Free Movement of Goods: Responsible, Irresponsible, or a Lack of Principles?' (2015) 38 *Fordham International Law Journal* 993; Sacha Prechal and Sybe De Vries, 'Seamless web of judicial protection in t he internal market?' (2009) 34 *European Law Review* 5;Sacha Prechal, 'Direct Effect Reconsidered, Redefined and Rejected' in Jolande M Prinssen and Annette Schrauwen (eds), *Direct Effect-Rethinking: A Classic of EC Legal Doctrine* (Europa Law Publishing 2002); Arthur Hartkamp, 'The Effect of the EC Treaty in Private Law: On Direct and Indirect Horizontal Effects of Primary Community Law' (2010) 3 *European Review of Private Law* 529; Stefan Enchelmaier, 'Horizontality: the application of the four freedoms to restrictions imposed by private parties' in Panos Koutrakos and Jukka Snell (eds), *Research Handbook on the Law of the EU's Internal Market* (Edward Elgal Publishing 2017).

116   Case 43-75 *Gabrielle Defrenne v Société anonyme belge de navigation aérienne Sabena*, ECLI:EU:C:1976:56.

117   Ibid, para 31.

Article 157 TFEU includes also the national courts, which have a duty to interpret national legislation, collective agreements but also private contracts in light of the fundamental principle of equal pay between men and women.[118] This cannot be regarded as an undue interference with the principle of private autonomy, since Article 157 TFEU is mandatory in nature and applies not only to the action of public authorities, but also extends to collective labour agreements and individual labour contracts.[119]

b)   *Walrave & Koch and Bosman: Horizontal Effect of Free Movement of Workers – Federation Exercising Regulatory Powers*

In the field of fundamental freedoms, the first case raising the question of the horizontal effect of the free movement of workers was *Walrave and Koch*.[120] The case concerned the compatibility of a rule of the International Cycling Union relating medium-distance world cycling championships behind motorcycles, according to which the pacemaker had to be of the same nationality as the strayer, with Articles 7, 48 and 59 EEC Treaty (today Articles 18, 45 and 56 TFEU). The Court, emphasising the *regulatory powers* of the *association* in question, found that the prohibition of discrimination on the basis of nationality enshrined in the abovementioned provisions does not apply only to the action of public authorities but extends likewise to rules of any other nature regulating in a *collective manner* gainful employment and the provision of services.[121] This extension was justified by the *effet utile* argument,[122] according to which the abolition of obstacles to freedom of movement between Member States would be compromised if the abolition of barriers of national origin could be neutralised by obstacles resulting from the exercise of their legal autonomy by associations or organisation which do not come under public law.[123] Furthermore, the Court put forward the uniform application argument[124] according to which working conditions are regulated not only

---

118   Ibid, para 37.
119   Ibid, paras 38-39.
120   Case 36-74 *B.N.O. Walrave and L.J.N. Koch v Association Union cycliste internationale*, ECLI:EU:C:1974:140.
121   Ibid, para 17.
122   Stefaan Van den Bogaert, 'Horizontality: The Court Attacks?' in Barnard and Scott (eds), *The Law of the Single European Market – Unpacking the Premises* (Hart Publishing 2002), p. 125.
123   Case 36-74 *Walrave and Koch*, para 18.
124   Stefaan Van den Bogaert, 'Horizontality: The Court Attacks?' in Barnard and Scott (eds), *The Law of the Single European Market – Unpacking the Premises* (Hart Publishing 2002), p. 125.

by means of legislation, but also by means of collective agreements or individual contracts and therefore limiting the prohibition of discrimination to acts of public authorities would risk creating inequality in their application.[125] Finally, the Court underlined the general wording[126] of the provisions in question, which made no distinction between the source of the restrictions to be abolished and were therefore deemed to be applicable to the dispute rule of the International Cycling Union.[127]

Two decades later, in the seminal *Bosman* judgment,[128] the Court reiterated that Article 45 TFEU applies horizontally to rules of *sporting associations regulating in a collective manner* the working conditions of athletes.[129] More importantly, it added that the horizontal effect of Article 45 TFEU does not concern only measures discriminating on the basis of nationality, but extends likewise to *non-discriminatory restrictions* on the free movement of workers. In other words, it expanded the 'material scope' of the horizontal effect of Article 45 TFEU. The case concerned the compatibility with EU law (in particular Article 45, 101 and 102 TFEU) of the FIFA and UEFA 'football transfer rules', according to which a professional football player was not free to move to a new club without the payment of a transfer fee, even if his contract with his previous club had expired. The Court repeated the *effet utile* and the *uniform application argument* it had previously advanced in *Walrave and Koch*.[130] Furthermore, it rejected the *justification argument* according to which only Member State are able to rely on limitations justified on grounds of public policy, public security or public health, holding that there is nothing to preclude individuals from relying on those justification grounds.[131] In this way, it firmly established that Article 45 TFEU was applicable to the FIFA and UEFA football transfer rules, which constituted a disproportionate restriction on the free movement of workers.[132]

---

125   Case 36-74 *Walrave and Koch*, para 19.
126   Stefaan Van den Bogaert, 'Horizontality: The Court Attacks?' in Barnard and Scott (eds), *The Law of the Single European Market – Unpacking the Premises* (Hart Publishing 2002), p. 125.
127   Case 36-74 *Walrave and Koch*, para 20-21.
128   Case C-415/93 *Union royale belge des sociétés de football association ASBL v Jean-Marc Bosman*, ECLI:EU:C:1995:463.
129   See Stefaan Van den Bogaert, 'Bosman: The Genesis of European Sports Law' in Miguel Poiares Maduro and Loïc Azoulai (eds), *The Past and Future of EU Law: The Classics of EU Law Revisited on the 50th Anniversary of the Rome Treaty* (Hart Publishing 2010), p. 493.
130   Case C-415/93 *Bosman*, paras 82-84.
131   Ibid, paras 85-86.
132   Ibid, para 114.

c) *Angonese: Horizontal Effect of Free Movement of Workers – Discriminatory Private Conduct*

Then came the *Angonese* judgment,[133] which expanded the 'personal scope' of the horizontal effect of Article 45 TFEU so as to cover not only associations with regulatory powers but also private individuals, but only in relation to measures discriminating on the basis of nationality (not restrictions). In particular, the case concerned Mr Angonese, a bilingual (Italian-German) Italian national, who was denied admission to a competition for a post with a private bank in Bolzano because of the fact that he did not possess a certificate of bilingualism which was issued only by the local authorities in Bolzano. The Court reiterated the *effet utile, uniform application* and *general wording* arguments it had previously presented in *Walrave and Koch*.[134] Furthermore, it repeated the *Defrenne* argument that provisions which are *mandatory in nature*, such as Article 45 TFEU, which lays down a fundamental freedom and which constitutes a specific expression of the general prohibition of discrimination under Article 18 TFEU, apply not only in the public but also in the private sphere.[135] On the basis of this reasoning, it ruled that the prohibition of discrimination on grounds of nationality laid down in Article 45 TFEU is applicable not only to public authorities but also to private persons, and actually to *all* private persons, not only the ones holding collective regulatory powers.

It has been argued that *Angonese* as well as *Defrenne* are characterised by a 'fundamental rights twist', in the sense that they both concern cases of the fundamental principle of non-discrimination in the employment sector.[136] This 'fundamental rights twist' is perhaps the reason why the Court was willing to accord an 'extended' horizontal effect to the non-discrimination principle so as to cover *all* private individuals, regardless of whether they exercise regulatory powers or not.[137] However, so far, this 'extended' horizontal effect concerns only discriminatory measures cases, not restrictions on the fundamental freedoms.

---

133 Case C-281/98 *Roman Angonese v Cassa di Risparmio di Bolzano SpA*, ECLI:EU:C:2000:296.
134 Ibid, paras 31-33.
135 Ibid, paras 30-36.
136 Sacha Prechal and Sybe De Vries, 'Seamless web of judicial protection in t he internal market?' (2009) 34 European Law Review 5, p. 17; Eleni Frantziou, 'The Horizontal Effect of the Charter of Fundamental Rights of the EU: Rediscovering the Reasons for Horizontality' (2015) 21 European Law Journal 657, p. 665.
137 Sacha Prechal and Sybe De Vries, 'Seamless web of judicial protection in the internal market?' (2009) 34 European Law Review 5, p. 17.

d) *Viking and Laval: Horizontal Effect of Freedom of Establishment and Services – Trade Unions*

In *Viking*[138] and *Laval*,[139] two landmark judgments in the field of social rights which sparked a contentious debate among scholars,[140] the Court recognised

---

138 Case C-438/05 *Viking*.
139 Case C-341/05 *Laval*.
140 See, in particular, Mark Freedland and Jeremias Prassl (eds), *Viking, Laval and Beyond* (Hart Publishing 2014); Andreas Bücker and Wiebke Warneck (eds), *Reconciling Fundamental Social Rights and Economic Freedoms After Viking, Laval and Rüffert* (Nomos 2011); Niamh Nic Shuibhne, 'Settling Dust? Reflections on the Judgments in Viking and Laval' (2010) 21 *European Business Law Review* 681; Taco van Peijpe, 'Collective Labour Law after Viking, Laval, Rüffert, and Commission v. Luxembourg' (2009) 25 *International Journal of Comparative Labour Law and Industrial Relations* 81; Claire Kilpatrick, 'Has Polycentric Strike Law Arrived in the UK? After Laval, After Viking, After Demir?' (2014) 30 *International Journal of Comparative Labour Law and Industrial Relations* 293; Loïc Azoulai, 'The Court of Justice and the social market economy: The emergence of an ideal and the conditions for its realization' (2008) 45 Common Market Law Review 1335; Jonas Malmberg and Tore Sigeman, 'Industrial actions and EU economic freedoms: The autonomous collective bargaining model curtailed by the European Court of Justice' (2008) 45 *Common Market Law Review* 1115; Ulf Bernitz and Norbert Reich, 'Case No. A 268/04, The Labour Court, Sweden (Arbetsdomstolen) Judgment No. 89/09 of 2 December 2009, Laval un Partneri Ltd. v. Svenska Byggnadsarbetareförbundet et al'. (2011) 48 *Common Market Law Review* 603; Stephanie Reynolds, 'Explaining the constitutional drivers behind a perceived judicial preference for free movement over fundamental rights' (2016) 53 *Common Market Law Review* 643; Tonia Novitz, 'The Internationally Recognized Right to Strike: A Past, Present and Future Basis upon Which to Evaluate Remedies for Unlawful Collective Action?' (2014) 30 *International Journal of Comparative Labour Law and Industrial Relations* 357; Gareth Davies, 'Freedom of Movement, Horizontal Effect, and Freedom of Contract' (2010) 20 *European Review of Private Law* 805; Kristina Lovén Seldén, 'Laval and Trade Union Cooperation: Views on the Mobilizing Potential of the Case' (2014) 30 *International Journal of Comparative Labour Law and Industrial Relations* 87; Claire Kilpatrick, 'Laval's regulatory conundrum: collective standard-setting and the Court's new approach to posted workers' (2009) 34 *European Law Review* 844; Phil Syrpis and Tonia Novitz, 'Economic and social rights in conflict: political and judicial approaches to their reconciliation' (2008) 33 *European Law Review* 411; Brian Bercusson, 'The Trade Union Movement and the European Union: Judgment Day' (2007) 13 *European Law Journal* 279; Damjan Kukovec, 'Law and the Periphery' (2015) 21 *European Law Journal* 406; Christian Joerges and Florian Rödl, 'Informal Politics, Formalised Law and the 'Social Deficit' of European Integration: Reflections after the Judgments of the ECJ in Viking and Laval' (2009) 15 *European Law Journal* 1; Diamond Ashiagbor, 'Unravelling the Embedded Liberal Bargain: Labour and Social Welfare Law in the Context of EU Market Integration' (2013) 19 *European Law Journal* 303; Catherine Barnard, 'Viking and Laval: An Introduction' (2007–2008) 10 *Cambridge Yearbook of European Legal Studies* 463; Mia Rönnmar, 'Free Movement of Services versus National Labour Law and Industrial Relations Systems: Understanding the Laval Case from a Swedish and Nordic Perspective' (2007–2008) 10 *Cambridge Yearbook of European Legal Studies* 493; Alan Dashwood,

the horizontal effect of the freedom of establishment under Article 49 TFEU and the freedom to provide services under Article 56 TFEU in relation to trade unions exercising their right to take collective action. The Court in effect agreed with Advocates General Maduro and Mengozzi that under certain conditions private action may very well obstruct the proper functioning of the Internal Market.[141] Reasoning along the lines of the case law on the horizontal application of the free movement of workers, in *Viking* the Court referred to its well-established case law in the field of non-discrimination and free movement of workers[142] and emphasized that Article 49 TFEU may be relied on by a private undertaking against a trade union or an association of trade unions participating in the drawing up of agreements seeking to regulate paid work collectively.[143] Furthermore, it clarified that it does not follow from the case law that the horizontal application concerns only quasi-public organisations or associations exercising a regulatory task and having quasi-legislative powers.[144] To the contrary, the Court emphasised that the prohibition on prejudicing a fundamental freedom applies to *all agreements intended to regulate paid labour collectively*.[145] In exercising their autonomous power to negotiate with employers the conditions of employment and pay of workers, the trade unions

---

'Viking and Laval: Issues of Horizontal Direct Effect' (2007–2008) 10 *Cambridge Yearbook of European Legal Studies* 525; Tonia Novitz, 'A Human Rights Analysis of the Viking and Laval Judgments' (2007–2008) 10 *Cambridge Yearbook of European Legal Studies* 541; Silvana Sciarra, 'Viking and Laval: Collective Labour Rights and Market Freedoms in the Enlarged EU' (2007–2008) 10 *Cambridge Yearbook of European Legal Studies* 563; Simon Deakin, 'Regulatory Competition after Laval' (2007–2008) 10 *Cambridge Yearbook of European Legal Studies* 581; Anne Davies, 'One Step Forward, Two Steps Back? The Viking and Laval Cases in the ECJ' (2008) 37 *Industrial Law Journal* 126; Alicia Hinarejos, 'Laval and Viking: The Right to Collective Action versus EU Fundamental Freedoms' (2008) 8 *Human Rights Law Review* 714; Catherine Barnard, 'Social dumping or dumping socialism?' (2008) 67 *The Cambridge Law Journal* 262; Phil Syrpis and Tonia Novitz, 'Economic and social rights in conflict: Political and judicial approaches to their reconciliation' (2008) 33 *European Law Review* 411.

141   Opinion of Advocate General Poiares Maduro in Case C-438/05 *The International Transport Workers' Federation and The Finnish Seamen's Union v Viking Line ABP and OÜ Viking Line Eesti*, ECLI:EU:C:2007:292, paras 35-38; Opinion of Advocate General Mengozzi in Case C-341/05 *Laval un Partneri Ltd v Svenska Byggnadsarbetareförbundet and Others*, ECLI:EU:C:2007:291, paras 156-161.

142   Case 43-75 *Defrenne*, paras 31 and 39; Case 36-74 *Walrave and Koch*, para 18; Case C-415/93 *Bosman*, para 83; Joined cases C-51/96 and C-191/97 *Christelle Deliège v Ligue francophone de judo et disciplines associées ASBL*, ECLI:EU:C:2000:199, para 47; Case C-281/98 *Angonese*, para 32; Case C-309/99 *Wouters and others*, para 120.

143   Case C-438/05 *Viking*, paras 60-61, 66.
144   Ibid, para 64.
145   Ibid, para 58.

participated in the conclusion of agreements seeking to regulate paid work collectively.[146] The power of the trade unions to collectively regulate employment was deemed as a sufficient condition to bring their actions within the scope of the freedom of establishment and services.

In the same vein, in *Laval* the Court underlined that compliance with Article 56 TFEU is also required in the case of rules which are not public in nature but which are designed to *regulate collectively* the provision of services[147] and concluded that Article 56 TFEU could be relied on by a company against a trade union striking in order to protect the workers against possible social dumping.[148] Thus, Articles 49 and 56 TFEU can be invoked not only against the State (as broadly construed in *Marshall*[149] and *Foster*[150]), but also against private entities exercising *regulatory powers*.[151] Whether the application of the freedom of establishment and services to private bodies exercising collective regulatory powers amounts to a recognition of a horizontal applicability of the freedoms to purely private scenarios is a question that remains to be answered.

e) *Dansk Supermarked, Van de Haar and Fra.bo: Horizontal Effect of Free Movement of Goods*

In the field of free movement of goods, the situation is rather different. The judgment in *Dansk Supermarked*[152] is often cited as a one-off case where the Court implicitly recognised the indirect horizontal effect of Article 34 TFEU.[153] In particular, Imerco ordered a British manufacturer to manufacture certain dinning china with the intention to sell them exclusively to its shareholder. The agreement prohibited the exportation of any item in Denmark. Notwithstanding this prohibition, Dansk Supermarked imported some of the items into Denmark and Imerco argued that Dansk Supermarked had infringed the Danish law on unfair competition. Dansk Supermarked invoked

---

146   Ibid, para 65.
147   Case C-341/05 *Laval*, para 98.
148   Ibid, para 99.
149   Case 152/84 *M. H. Marshall v Southampton and South-West Hampshire Area Health Authority (Teaching)*, ECLI:EU:C:1986:84, para 49.
150   Case C-188/89 *A. Foster and others v British Gas plc.*, ECLI:EU:C:1990:313, para 17.
151   Paul Craig and Gráinne De Búrca, *EU Law: Text, Cases and Materials* (Oxford University Press 2011), p. 799.
152   Case 58/80 *Dansk Supermarked A/S v A/S Imerco*, ECLI:EU:C:1981:17.
153   Arthur Hartkamp, Carla Sieburgh and Wouter Devroe, *Cases, Materials and Text on European Law and Private Law* (Hart Publishing 2017), p. 174; Stefaan Van den Bogaert, 'Horizontality: The Court Attacks?' in Barnard and Scott (eds), *The Law of the Single European Market – Unpacking the Premises* (Hart Publishing 2002), p. 130 and the literature cited in footnote 35 Chapter 1.

the principle of mutual recognition enshrined in Article 34 TFEU as a defence and the Court indeed interpreted the pertinent Danish legislation in light of Article 34 TFEU, ruling that '[...] it is impossible in any circumstances for agreements between individuals to derogate from the mandatory provisions of the Treaty on the free movement of goods. It follows that an agreement involving a prohibition on the importation into a Member State of goods lawfully marketed in another Member State may not be relied upon or taken into consideration in order to classify the marketing of such goods as an improper or unfair commercial practice'.[154] However, this judgment has not been cited in subsequent case law and therefore it is questioned whether it is still good law.[155]

To the contrary, in *Van de Haar*,[156] which concerned the sale of tobacco products to persons other than resellers at prices lower than those appearing on the excise label, the Court excluded the application of Article 34 TFEU to private agreements, advancing the well-known argument according to which the conduct of private undertakings is regulated by the competition law provisions whereas the conduct of public authorities is regulated by the free movement provisions. In particular, the Court held that Article 101 TFEU belongs to the rules on competition which are addressed to undertakings and association of undertakings and which are intended to maintain effective competition in the common market.[157] On the other hand, Article 34 TFEU belongs to the rules which seek to ensure the free movement of goods and, to that end, to eliminate measures taken by Member States which might in any way impede such free movement.[158] In the same vein, in *Vlaamse Reisbureaus*,[159] the Court held that Article 34 TFEU concerns only public measures and not the conduct of undertakings.[160]

However, in 2012 came the *Fra.bo* judgment,[161] which is regarded as recognising the horizontal effect of the free movement of goods, albeit only in

---

154 Case 58/80 *Dansk Supermarked A/S v A/S Imerco*, para 17.
155 Stefaan Van den Bogaert, 'Horizontality: The Court Attacks?' in Barnard and Scott (eds), *The Law of the Single European Market – Unpacking the Premises* (Hart Publishing 2002), p. 131.
156 Joined cases 177 and 178/82 *Criminal proceedings against Jan van de Haar and Kaveka de Meern BV*, ECLI:EU:C:1984:144.
157 Ibid, para 11.
158 Ibid, para 12.
159 Case 311/85 *ASBL Vereniging van Vlaamse Reisbureaus v ASBL Sociale Dienst van de Plaatselijke en Gewestelijke Overheidsdiensten*, ECLI:EU:C:1987:418.
160 Ibid, para 30.
161 Case C-171/11 *Fra.bo SpA v Deutsche Vereinigung des Gas- und Wasserfaches eV (DVGW) – Technisch-Wissenschaftlicher Verein*, ECLI:EU:C:2012:453.

relation to private-law bodies entrusted with standardisation and certification activities. The Court ruled that a private-law body in charge of drawing up technical standards for products used in the drinking water supply sector and of cerifying products on the basis of these standards, is subject to the free movement of goods in the light of the legislative and regulatory context in which this body operates.[162] The underlying reason why the Court ruled in favour of the horizontal application of Article 34 TFEU *in casu* was that 'a body such as the DVGW, by virtue of its authority to certify the products, in reality holds the power to regulate the entry into the German market of products such as the copper fittings at issue in the main proceedings'.[163]

f)   *AMS and Egenberger: Horizontal Effect of the Charter*
The question of horizontality has been raised also in relation to the EU Charter of Fundamental Rights,[164] which with the entry into force of the Lisbon Treaty has been elevated into primary law with the same legally binding force as the Treaties. The starting point of every discussion about possible horizontality of the Charter is Article 51 (1) of the Charter which stipulates that 'The provisions of this Charter are addressed to *the institutions and bodies of the Union* with due regard for the principle of subsidiarity and to *the Member States* only when they are implementing Union law [...]'. The absence of any mention of private individuals has been interpreted as an argument against the horizontal applicability of the Charter.[165]

---

162   Ibid, para 26.
163   Ibid, para 31.
164   Eleni Frantziou, 'The Horizontal Effect of the Charter of Fundamental Rights of the EU: Rediscovering the Reasons for Horizontality' (2015) 21 European Law Journal 657; Dorota Leczykiewicz, Saša Sever Dorota Leczykiewicz, 'Horizontal application of the Charter of Fundamental Rights' (2013) 38 *European Law Review* 479; Saša Sever, 'Horizontal Effect and the Charter' (2014) 10 *Croatian Yearbook of European Law and Policy* 39; Schim Seifert, 'L'effet horizontal des droits fondamentaux' (2012) 48 *Revue Trimestrielle de Droit Européen* 801.
165   Eleni Frantziou, 'The Horizontal Effect of the Charter of Fundamental Rights of the EU: Rediscovering the Reasons for Horizontality' (2015) 21 European Law Journal 657, p. 659 citing *Opinion of Advocate General Trstenjak in Case C-282/10 Maribel Dominguez v Centre informatique du Centre Ouest Atlantique and Préfet de la région Centre* ECLI:EU:C:2011:559, paras 80-88; Koen Lenaerts, 'Exploring the Limits of the EU Charter of Fundamental Rights' (2012) 8 *European Constitutional Law Review* 375, footnote 11; Julianne Kokott and Christoph Sobotta, *The Charter of Fundamental Rights of the European Union after Lisbon* (EUI Working Papers, Academy of European Law (2010) No 2010/06, 2010), p. 14.

However, it has been counterargued that Article 51 (1) of the Charter does not explicitly exclude the horizontal effect of the Charter[166] and, furthermore, the Court, in *Defrenne,* expressly rejected a strict textual interpretation of the Treaties, ruling that 'the fact that certain provisions [...] are formally addressed to the Member States does not prevent rights from being conferred at the same time on any individual who has an interest in the performance of the duties thus laid down'.[167] By the same token, the Court could reject a similar strict textual interpretation of the Charter.

However, until very recently, the case law of the Court was pointing towards the opposite direction. In *AMS*,[168] the Court refused to accord horizontal effect to the Charter. In particular, the case concerned the wrongful implementation of Directive 2002/14 establishing a general framework for informing and consulting employees into the French legal order, and more specifically, the exclusion of certain categories of employees from the fundamental right to information and consultation. The Court reiterated its well-established case law that directives cannot be applied horizontally in a dispute between private individuals and found that, in the case at hand, indirect effect (duty of consistent/harmonious interpretation) was not possible, as it would entail a *contra legem* interpretation of the national legislation. Finally, the Court ruled that Article 27 of the Charter protecting the fundamental workers' right to information and consultation within the undertaking does not create a right specific enough to be directly invoked in a dispute between private individuals in order to assess the compliance with EU law of a national measure implementing the directive.[169]

Scholars seem unsatisfied with this judgment and have criticised the Court for not embarking on a much-needed interpretation of the content of Article 27 of the Charter and for not following an approach similar to the one adopted in *Mangold*[170] and *Kücükdeveci*,[171] in which the Court resorted to the use of the 'general principles' mechanism in order to grant direct horizontal effect to the principle of non-discrimination as enshrined in Article 21 of the Charter and

---

166   Eleni Frantziou, 'The Horizontal Effect of the Charter of Fundamental Rights of the EU: Rediscovering the Reasons for Horizontality' (2015) 21 European Law Journal 657, p. 659.
167   Case 43-75 *Defrenne*, para 31.
168   Case C-176/12 *Association de médiation sociale v Union locale des syndicats CGT and Others,* ECLI:EU:C:2014:2.
169   Ibid, paras 45-46, 51.
170   Case C-144/04 *Werner Mangold v Rüdiger Helm,* ECLI:EU:C:2005:709.
171   Case C-555/07 *Seda Kücükdeveci v Swedex GmbH & Co. KG.,* ECLI:EU:C:2010:21.

given specific expression in Directive 2000/78/EC establishing a general framework for equal treatment in employment and occupation.[172]

In his Opinion regarding the horizontal application of Article 31 (2) of the Charter (in particular the right to an annual period of paid leave), Advocate General Bot expressed the view that in *AMS*, the Court implicitly recognised 'the *summa divisio* between the principles proclaimed by the Charter, the enforceability of which is limited and indirect, and the rights recognised by the Charter, which, fore their part, are fully and directly enforceable'.[173] He furthermore considered that the recognition of horizontal effect of the Charter is not contrary to Article 51 of the Charter, 'since that recognition is intended to ensure that Member States, to which the provisions of the Charter apply, respect the fundamental rights recognised therein when implementing EU law'.[174] In fact, he argued that Article 52 (5) of the Charter expressly permits the possibility of relying directly on a Charter provision recognising a 'principle' before a national court for the purpose of reviewing the legality of national measures implementing EU law.[175]

Very recently, in *Egenberger*,[176] the Court re-evaluated its position and recognised that not only Article 21 of the Charter but also Article 47 of the Charter are capable of being horizontally applicable in a dispute between private individuals. In particular, the case concerned a dispute between Ms Vera Egenberger and Evangelisches Werk für Diakonie und Entwicklung eV concerning a claim by Ms Egenberger for compensation for discrimination on grounds of religion allegedly suffered by her in a recruitment procedure. The Court convincingly held that:

---

[172] Eleni Frantziou, 'The Horizontal Effect of the Charter of Fundamental Rights of the EU: Rediscovering the Reasons for Horizontality' (2015) 21 European Law Journal 657, p. 667 citing Eleni Frantziou, 'Case C-176/12 Association de Médiation Sociale: Some Reflections on the Horizontal Effect of the Charter and the Reach of Fundamental Employment Rights in the European Union' (2014) 10 *European Constitutional Law Review* 332; Nicole Lazzerini, 'Case C-176/12, Association de Médiation Sociale v. Union Locale des Syndicats CGT and Others, Judgment of the Court of Justice (Grand Chamber) of 15 January 2014' (2014) 51 *Common Market Law Review* 907; Cian C. Murphy, 'Using the EU Charter of Fundamental Rights Against Private Parties after Association De Médiation Sociale" (2014) *European Human Rights Law Review* 170.

[173] *Opinion of Advocate General Bot in Joined Cases C569/16 and C570/16 Stadt Wuppertal v Maria Elisabeth Bauer and Volker Willmeroth* ECLI:EU:C:2018:337, para 70.

[174] Ibid, para 77.

[175] Ibid, para 68.

[176] Case C-414/16 *Vera Egenberger v Evangelisches Werk für Diakonie und Entwicklung e.V.*, ECLI:EU:C:2018:257.

a national court hearing a dispute between two individuals is obliged, where it is not possible for it to interpret the applicable national law in conformity with Article 4(2) of Directive 2000/78, to ensure within its jurisdiction the judicial protection deriving for individuals from Articles 21 and 47 of the Charter and to guarantee the full effectiveness of those articles by disapplying if need be any contrary provision of national law.[177]

A careful analysis of this statement reveals that the Court advances first the *indirect* horizontal effect of Article 21 and 47 of the Charter, i.e. the duty of harmonious interpretation, and if this fails, national courts are obliged to resort to the *direct* horizontal effect of the provisions in question. Scholars have welcomed this jurisprudential development as affirming unequivocally that the rights to non-discrimination and to effective judicial protection enshired in Article 21 and 47 of the Charter respectively are capable of producing direct horizontal effect and as offering a methodologically comprehensive account of how such an interpretation can be reached.[178] Similarly, in the *IR v JQ* case, the Court emphasised that:

> a national court cannot validly claim that it is impossible for it to interpret a provision of national law in a manner that is consistent with EU law merely because that provision has consistently been interpreted in a manner that is incompatible with EU law.[179]

Rather, if it considers that it is impossible to interpret the national provision in a manner compatible with EU law, it is:

> under an obligation to provide [...] the legal protection which individuals derive from EU law and to ensure the full effectiveness of that law, disapplying if need be any provision of national legislation contrary to the principle prohibiting discrimination on grounds of religion or belief.[180]

---

177   Ibid, para 82.
178   Eleni Frantziou, 'Mangold Recast? The ECJ's Flirtation with Drittwirkung in Egenberger' (*European Law Blog*, 24 April 2018) <http://europeanlawblog.eu/2018/04/24/mangold-recast-the-ecjs-flirtation-with-drittwirkung-in-egenberger/> accessed 31-01-2019.
179   Case C-68/17 *IR v JQ*, ECLI:EU:C:2018:696, para 65.
180   Ibid, para 68.

Finally, in the recent *Bauer* case,[181] the Court went so far as to regcognise the horizontal effect of Article 31 (2) of the Chater. In particular, the Court held that:

> the right to a period of paid annual leave, affirmed for every worker by Article 31(2) of the Charter, is thus, as regards its very existence, both mandatory and unconditional in nature [...]. It follows that that provision is sufficient in itself to confer on workers a right that they may actually rely on in disputes between them and their employer in a field covered by EU law and therefore falling within the scope of the Charter.[182]

Therefore, it concluded that:

> in the event that the referring court is unable to interpret the national legislation at issue in a manner ensuring its compliance with Article 31(2) of the Charter, it will be required [...] to ensure, within its jurisdiction, the judicial protection for individuals flowing from that provision and to guarantee the full effectiveness thereof by disapplying if need be that national legislation.[183]

3 Horizontal Effect of Article 63 TFEU

So far, the Court has not dealt explicitly with the question of the horizontal application of Article 63 TFEU. It has been argued that the majority of the capital case law concerns the field of taxation, a quintessentially vertical issue, and this is why the question of horizontality of the free movement of capital has not been answered until now.[184] Furthermore, in the field of golden shares, national governments acting in their capacity as shareholders have tried to escape from judicial scrutiny by arguing that the contested measure does not constitute a 'State measure' and therefore does not fall within the scope of the free movement of capital, an argument which implies that Member States oppose the idea of granting horizontal effect of Article 63 TFEU. However, until now, the Court has rejected this argument on the basis of a broad interpretation of the notion of 'State measure' covering all measures taken by public authorities even when acting in their private capacity. This has allowed the Court to

---

181 Case C-569/16 *Stadt Wuppertal v Maria Elisabeth Bauer and Volker Willmeroth v Martina Broßonn,* ECLI:EU:C:2018:871.
182 Ibid, Para 85.
183 Ibid, Para 91.
184 Catherine Barnard, *The Substantive Law of the EU: The Four Freedoms* (Oxford University Press 2016), p. 526.

treat these situations as vertical and to review the compatibility of those measures with the fundamental freedoms, without having to give an explicit answer to the question whether Article 63 TFEU is horizontally applicable. However, in light of the multilevel regulatory regime governing corporate governance systems and financial operations (consisting of not only national legislation but also of *private* instruments, such as shareholders' agreements, articles of associations, codes of conduct etc.), it seems reasonable to predict that sooner or later the Court will be faced with the question whether Article 63 TFEU is horizontally applicable. Drawing from the evolution of the case law on the horizontal application of the other fundamental freedoms (especially workers, services and establishment), the Court might in fact be inclined to recognise the horizontal effect of the free movement of capital (at least in its indirect form). Although the fears regarding the possible intrusion into private autonomy resulting from such a recognition might be well-founded, it is argued here that granting horizontal effect to the free movement of capital can actually be regarded as a methodologically consistent approach aiming at advancing the *effectiveness* of EU law, especially in a field dominated by private corporations and financial institutions which can exercise quasi-regulatory powers over other market participants. Besides, it is suggested that the far-reaching effect of a possible recognition of horizontal effect of Article 63 TFEU can be thwarted by a contraction of the *material* scope of Article 63 TFEU (i.e through a more restrictive interpretation of the notion of 'capital restrictions').

a) *The Case Law Regarding the Horizontal Effect of Article 63 TFEU*
In the *Eurobond* case,[185] the Commission initiated infringement proceedings against Belgium arguing that the prohibition contained in a Royal Decree on the acquisition by persons resident in Belgium of securities of a public loan issued in German marks constituted a restriction on the free movement of capital. The Royal Decree in question provided for a waiver of withholding tax on interest payable on the loan. This meant that if Belgian residents were able to subscribe to this loan, they could take advantage of the waiver in order to evade tax on the interest received. The prevention of tax evasion was according to the Belgian Government the underlying purpose of the contested measure. The Government started its defence by arguing that the contested measure had been taken by the Belgian State not in its capacity as a public authority, but *in its capacity as a private operator* and thus it did not fall within the scope of Article 63 TFEU. Essentially, the Belgian Government tried to escape from

---

185   Case C-478/98 *Commission v Belgium*.

the scrutiny of the Court by arguing that it had acted as a *normal private market operator*. The Court dismissed the argument on the facts, as the waiver of withholding tax on interest payable on the loan *contained in the Royal Decree* constituted a *regulatory* measure, which only the State in its capacity as public authority was authorised to take.[186] This waiver together with the prohibition imposed on Belgian residents was clearly adopted by the Belgian State acting as a public authority exercising its regulatory powers on matters of fiscal policy.[187] Consequently, the Court concluded that in the case at hand Article 63 TFEU was *vertically* applicable, as the contested measure had been adopted by the State in its capacity as a public authority. Thus, it did not deal explicitly with the question of horizontal applicability of the free movement of capital.

The question was brought up again some years later in the *Dutch Golden Shares* case.[188] The Court was called upon to appraise the compatibility with the free movement of capital of the golden shares that the Kingdom of the Netherlands had retained in the privatised companies Koninklijke KPN NV and TPG NV. The golden shares were maintained in the memorandum and the articles of association of the companies and had the form of special rights to approve certain decisions of the competent organs of the companies in question. The Dutch Government argued that the shares at issue could not qualify as 'State measures', as it did not hold them in its capacity as a public authority, but instead *as a private shareholder without departing from normal national company law*.

Advocate General Maduro disagreed with the argument put forward by the Dutch Government. He expressed the view that the free movement rules imposed obligations on the Member States regardless of whether they acted in their capacity as public authorities or as entities under private law.[189] He further explained that the crucial factor rendering Member States subject to the free movement rules was not their *functional* capacity as a public authority, but their *organic* capacity as signatories of the Treaty. He therefore argued that the free movement of capital was applicable even when the public authorities were acting like any other shareholder under general company law. Legislation enabling some shareholders to obtain certain special rights in order to shield

---

186   Ibid, para 22.
187   Ibid, paras 24-25.
188   Joined cases C-282/04 and C-283/04 *Commission v The Netherlands (golden shares)*.
189   *Opinion of Advocate General Maduro in Joined cases C-282/04 and C-283/04 Commission v The Netherlands (golden shares)*, ECLI:EU:C:2006:234, para 22.

them from the market process could itself constitute a restriction on the free movement of capital.[190]

The Court followed the Advocate's General suggestion to qualify the golden shares in question as 'State measures' despite the fact that they were adopted by the State in its private capacity as a shareholder. Thus, it avoided the question of horizontal application of Article 63 TFEU. It concluded that the contested golden shares could be classified as 'State measures', as the introduction of the special shares into the memorandum and the articles of association of KPN and TPG was the result of decisions taken by the Netherlands State in the course of the privatisation of the companies with a view to reserving a certain number of special rights under the companies' statutes.[191]

Similarly, in the seminal *Volkswagen* case,[192] the Court refrained from explicitly ruling on the crucial question of horizontal direct effect of Article 63 TFEU. The provisions of the German Volkswagen Law concerning the capping of voting rights at 20% and the fixing of the blocking minority at 20%, and the right of the Federal State and the Land of Lower Saxony to appoint each two representatives to the supervisory board, were found to be contrary to Article 63 TFEU. In its defence Germany argued that the Volkswagen Law merely reproduced an agreement concluded in 1959 between the workers and the trade unions in the form of a private contract.[193] This agreement had deep historical roots and it served social and political considerations: the privatisation of Volkswagen relinquished any claims to ownership rights of the workers over the company and thus, the underlying purpose of the agreement was to secure the assurance of workers' protection against any large shareholder, which might gain control of the company.[194]

The Court rejected this argument on the grounds that the incorporation of an agreement into national legislation sufficed for it to be considered as a 'State

---

[190] Ibid, para 24. See also *Opinion of Advocate General Maduro in Case C-446/03 Marks & Spencer*, ECLI:EU:C:2005:201, paras 37-40; *Opinion of Advocate General Maduro in Joined Cases C-94/04 and C-202/04 Federico Cipolla v Rosaria Fazari*, ECLI:EU:C:2006:76, paras 55-56;*Opinion of Advocate General Maduro in Joined Cases C-158/04 and C-159/04 Alfa Vita Vassilopoulos AE*, ECLI:EU:C:2006:212, paras 54-55. For an interesting comment see Stefan Grundmann and Florian Möslein, 'Golden Shares – State Control in Privatised Companies: Comparative Law, European Law and Policy Aspects' (2001–2002) 4 EUREDIA 623.

[191] Joined cases C-282/04 and C-283/04 *Commission v The Netherlands (golden shares)*, para 22.

[192] Case C-112/05 *Commission v Germany (golden shares – Volkswagen I)*.

[193] Ibid, para 22.

[194] Ibid.

measure' for the purposes of the free movement of capital.[195] It emphatically underlined that 'the exercise of legislative power by the national authorities duly authorised to that end is a manifestation *par excellence* of State power'.[196] Furthermore, the provisions of the contested law could no longer be amended solely at the will of the parties to the initial agreement. To the contrary, any modification required the adoption of new legislation in accordance with the procedure prescribed by the German Constitution.[197] Thus, the Court concluded that the Volkswagen Law was a 'State measure' for the purposes of the free movement of capital.[198]

Nevertheless, in one of the first *Portuguese Golden Shares* case,[199] the Court seemed to rule out the view that even when the State acts as a normal *shareholder* Article 63 TFEU is still applicable. The case concerned national legislation granting to the Portuguese State and to other public shareholders golden shares in the company EDP – Energias de Portugal, the principal licensed distributor of electricity in Portugal and the undertaking acting as last resort supplier. The special rights at stake included (a) the right of veto in respect of certain resolutions of the general meeting of the company's shareholders; (b) the right to appoint a director, where the State has voted against the nominees successfully elected as directors, and (c) the exemption of the State from the voting ceiling of 5% laid down in relation to the casting of votes.

Despite the fact that the Portuguese State admittedly conceded that the contested golden shares qualified as 'State measures' and thus focused primarily on the absence of any hindrance to the market access of foreign investors, the Court in an *obiter dictum* in paragraph 62, implied that there might be no restriction on capital movements when the State acts as any other *shareholder* and introduces special rights which are available to *all* shareholders. In particular, it found that the right to appoint a director constituted a restriction on the free movement of capital since it departed from general company law and was laid down by a national legislative measure for the sole benefit of the public authorities.[200] However, it made a very interesting general statement recognising that such a right to appoint a director can be conferred by legislation as a right of a qualified minority on the condition that it is accessible to *all* shareholders and not reserved exclusively to the State.[201] It has been argued

---

195 Ibid, para 26.
196 Ibid, para 27.
197 Ibid, para 28.
198 Ibid, para 29.
199 Case C-543/08 *Commission v Portugal (golden shares – EDP)*.
200 Ibid, para 60.
201 Ibid, para 62.

that this excerpt should be interpreted in the sense that if the Member State just makes use of the rights available for all shareholders, it may not impinge upon Article 63 TFEU.[202]

The aforementioned case law reveals that the qualification of a measure as 'State measure' is sometimes confused with the finding of a 'restriction'. In principle, these should be treated as two distinct steps in the legal reasoning, as the first one concerns primarily the question whether the case concerns a vertical situation in which an individual can bring a claim against the State, whereas the latter concerns the question whether the contested measure obstructs the free movement of capital. However, more often than not, in the capital case law these two distinct questions are treated as one. While this is perhaps understandable from a judicial economy perspective, it nevertheless reveals the strikingly broad interpretation of 'capital restrictions' adopted by the Court, which covers virtually all measures that qualify as 'State measures'.

b) *Scholarly Opinions on the Horizontal Effect of Article 63 TFEU*

Scholars have expressed different views regarding the horizontal effect of Article 63 TFEU, both in relation to the question whether Article 63 TFEU applies when the State acts as a shareholder/market participant under private law ('extended vertical effect') and in relation to the *stricto sensu* horizontal effect of Article 63 TFEU covering acts of private parties.

Commenting on the *Volkswagen* case, Catherine Barnard argues that if the Court considered that Article 63 TFEU was horizontally applicable, it would have rejected Germany's argument that Volkswagen Law merely reproduced a private agreement on that ground.[203] In other words, it would have said that despite its private nature, this agreement is still caught by Article 63 TFEU. The fact that it chose to classify the measure at issue as a *State measure* is an indication of its unwillingness to grant horizontal direct effect to Article 63 TFEU.

Conversely, Jonathan Rickford, who interprets the Court's rulings in *Viking* and *Laval* as endorsing the concept of horizontal effect of Articles 49 and 56

---

202 Karsten Engsig Sørensen, 'Company Law as a Restriction to Free Movement – Examination of the Notion of 'Restriction' Using Company Law as the Frame of Reference' (2014) 11 *European Company Law* 178 at p. 186. See also the cited books Stefan Grundmann, *European Company Law – Organization, Finance and Capital Markets* (Intersentia 2012); Alan Dashwood and others, *Wyatt and Dashwood's European Union Law* (Hart Publishing 2011).
203 Catherine Barnard, *The Substantive Law of the EU: The Four Freedoms* (Oxford University Press 2016), p. 526.

TFEU, contends that the same applies to capital as well.[204] Firstly, he espouses the 'extended vertical effect' of Article 63 TFEU, arguing that there is no doubt that the obligation not to obstruct capital movements binds Member States not only when they exercise their sovereign powers under public law, but also when they act *in their private capacity under private law*.[205] This view is reinforced by the principle of sincere cooperation enshrined in Article 4 (3) TFEU, according to which Member States are obliged to abstain from any measure that could jeopardise the attainment of the objectives of the Treaty.[206] He agrees with Advocate General Maduro in KPN where he famously stated that 'Member States are subject to the rules on free movement, of which they are clearly addressees, not on account of their *functional* capacity as public authority, but on account of their *organic* capacity as signatory of the Treaty'.[207]

Secondly, he ponders over the extent to which private persons are bound by the free movement of capital and, drawing from *Angonese*, he thinks that there is reason to believe that a discriminatory practice by a private individuals might be caught by Article 63 TFEU. At the same time, he draws a parallel with the *Viking* and *Laval* rulings on the basis of which he contends that, by the same token, the free movement of capital applies to private persons exercising regulatory powers.[208] In other words, he considers that where a private party is *entrusted with public functions* under private law, the free movement of capital applies because that private party acts *as a surrogate for the State*.[209] As an illustration of this configuration he refers to three examples of *private acts with a public purpose* which might be subject to the scrutiny of the free movement of capital: (1) the private law golden share in the UK Reuters Trust aiming at ensuring that control changes in the company will not jeopardise

---

204   Jonathan Rickford, 'Protectionism, Capital Freedom and the Internal Market' in Bernitz and Ringe (eds), *Company Law and Economic Protectionism – New Challenges to European Integration* (Oxford University Press 2010), p. 77.
205   Jonathan Rickford, 'Free movement of capital and protectionism after Volkswagen and Viking Line' in Tison and Wymeersch (eds), *Perspectives in Company Law and Financial Regulation – Essays in Honour of Eddy Wymeersch* (Cambridge University Press 2009), p. 83–84.
206   Jonathan Rickford, 'Protectionism, Capital Freedom and the Internal Market' in Bernitz and Ringe (eds), *Company Law and Economic Protectionism – New Challenges to European Integration* (Oxford University Press 2010), p. 78.
207   *Opinion of Advocate General Maduro in Joined cases C-282/04 and C-283/04 Commission v The Netherlands (golden shares)*, para 22.
208   Jonathan Rickford, 'Free movement of capital and protectionism after Volkswagen and Viking Line' in Tison and Wymeersch (eds), *Perspectives in Company Law and Financial Regulation – Essays in Honour of Eddy Wymeersch* (Cambridge University Press 2009), p. 86.
209   Ibid, p. 87.

the editorial independence; (2) certain company law arrangements in Nordic countries offering voting shares with enhanced powers exercisable for the benefit not of the shareholders but of the company in the widest sense, including its continuity, the protection of its workers and the interests of the society as a whole; and (3) the powers of company boards in certain Member States to frustrate the success of takeover bids from companies with a less open structure than their own (a possibility which is stems from the fact that the 'board neutrality rule' under Article 9 of Directive 2004/25/EC on Takeovers[210] is *optional* under Article 12 thereof). He regards these private acts as subject to the Internal Market scrutiny because of the fact that they have a *public purpose* and the private parties exercising them act as *surrogate for the State*. However, he expresses doubts as to whether private parties engaging for purely private purposes in conduct which falls short of discrimination are bound by the free movement of capital.[211]

Similarly, Wolf-Georg Ringe strongly advocates the 'extended vertical effect' of Article 63 TFEU, arguing that there is 'no escape into private law' for the Member States.[212] All State action, regardless of whether it is based on public authority or not, should be classified as 'State measure' and should therefore be subject to the free movement of capital.[213] He effectively agrees with Advocate General Maduro that 'Member States, when operating as a market participant, may be subject to constraints that do not apply to other market participants'[214] and he compares golden shares with the area of public procurement where the State, even when acting under private law, is subject to additional and more restrictive requirements of transparency and accountability which do not bind private parties.[215] Similarly, he considers that, despite the 'private market

---

210 'Directive 2004/25/EC of the European Parliament and of the Council of 21 april 2004 on takeover bids' (2004) *OJ L 142, 30.4.2004, p. 12–23*.
211 Jonathan Rickford, 'Free movement of capital and protectionism after Volkswagen and Viking Line' in Tison and Wymeersch (eds), *Perspectives in Company Law and Financial Regulation – Essays in Honour of Eddy Wymeersch* (Cambridge University Press 2009), p. 87.
212 Wolf-Georg Ringe, 'Company Law and Free Movement of Capital' (2010) 69 Cambridge Law Journal 378, p. 396. See also Wolf-Georg Ringe, 'Case C-112/05, Commission v. Germany ("vw law"), Judgment of the Grand Chamber of 23 October 2007, nyr'. (2008) 45 Common Market Law Review 37; Wolf-Georg Ringe, 'Is Volkswagen the New Centros? Free movement of Capital's Impact on Company Law' in Prentice and Reisberg (eds), *Corporate Finance Law in the UK and EU* (Oxford University Press 2011).
213 Wolf-Georg Ringe, 'Company Law and Free Movement of Capital' (2010) 69 Cambridge Law Journal 378, p. 397–398.
214 *Opinion of Advocate General Maduro in Joined cases C-282/04 and C-283/04 Commission v The Netherlands (golden shares)*, para 22.
215 Wolf-Georg Ringe, 'Company Law and Free Movement of Capital' (2010) 69 Cambridge Law Journal 378, p. 397.

actor' test, the very existence of State aid rules reveals that the State is treated with more suspicion than private parties.

In relation to the *stricto sensu* horizontal effect of Article 63 TFEU, he draws from the settled case law in the other fields (*Bosman, Viking, Laval, Defrenne, Angonese*) and concludes that when powerful federations act in a quasi-regulatory manner, they are subject to the free movement rules because the effect of their action can be equalised with the effect of State legislation (the 'private governance' argument).[216] At the same time, because of its eminent status as a fundamental value, the principle of non-discrimination is applied horizontally even when there is no private governance.[217] In the context of the interaction between company law and free movement of capital, Ringe ponders the question whether a commercial company, which collectively decides for all investors, fulfils the 'private governance' test (which has traditionally be linked to the 'intermediary powers' of federations and trade unions issuing collective rules) and thus can be subject to the Treaty provisions on the free movement of capital.[218] In this respect, he estimates that decisions of a single company will not necessarily cross this threshold in the absence of any particular circumstances.[219]

By contrast, Andrea Biondi follows a more nuanced approach in relation to the 'extended vertical effect' of Article 63 TFEU.[220] He considers that the golden shares case law carries an element of risk in the sense that every action attributable to the State might be caught by capital scrutiny, leaving thus very limited leeway for Member States to organise their economic and industrial policies and to pursue public policy objectives.[221] Inspired by state aid law, he suggests that this risk might be prevented through the adoption of a 'private market investor' principle, whereby State conduct is immune from scrutiny if proven to be subject to the normal rules of the operation of the market.[222]

Carsten Gerner-Beuerle agrees with the other scholars that the vertical effect of Article 63 TFEU covers not only regulatory acts of the State (*ius imperii*), but also acts taken by the State in the course of its operation as a

---

216 Ibid, p. 392.
217 Ibid, p. 392–393.
218 Ibid.
219 Ibid.
220 Andrea Biondi, 'When the State is the Owner – Some Further Comments on the Court of Justice 'Golden Shares' Strategy' in Bernitz and Ringe (eds), *Company Law and Economic Protectionism: New Challenges to European Integration* (Oxford University Press 2010).
221 Ibid, p. 97.
222 Ibid, p. 101.

normal shareholder without *ius imperii*.[223] However, in the latter scenario, only measures discriminating between domestic and foreign investment should fall within the scope of the free movement of capital.[224] In relation to the horizontal application of Article 63 TFEU, he expresses his fear that if the Court accords horizontal effect to Article 63 TFEU, this could potentially open the door to an avalanche of claims challenging any type of control enhancing mechanisms contained in a company's Articles of Association as capital restrictions.[225] However, from a conceptual point of view, it is not self-evident why the free movement of capital should restrict the private autonomy of companies opting to include control enhancing mechanisms in their Articles of Association.[226] Furthermore, while it is true that some control enhancing mechanisms might have a deterrent effect on foreign investment, it cannot be excluded that a possible prohibition on them might actually have the same deterrent effect on foreign investment.[227] Indeed, some investors might be discouraged by the existence of control enhancing mechanisms in the undertaking concerned, while some others might be discouraged by their very absence. Moreover, convincing statistical evidence might be required in order to assess the deterrent effect private actions might have on cross-border investment and it is questionable whether the Court is well-equipped to devise and employ such evidence.[228] He therefore concludes that, apart from cases of flagrant discrimination like the one in *Angonese* and *Defrenne*, which however are of limited practical use in the capital case law, special rights included in the Articles of Association of a company without any involvement of public authorities should not fall within the scope of Article 63 TFEU.[229]

Finally, Harm Schepel believes that the Court will sooner or later recognise the horizontal direct effect of Article 63 TFEU, since the *Walrave* rationale of *effet utile and uniform application* apply *a fortiori* in the field of free movement of capital due to the nature of the rules defining the corporate governance systems of the Member States in the EU.[230] These rules include a transnational

---

223　Carsten Gerner-Beuerle, 'Shareholders Between the Market and the State. The VW Law and other Interventions in the Market Economy' (2012) 49 Common Market Law Review 97, p. 131.
224　Ibid, p. 131.
225　Ibid, p. 133.
226　Ibid, p. 134.
227　Ibid, p. 134.
228　Ibid, p. 135.
229　Ibid, p. 136.
230　Harm Schepel, 'Constitutionalising the Market, Marketising the Constitution, and to Tell the Difference: On the Horizontal Application of the Free Movement Provisions in EU Law' (2012) 18 European Law Journal 177.

patchwork of private agreements, a number of codes, a plethora of different rules included in the Articles of Association of companies as well as diverging mandatory and optional rules of national company law.[231] However, it is argued that the recognition of horizontal effect of Article 63 TFEU together with the strikingly broad interpretation of capital restrictions will most likely place all company law structures deviating from the one share/one vote principle and from the principle of shareholders' primacy under judicial review for conformity with the free movement of capital.[232]

c) *Granting Horizontal Effect to Article 63 TFEU*

The aforementioned scholarly contributions provide a thorough analysis of all the legal, political and social dimensions of ascribing horizontal effect to Article 63 TFEU and reveal the intricate legal issues arising from a possible horizontality of the free movement of capital in view of the multifaceted nature of the various corporate governance arrangements that exist in the Member States. It is submitted here that, for reasons of legal consistency, if one accepts that when the State acts in its private capacity as a normal shareholder its actions are not caught by the free movement of capital by virtue of the private market operator test, then *a fortiori* it should be acknowledged that private parties are not bound by Article 63 TFEU. If, however, one accepts that the free movement of capital binds the State even when it acts as a shareholder, the same should apply to all private parties, especially when given their dominant position they exercise quasi-regulatory powers over other market participants. It is thus argued that when acting in their private capacity as market participants, both the State and private parties should operate under equal conditions. The more restrictive requirements imposed on the State in the field of public procurement through the adoption of specific secondary legislation, cannot justifiably be extrapolated to the free movement of capital.

Private parties are important market operators and their actions can have far-reaching economic and social implications, especially when they hold a dominant position in the market which gives them the power to impose conditions on other market participants (such as consumers, creditors, suppliers, other competitors etc.). This is all the more true if one accepts the theory of

---

[231] Carsten Gerner-Beuerle, 'Shareholders Between the Market and the State. The VW Law and other Interventions in the Market Economy' (2012) 49 Common Market Law Review 97, p. 193.

[232] Harm Schepel, 'Constitutionalising the Market, Marketising the Constitution, and to Tell the Difference: On the Horizontal Application of the Free Movement Provisions in EU Law' (2012) 18 European Law Journal 177, p. 193.

horizontality of fundamental rights which regards private individuals as not existing in a legal vacuum, but as part of a solidaristic society in which individuals are responsible for their actions towards other individuals. To reject horizontality on the basis of the argument of self-regulation of the market and respect of private autonomy, although admittedly appealing, disregards firstly the shortcomings of self-regulation and secondly the fact that private autonomy is in any case regulated by national legislation.

It should be noted, however, that the fears expressed by some scholars above are well-founded. Indeed, it seems that the golden shares case law amounts to a 'quality control' review of all company law arrangements and this could perhaps be exacerbated if the Court accords horizontal effect to Article 63 TFEU, as this would bring under judicial scrutiny *all* (both public and private) corporate governance instuments derogating from the *principle of proportionality between ownership and control* and the *principle of shareholders' primacy*. However, despite the undisputed merits of this argument, it is claimed here that this intrusive function of the free movement of capital can be thwarted by a more restrictive interpretation of the notion of 'capital restrictions', not by refusing to grant horizontal effect.

Indeed, horizontal effect relates more to the question whether private parties can judicially invoke their free movement rights against other private parties. This is different from the question whether the substantive content of the specific private act constitutes indeed a restriction on capital movements. Concerns over the potentially invasive effect of the free movement of capital for the corporate governance systems of Member States are more adequately adressed in the following steps of the legal reasoning, i.e. the one concerning whether the measure in question constitutes a capital restriction and the next one concerning possible justification of that restriction.

The same holds true for concerns relating to the potential interference with private autonomy and with the freedom to conduct a business under Article 16 of the Charter as a result of the horizontal application of the free movement provisions. In particular, it has been argued that if all free movement provisions were attributed full horizontal effect this would negate the freedom to conduct a business under Article 16 of the Charter.[233] To resolve the conflict between free movement rights and freedom to conduct a business, a 'double proportionality' test is proposed under which the realisation of both must be presumed to constitute a legitimate objective.[234] On the basis of this test, it is

---

233 Rufat Babayev, 'Private Autonomy at Union Level: On Article 16 CFREU and Free Movement Rights' (2016) 53 *Common Market Law Review* 979.
234 Ibid, p. 1000.

argued that when there is no 'dominance' (i.e. when the private actors in question do not exert power the outcome of which other private actors are not able to avoid), the 'minor' interference with free movement rigths cannot justify the 'major' interference with the freedom to conduct a business.[235] Conversely, when there is 'dominance' (i.e when the private actors impose obligations which other private actors cannot avoid), the 'major' interference with the free movement rights can justify the 'minor' interference with the freedom to conduct a business.[236]

B *Public Interest Objectives as Justification Grounds in the Golden Shares Case Law*

The Court has recognised that, in principle, the free movement of capital may be restricted by national measures justified on the grounds set out in Article 65 TFEU or by overriding reasons in the general interest to the extent that there is no harmonisation at the EU level providing for measures necessary to ensure the protection of those interests.[237] Member States have also attempted to justify capital restrictions on the basis of other Treaty provisions, such as Article 106 (2) TFEU and Article 345 TFEU. In the absence of harmonisation, the Court, in principle, accepts that it is for the Member States to decide the degree of protection they wish to afford to such legitimate interests and the way such protection is to be achieved, while ensuring that they respect the principle of proportionality.[238] However, in all but one golden shares case (the *Belgian* case), the above-mentioned justification grounds have been rejected either due to a lack of evidence proving that the special shareholding in question is actually suitable and necessary in order to pursue the legitimate objective invoked or due to a failure to comply with the principle of legal certainty. This stems partly from the principle according to which fundamental freedoms must be interpreted widely, whereas exceptions must be construed narrowly. But it also stems from the ideological premise according to which golden shares are protectionist measures and as such they are inherently incompatible with the Internal Market. The following section provides a typology of the justification grounds unsuccessfully that have been invoked by the Member States.

---

235 Ibid, p. 1004.
236 Ibid.
237 Joined cases C-463/04 and C-464/04 *Federconsumatori (AEM/Edison)*, para 39.
238 Ibid, para 40.

1 The Objective of Safeguarding Energy Supplies in the Event of a Crisis as Covered by Public Security under Article 65 (1) (b) TFEU

One of the most frequently used legitimate objectives in the golden shares case law is the *safeguarding of energy supplies in the event of a crisis*.[239] This is because most of the privatised undertakings in which the Member States maintain special rights are active in the *energy sector*. For instance, in one of the early golden shares cases, the French Government argued that the prior administrative authorisation scheme for the acquisition of shares in privatised undertakings was essential in order to safeguard supplies of petroleum products in the event of a crisis, which, in *Campus Oil*,[240] had been recognised as an objective covered by the concept of *public security*.[241] In this regard, the Court recognised that the objective of safeguarding supplies of petroleum products fell within the ambit of a legitimate public interest which could justify an obstacle to the free movement of goods and the same could apply to obstacles to the free movement of capital, inasmuch as public security was also one of the justification grounds referred to in Article 65 (1) (b) TFEU.[242] Similarly, in the *Belgian golden shares* case, the Court accepted that the national opposition scheme in question could be justified on grounds of safeguarding energy supplies in the event of a crisis, which fell within the ambit of public security as a derogation ground under Article 65 (1) (b) TFEU.[243]

At the same time, however, the Court has clarified that public security as a derogation from the fundamental freedoms must be interpreted strictly, with the result that its scope cannot be determined unilaterally by each Member State without any control by the institutions of the European Union.[244] It can be relied on only if there is a genuine and sufficiently serious threat to a fundamental interest of society.[245] Merely making a general statement asserting

---

239 Case C-367/98 *Commission v Portugal (golden shares)*, ECLI:EU:C:2002:326; Case C-483/99 *Commission v France (golden shares – Société Nationale Elf-Aquitaine)*; Case C-503/99 *Commission v Belgium (golden shares)*; Case C-463/00 *Commission v Spain (golden shares)*; Case C-174/04 *Commission v Italy (golden shares)*; Case C-274/06 *Commission v Spain (golden shares)*; Case C-207/07 *Commission v Spain (golden shares in the energy sector)*; Case C-326/07 *Commission v Italy (golden shares)*; Case C-543/08 *Commission v Portugal (golden shares – EDP)*; Case C-212/09 *Commission v Portugal (golden shares – GALP Energia SGPS SA)*; Case C-244/11 *Commission v Greece (golden shares)*.
240 Case 72/83 *Campus Oil*, paras 34-35.
241 Case C-483/99 *Commission v France (golden shares – Société Nationale Elf-Aquitaine)*, para 28.
242 Ibid, para 47.
243 Case C-503/99 *Commission v Belgium (golden shares)*, para 46.
244 Case C-212/09 *Commission v Portugal (golden shares – GALP Energia SGPS SA)*, para 83.
245 Case C-207/07 *Commission v Spain (golden shares in the energy sector)*, para 47; Case C-244/11 *Commission v Greece (golden shares)*, para 67.

the relevance of the safequarding of enegy supplies as a legitimate objective is not sufficient to meet the required standard of proof.[246] Thus, in *Commission v Portugal* (*EDP – Energias de Portugal*) the Court rejected Portugal's argument that a State could legitimately equip itself with the means required to guarantee the fundamental interest of security of energy supplies even if there was no imminent threat.[247] In particular, the Portuguese government had argued that since the risk of serious threats to the security of energy supply could not be excluded and since such threats were by definition sudden and, in the majority of cases, unforeseeable, it was the duty of the Member State concerned to ensure that adequate mechanisms were put in place to enable it to react rapidly and effectively to guarantee that the security of that supply was not interrupted.[248] While acknowledging the merit of this argument, the Court nevertheless rejected the justification on the ground that the Portuguese government had done no more than raise the ground relating to the security of the energy supply, without stating clearly the exact reasons why it considered that the special rights at issue would make it possible to prevent such an interference with a fundamental interest of society.[249]

2 The Objective of Ensuring Availability of the Telecommunications Network in the Event of a Crisis as Covered by Public Security under Article 65 (1) (b) TFEU

By analogy, in the field of telecommunications, it has been accepted that the objective of ensuring availability of the telecommunications network in case of crisis, war or terrorism may constitute a ground of public security under Article 65 (1) (b) TFEU.[250]

3 The Objective of Guaranteeing a Service of General Interest as an Overriding Reason in the Public Interest

In the *Dutch golden shares* case, the Court acknowledged that the guarantee of a service of general interest, such as universal postal service, may constitute an overriding reason in the general interest capable of justifying an obstacle to

---

246 Niamh Nic Shuibhne and Marsela Maci, 'Proving Public Interest: The Growing Impact of Evidence in Free Movement Case Law' (2015) 50 *Common Market Law Review* 965, p. 980.
247 Case C-543/08 *Commission v Portugal (golden shares – EDP)*, para 86.
248 Ibid, para 86.
249 Ibid, para 87.
250 Case C-171/08 *Commission v Portugal (golden shares – Portugal Telecom SGPS SA)*, para 72.

the free movement of capital.[251] In *Federconsumatori*, the Court held that 'it is undeniable that certain concerns may justify the retention by Member States of a degree of influence within undertakings that were initially public and subsequently privatised, where those undertakings are active in fields involving the provision of services in the public interest or strategic services'.[252]

4   Article 106 (2) TFEU

In *Commission v Portugal (GALP Energia SGPS SA)*, the Portuguese governement argued that the right to veto certain important decisions of the company and the right to appoint the chairman of the Board of Directors were required under Article 106 (2) TFEU in order to enable GALP to carry out appropriately its tasks of managing services of general economic interest entrusted to it by the State.[253] The Court rejected this argument on the basis of the fact that the national provisions in question did not involve the granting of special or exclusive rights to GALP or the classification of GALP's activities as services of general economic interest, but were concerned with the lawfulness of attributing to the Portuguese State, as a shareholder of that company, special rights in connection with golden shares which it holds in the share capital of GALP.[254] Moreover, the Court emphasised that the Portuguese government had not provided any reasons why the performance of services of general economic interest would be jeopardised if the special rights in question were abolished.[255] Therefore, Article 106 (2) TFEU was not applicable *in casu*.[256] The same conclusion was reached in *Commission v Portugal (EDP)*.[257]

---

251   Joined cases C-282/04 and C-283/04 *Commission v The Netherlands (golden shares)*, para 38 citing Joined cases C388/00 and C429/00 *Radiosistemi Srl v Prefetto di Genova*, ECLI:EU:C:2002:390, para 44.
252   Joined cases C-463/04 and C-464/04 *Federconsumatori (AEM/Edison)*, para 41.
253   Case C-212/09 *Commission v Portugal (golden shares – GALP Energia SGPS SA)*, para 80.
254   Ibid, para 93.
255   Ibid, para 94.
256   Ibid, para 95.
257   Case C-543/08 *Commission v Portugal (golden shares – EDP)*, paras 93-96. Similarly, in the recent *Commission v Hungary*, the Court found that a national monopoly of mobile payment services constitutes a restriction of the freedom to provide services that could not be justified on Article 106 (2) TFEU, as Hungary failed to prove why the performance of the particular task with which the service concerned was entrusted required the creation of a monopoly by granting exclusive rights to the undertaking in question. See Case C-171/17 *Commission v Hungary*, ECLI:EU:C:2018:881, para 93.

5 Protection of Workers and of Minority Shareholders

In *Commission v Germany (Volkswagen I)*, which epitomizes the conflict between internal market and social objectives,[258] the Court accepted that the protection of workers[259] and the protection of minority shareholders[260] could be regarded as overriding reasons in the public interests capable of justifying a restriction on capital movements.[261] However, it found that Germany had failed to explain how the special rights in question could protect the workers and the minority shareholders.[262]

6 Economic Rule

The Court has applied the economic rule in the golden shares case law and has ruled that economic considerations cannot justify a restriction on capital movements. In particular, in the first *Portuguese golden shares* case, the Portuguese Government claimed that its legislation, imposing a cap on foreign investment and an authorisation procedure for the acquisition of shares, was justified by overriding requirements of the general interest, since it was intended to safeguard its financial interests and the economic policy objectives pursued by

---

258 Jonathan Rickford, 'Protectionism, Capital Freedom and the Internal Market' in Bernitz and Ringe (eds), *Company Law and Economic Protectionism – New Challenges to European Integration* (Oxford University Press 2010), p. 67.

259 Case 279/80 *Criminal proceedings against Alfred John Webb*, ECLI:EU:C:1981:314, para 19; Case C-288/89 *Stichting Collectieve Antennevoorziening Gouda and others v Commissariaat voor de Media*, ECLI:EU:C:1991:323, paras 13–14; Case C-106/16 *Polbud – Wykonawstwo sp. z o.o.*, ECLI:EU:C:2017:804, para 54; Joined cases C-369/96 and C-376/96 *Criminal proceedings against Jean-Claude Arblade and Arblade & Fils SARL and Bernard Leloup, Serge Leloup and Sofrage SARL*, ECLI:EU:C:1999:575, para 36; Case C-411/03 *SEVIC Systems AG*, ECLI:EU:C:2005:762, para 28; Case C-438/05 *Viking*, para 77; Case C-201/15 *AGET Iraklis*, para 73. Similarly, it has also been accepted that the encouragement of employment and recruitment which, being designed in particular to reduce unemployment, constitutes a legitimate aim of social policy. See, Case C-208/05 *ITC Innovative Technology Center GmbH v Bundesagentur für Arbeit*, ECLI:EU:C:2007:16, para 38; Case C-385/05 *Confédération générale du travail and Others*, ECLI:EU:C:2007:37, para 28; Case C-379/11 *Caves Krier Frères Sàrl v Directeur de l'Administration de l'emploi*, ECLI:EU:C:2012:798, para 51. See also Catherine Barnard, 'The Worker Protection Justification: Lessons from Consumer Law' in Panos Koutrakos, Niamh Nic Shuibhne and Phil Syrpis (eds), *Exceptions from EU Free Movement Law: Derogation, Justification and Proportionality* (Hart Publishing 2016), p. 106–130; Sophie Robin-Olivier, 'Bargaining in the shadow of free movement of capital' (2012) 8 *European Review of Contract Law* 167.

260 Case C-106/16 *Polbud*, para 54; Case C-411/03 *SEVIC Systems*, para 28; Case C-208/00 *Überseering BV v Nordic Construction Company Baumanagement GmbH (NCC)*, ECLI:EU:C:2002:632, para 92.

261 Case C-112/05 *Commission v Germany (golden shares – Volkswagen I)*, paras 72-80.

262 Ibid, paras 74-77.

the pre-privatisation process, such as choosing a strategic partner where the activities of the undertaking were to assume an international dimension, or strengthening the competitive structure of the market concerned, or modernising and increasing the efficiency of means of production.[263] Not surprisingly, the Court replied that neither the *general financial interests* of a Member State nor the *economic policy objectives* could constitute adequate justification, as according to settled case law economic grounds can never serve as justification for obstacles prohibited by the Treaty.[264] In the same vein, in *Commission v Italy*, the Court held that an interest in strengthening the competitve structure of the market could not constitute valid justification for restrictions on the free movement of capital.[265] Finally, in *Commission v Portugal (Portugal Telecom SGPS SA)*, the Court found that an interest in ensuring the conditions of competition on a particular market and the need to prevent a possible disruption of the capital market could not constitute valid justifications for restrictions on the free movement of capital.[266]

C *Proportionality in the Golden Shares Case Law*

The proportionality test applied by the Court in its case law on the fundamental freedoms consists of two separate steps: 1) whether the national measure in question is sutable/appropriate to achieve the legitimate objective pursued (suitability test); and 2) whether it is necessary to achieve this objective, i.e. whether there are other less restrictive means capable of attaining the objective in question (necessity test).[267] In order to prove that the contested national measure is compatible with the principle of proportionality, Member States are required to provide sufficient evidence capable of substantiating this conclusion.[268] In view of the general rule that exceptions from the fundamental freedoms are to be construed narrowly, the burden of proof of the Member States – although admittedly not strictly defined[269] – is in practice very high

---

263 Case C-367/98 *Commission v Portugal (golden shares)*, para 31.
264 Ibid, para 52.
265 Case C-174/04 *Commission v Italy (golden shares)*, para 37.
266 Case C-171/08 *Commission v Portugal (golden shares – Portugal Telecom SGPS SA)*, paras 70-71.
267 In the majority of the cases, proportionality *stricto sensu*, as the third step in the traditional proportionality assessment stemming from German Constitutional Law, is not applied by the Court. See Paul Craig and Gráinne De Búrca, *EU Law: Text, Cases and Materials* (Oxford University Press 2011), p. 551.
268 Case C-542/09 *Commission v Netherlands (access to education)*, ECLI:EU:C:2012:346, para 82.
269 Niamh Nic Shuibhne and Marsela Maci, 'Proving Public Interest: The Growing Impact of Evidence in Free Movement Case Law' (2015) 50 Common Market Law Review 965, p. 975.

and often difficult to be met. The Court is usually strict in the review of the justifications invoked by the Member States and quite tough when assessing the proportionality of the contested measure.[270]

The golden shares case law provides a typical example of rigorousness in the application of the standard of proof in the proportionality assessment. The Court requires a high degree of evidence in order to establish the legal claim that the contested special rights are justified and proportionate to the objective pursued. The intensity of the judicial review comes as no surprise as it reflects the underlying rationale that golden shares are inherently incompatible with free movement of capital and it confirms the generally strict jurisprudential approach to proportionality in Internal Market litigation. What is more interesting, however, is the additional step that emerges from the proportionality assessment of golden shares and characterises the capital case law in general. This additional step examines the compatibility with the principle of legal certainty and it is governed by a procedural rather than substantive rationality.

Procedural elements of proportionality such as policy coherence, consistency and transparency are discerned in other fields of Internal Market case law, primarily the ones touching upon morally contientious issues. Floris de Witte argues that in these fields the 'procedural proportionality' test is used to rationalise the process of national legislation and is more respectful of the normative policy aims of the Member States.[271] The 'procedural proportionality' test is juxtaposed with the 'substantive proportionality' test which seeks to rationalise the content of national legislation, leaving little normative leeway for Member States.[272] It is argued that for morally and ethically contentious questions, the 'procedural proportionality' test is better suited, as it respects the substance of national moral and ethical choices and focuses only on teasing out discriminatory or protectionist biases by assessing the normative coherence of national policies, the consistent application of sanctions and the legislative transparency.[273]

The main field in which the 'procedural proportionality' test has been widely applied is gambling, a field in which the process of market liberalisation has not been very successful and Member States continue to enjoy a wide

---

270   Catherine Barnard, 'Derogations, Justifications and the Four Freedoms: Is State Interest Really Protected?' in Catherine Barnard and Okeoghene Odudu (eds), *The Outer Limits of European Union Law* (Hart Publishing 2009), p. 299.
271   Floris De Witte, 'Sex, Drugs & EU Law: The Recognition of Moral and Ethical Diversity in EU Law' (2013) 50 *Common Market Law Review* 1545, p. 1566.
272   Ibid.
273   Ibid, p. 1573.

margin of discretion in defining their regulatory framework. It has been argued that the relaxation of the internal market requirements in the gambling cases comes down to virtual dismantling.[274] In particular, in its gambling case law,[275] the Court has granted a general margin of appreciation to the Member States in choosing how to regulate gambling services and has accepted a whole array

---

274   Stefaan Van den Bogaert and Armin Cuyvers, ' "Money for nothing": The case law of the EU Court of Justice on the regulation of gambling' (2011) 48 *Common Market Law Review* 1175, p. 1208; Alan Littler, 'Regulatory perspectives on the future of interactive gambling in the internal market' (2008) 33 *European Law Review* 211; Allan Littler, *Member States versus the European Union – The Regulation of Gambling* (Brill Academic Publishers 2011). See also the annotations: Marek Szydło, 'Continuing the judicial gambling saga in Berlington' (2016) 53 *Common Market Law Review* 1089; Thomas Beukers, 'Case C-409/06, Winner Wetten GmbH v. Bürgermeisterin der Stadt Bergheim, Judgment of the Court (Grand Chamber) of 8 September 2010, not yet reported' (2011) 48 *Common Market Law Review* 1985; Armin Cuyvers, 'Joined Cases C-338/04, C-359/04 and C-360/04, Massimiliano Placanica, Christian Palazzese and Angelo Sorricchio (Placanica)' (2008) 45 *Common Market Law Review* 515; Vassilis Hatzopoulos, 'Case C-275/92, Her Majesty's Customs and Excise v. Gerhart and Jorg Schindler, [1994] ECR 1-1039' (1995) 32 *Common Market Law Review* 841.

275   Case C-275/92 *Schindler*; Case C-124/97 *Markku Juhani Läärä, Cotswold Microsystems Ltd and Oy Transatlantic Software Ltd v Kihlakunnansyyttäjä (Jyväskylä) and Suomen valtio (Finnish State)*, ECLI:EU:C:1999:435; Case C-67/98 *Questore di Verona v Diego Zenatti*, ECLI:EU:C:1999:514; Case C-6/01 *Associação Nacional de Operadores de Máquinas Recreativas (Anomar) and Others v Estado português*, ECLI:EU:C:2003:446; Case C-243/01 *Criminal proceedings against Piergiorgio Gambelli and Others*, ECLI:EU:C:2003:597; Case C-338/04 *Criminal proceedings against Massimiliano Placanica, Christian Palazzese and Angelo Sorricchio*, ECLI:EU:C:2007:133; Case C-409/06 *Winner Wetten GmbH v Bürgermeisterin der Stadt Bergheim*, ECLI:EU:C:2010:503; Case C-42/07 *Liga Portuguesa de Futebol Profissional and Bwin International*, ECLI:EU:C:2009:519; Case C-316/07 *Markus Stoß, Avalon Service-Online-Dienste GmbH and Olaf Amadeus Wilhelm Happel*, ECLI:EU:C:2010:504; Case C-46/08 *Carmen Media Group Ltd v Land Schleswig-Holstein and Innenminister des Landes Schleswig-Holstein*, ECLI:EU:C:2010:505; Case C-64/08 *Criminal proceedings against Ernst Engelmann*, ECLI:EU:C:2010:506; Case C-203/08 *Sporting Exchange Ltd v Minister van Justitie*, ECLI:EU:C:2010:307; Case C-258/08 *Ladbrokes Betting & Gaming and Ladbrokes International*, ECLI:EU:C:2010:308; Case C-447/08 *Criminal proceedings against Otto Sjöberg and Anders Gerdin* ECLI:EU:C:2010:415; Case C-347/09 *Criminal proceedings against Jochen Dickinger and Franz Ömer*, ECLI:EU:C:2011:582; Case C-186/11 *Stanleybet International Ltd, William Hill Organization Ltd, William Hill plc, Sportingbet plc v Ipourgos Oikonomias kai Oikonomikon Ipourgos Politismou*, ECLI:EU:C:2013:33; Case C-463/13 *Stanley International Betting and Stanleybet Malta*, ECLI:EU:C:2015:25; Case C-98/14 *Berlington Hungary Tanácsadó és Szolgáltató kft and Others v Magyar Állam*, ECLI:EU:C:2015:386; Case C-336/14 *Criminal proceedings against Sebat Ince*, ECLI:EU:C:2016:72; Case C-375/14 *Criminal proceedings against Rosanna Laezza*, ECLI:EU:C:2016:60; Case C-3/17 *Sporting Odds Limited v Nemzeti Adó- és Vámhivatal Központi Irányítása*, ECLI:EU:C:2018:130 (Court of Justice).

of public interest objectives capable of justifying restrictions on the fundamental freedoms (such as the fight against gaming addiction, the reduction of gambling opportunities, the fight against crime, the general need to preserve public order, protection of consumers of games of chance against fraud on the part of operators etc). At the same time it has refined the suitability test so as to include the requirement of consistency: restrictions on gaming activities are suitable to achieve their public interest objectives only insofar as these objectives are being pursued 'in a consistent and systematic manner'.[276] The consistency test *prima facie* imposes an additional procedural requirement in the proportionality assessment: Member States must not take, facilitate or tolerate measures that would run counter to the achievement of the legitimate objectives pursued.[277] In practice, however, the consistency test means that if the legitimate objectives are pursued in a 'consistent and systematic manner', the national regulatory framework on gambling will generally pass the proportionality assssement, without really examining the substantive content of the legislation in question and without really applying the suitability and necessity test as applied in other fields of Internal Market litigation. This is all the more true when considering that the necessity requirement plays virtually no role in assessing the regulation of gambling services.[278] Member States have a sufficient degree of latitude to set the level of protection desired according to the national scale of values and it is up to them 'to assess not only whether it is necessary to restrict the activities of lotteries but also whether they should be prohibited'.[279] Overall, it has been argued that consistency makes restrictions more easily acceptable: a measure as restrictive as a public monopoly, which however forms part of a consistent policy, is easier to justify than a far less restrictive licensing requirement fraught with inconsistencies.[280]

---

276 Case C-169/07 *Hartlauer Handelsgesellschaft mbH v Wiener Landesregierung and Oberösterreichische Landesregierung*, ECLI:EU:C:2009:141, para 55; Case C-42/07 *Liga Portuguesa*, para 61.

277 European Commission, *Commission Staff Working Document: Online gambling in the Internal Market* (SWD(2012) 345 final, 2012), p. 35.

278 Stefaan Van den Bogaert and Armin Cuyvers, '"Money for nothing": The case law of the EU Court of Justice on the regulation of gambling' (2011) 48 Common Market Law Review 1175, p. 1207.

279 Case C-275/92 *Schindler*, para 61; Case C-124/97 *Läärä*, para 39; Case C-67/98 *Zenatti*, para 33; Case C-6/01 *Anomar*, para 87; Case C-243/01 *Gambelli*, para 63.

280 Gjermund Mathisen, 'Consistency and Coherence as Conditions for Justification of Member State Measures Restricting Free Movement' (2010) 47 Common Market Law Review 1021, p. 1047.

It has been argued that this 'light-touch proportionality review' in the gambling case law offers a perfect example of how free movement should operate in areas which fall within the competence of the Member States.[281] At the same time, however, it is noted that, below the surface, Member States are primarily concerned with the economic imperative of maximising tax revenues,[282] but – because of the rule that economic objectives cannot justify restriction on the fundamental freedoms – they invoke social, moral and cultural values as justification grounds for their restrictive regulatory choices.[283] The Court, in applying the requirement of *coherence* and *consistency* of the national gambling policy in the proportionality assessment, holds Member States accountable for their own regulatory framework on gambling services.[284] In this way, the Court not only respects the regulatory choices of the Member States (ranging from national monopolies to complete liberalisation), but it also enforces the domestic normative aspirations against the Member States themselves, forcing them to take seriously the social, moral and cultural objectives they claim to pursue.[285] From a constitutional perspective, this approach offers an interesting and convincing example of an adjudicative method that respects both the division of competences between the EU and its Member States and the specific regulatory and normative choices made on the national level.[286]

The procedural proportionality test has also been described as 'good governance' model by Jotte Mulder.[287] In particular, it has been argued that three models of adjudication can be distinguished in the internal market case law: 1) The *substantive efficiency model*, which examines the substantive content of a measure and its necessity (a representative example can be found the Beer Purity case[288]); 2) The *margin of appreciation model*, which grants a margin of discretion to the Member States when the restriction is considered to be 'sensitive', i.e. primarily when fundamental rights or fundamental values are being invoked in order to justify a restriction on the fundamental freedoms (such as

---

281 Floris De Witte, 'The constitutional quality of the free movement provisions: looking for context in the case law on Article 56 TFEU' (2017) 42 *European Law Review* 313, p. 332.
282 Des Laffey, Vincent Della Sala and Kathryn Laffey, 'Patriot games: the regulation of online gambling in the European Union' (2016) 23 *Journal of European Public Policy* 1425.
283 Floris De Witte, 'The constitutional quality of the free movement provisions: looking for context in the case law on Article 56 TFEU' (2017) 42 *European Law Review* 313, p. 332.
284 Ibid, p. 336.
285 Ibid, p. 336.
286 Ibid, p. 339.
287 Jotte Mulder, 'Responsive Adjudication and the 'Social Legitimacy' of the Internal Market' (2016) 22 *European Law Journal* 597, p. 599.
288 Case 178/84 *Commission v Germany (Beer Purity)*, ECLI:EU:C:1987:126.

the *Schmidberger* case[289]); 3) The *good governance model*, which reviews the procedural aspects of the contested measure, focusing on principles of transparency, coherence and consistency (for instance, the aforementioned gambling case law).[290]

Applying this theoretical framework in the *Volkswagen* case,[291] it has been argued that the judicial scrutiny of the Volkswagen law should have been based on principles of good governance (i.e. coherence and transparency of the decision making process, availability of judicial remedies, and broader coherence of the Germany policy) and not on substantive efficiency.[292] The application of the *good governance model* would not necessarily have led to a different outcome of the case, but it would have allowed diverging corporate governance models to co-exist in accordance with good governance standards, i.e. it would have respected *national regulatory diversity* while stimulating *EU procedural unity*.[293]

The application of the good governance model in the golden shares case law is very interesting and indeed worthy of further consideration. A proportionality assessment based on the procedural standards of the legal instruments granting golden shares in privatised undertakings can guarantee an objective judicial review that respects national regulatory diversity in a sensitive field that is not harmonised at the EU level, whilst at the same time ensuring compliance with procedural requirements that create a *transparent* legal framework protecting the *legitimate expectations* of foreign investors and providing *effective judicial remedies* against arbitrary decisions of public authorities. The adoption of a *good governance adjudicative model* shifts the discussion away from politically and ideologically fraught questions (such as the conflict between liberal market economy and coordinated market economy, or the conflict between a corporate governance model that advances shareholders' primacy or one that promotes other stakeholders' interests) to procedural questions which can be objectively reviewed by the Court.

The judicial scrutiny of procedural requirements such as compliance with the principle of legal certainty, transparency, consistency of national policies

---

289   Case C-112/00 *Eugen Schmidberger, Internationale Transporte und Planzüge v Republik Österreich*, ECLI:EU:C:2003:333.
290   Jotte Mulder, 'Responsive Adjudication and the 'Social Legitimacy' of the Internal Market' (2016) 22 European Law Journal 597, p. 606–613.
291   Case C-112/05 *Commission v Germany (golden shares – Volkswagen I)*.
292   Jotte Mulder, 'Responsive Adjudication and the 'Social Legitimacy' of the Internal Market' (2016) 22 European Law Journal 597, p. 616.
293   Ibid, p. 616, 617.

and availability of effective judicial remedies falls undoubtedly within the competence of the Court and can effectively promote *procedural uniformity* in the EU, which can in turn significantly facilitate cross-border investment. In fact, it can be argued that the existence of procedural discrepancies and the lack of transparency often pose more obstacles to cross-border capital flows than the mere participation of the State in the shareholding of privatised undertakings. This is why the application of the *good governance model* in the proportionality assessment of the golden shares case law offers a better adjudicative approach, one that provides all the procedural guarantees necessary for the promotion of foreign investment, whilst at the same time respecting the discretion of the Member States in the field of corporate governance and promoting a 'pluralism of values' in the EU.[294]

The Court has indeed been responsive to concerns relating to compliance with procedural standards in order to incentivise and facilitate foreign investment and has developed an additional step in the proportionality assessment that examines the compatibility of the measure in question with the fundamental principle of legal certainty. This additional step reflects the broader discussion about the protection of *legitimate expectations* of foreign investors as part of the *Fair and Equitable Treatment* standard in international investment law.[295] In EU law, the protection of legitimate expectations is usually framed as compliance with the principle of legal certainty. The Court has examined legal certainty as an additional step in the proportionality assessment in the *Beglian* golden shares case,[296] which is actually the only case where the Court found that the special rights that the Belgian government had retained in the undertakings concerned were justified by public interest objectives in accordance with the principle of proportionality. In particular, the contested Belgian legislation gave the Belgian government the right to oppose (a) any transfer

---

294   Niamh Nic Shuibhne, 'Margins of appreciation: national values, fundamental rights and EC free movement law' (2009) 34 *European Law Review* 230, p. 255.
295   Nicolas Angelet, *Fair and Equitable Treatment*, (Max Planck Encyclopedia of Public International Law, 2011); Stephen Vasciannie, 'The Fair and Equitable Treatment Standard in International Investment Law and Practice' (1999) 70 *British Yearbook of International Law* 99; Barnali Choudhury, 'Evolution or Devolution? – Defining Fair and Equitable Treatment in International Investment Law' (2005) 6 *Journal of World Investment and Trade* 297; Rudolf Dolzer, 'Fair and Equitable Treatment – A Key Standard in Investment Treaties' (2005) 39 *The International Lawyer* 87; Elizabeth Snodgrass, 'Protecting Investors' Legitimate Expectations – Recognizing and Delimiting a General Principle' (2006) 21 *ICSID Review – Foreign Investment Law Journal* 1; Ioana Tudor, *The Fair and Equitable Treatment Standard in the International Law of Foreign Investment* (Oxford University Press 2008).
296   Case C-503/99 *Commission v Belgium (golden shares)*.

of strategic assets of SNTC and Distrigaz and (b) certain management decisions regarded as contrary to the guidelines for the country's energy policy. The Court found that this 'opposition procedure' was justified by the objective of safeguarding supplies of petroleum products in the event of a crisis, and more importantly, it was in conformity with the principle of proportionality. In particular, the Court noted that the opposition procedure was predicated on the principle of respect for the *decision-making autonomy of the undertaking* concerned.[297] Moreover, the public authorities were obliged to adhere to *strict time limits* and the opposition regime was limited only to certain decisions concerning the *strategic assets* of the companies in question.[298] Finally, the responsible Minister could oppose only when there was a *threat* to the objectives of the energy policy and only on the condition that any such opposition was supported by a *formal statement of reasons* and could be the subject of an *effective review* by the courts.[299] Accordingly, the Court concluded that the opposition scheme was consistent with the principle of proportionality, since it was based on *objective criteria* which were *subject to judicial review*,[300] enabling thus Belgium to intervene with a view to ensuring compliance with the public service obligations incumbent on SNTC and Distrigaz, whilst at the same time observing the requirements of legal certainty.[301]

The *Belgian* case offers a prime example of how the principle of legal certainty can operate in the golden shares case law so as to respect the regulatory autonomy of the Member States in the field of corporate governance and property ownership whilst at the same time applying procedural standards that can guarantee the protection of foreign investment. Ever since the *Belgian* case, the Court has attempted to apply the same standard of judicial review to most of the golden shares cases, but on no occasion was the restriction found to be justified. It is true that in some instances the Court might have been strict in the application of the standard of proof, requiring further (and often vaguely defined) evidence in order to prove that the special rights in question actually pursue the objective invoked by the government.[302] However, the fact still

---

297 Ibid, para 49.
298 Ibid, para 50.
299 Ibid, para 51.
300 Johannes Adolff, 'Turn of the Tide?: The "Golden Share" Judgments of the European Court of Justice and the Liberalization of the European Capital Markets' (2002) 3 *German Law Journal* 20.
301 Case C-503/99 *Commission v Belgium (golden shares)*, para 52.
302 Joined cases C-282/04 and C-283/04 *Commission v The Netherlands (golden shares)*, paras 39-40, in which the Court held that the Dutch golden shares went beyond what was necessary in order to safeguard the solvency and continuity of the provider of the universal

remains that in the majority of the golden shares cases the Court rejected the justification because of the rather general and imprecise manner in which the conditions were formulated, which, in turn, confered on the national authorities 'a latitude so discretionary in nature that it [could not] be regarded as proportionate to the objectives pursued'.[303] It is surprising that the Member States did not try to comply with the procedural requirements of legal certainty set out in the *Belgian* case or failed to prove compliance with these requirements.

Given the general application of the procedural proportionality test (based on the *Belgian* case) in the golden shares case law, it is surprising why the Court did not use the same standard of judicial review in the *Volkswagen* case. The two justification grounds invoked by the German government (i.e. the protection of workers and the protection of minority shareholders) were rejected by the Court due to lack of evidence. In particular, the Court found that 'the Federal Republic of Germany [had] not shown why, in order to protect the general interests of minority shareholders, it [was] appropriate or necessary to maintain such a position for the benefit of the Federal and State authorities'[304] and 'failed to explain, beyond setting out general considerations as to the risk that shareholders [might] put their personal interests before those of the workers, why the provisions of the VW Law criticised by the Commission [were] appropriate and necessary to preserve the jobs generated by Volkswagen's activity'.[305]

---

postal service, because of the fact that they were not limited to the company's activities as provider of a universal postal service. However, it should be noted that this was not the only reason why the Court rejected the invoked justification. It also found that the special rights in question were not based on any precise criterion and did not have to be backed by any statement of reasons, which made any effective judicial review impossible. See also Case C-174/04 *Commission v Italy (golden shares)*, para 40, in which the Court rejected the justification on the ground that the Italian Government had not explained why it was necessary for the shares of undertakings operating in the energy sector in Italy to be held by private shareholders or by public shareholders quoted on regulated financial markets for the undertakings concerned to be able to guarantee sufficient and uninterrupted supplies of electricity and gas in the Italian market.

303 Case C-212/09 *Commission v Portugal (golden shares – GALP Energia SGPS SA)*, paras 88-90; Case C-543/08 *Commission v Portugal (golden shares – EDP)*, paras 90-92; Case C-171/08 *Commission v Portugal (golden shares – Portugal Telecom SGPS SA)*, paras 75-77; Case C-244/11 *Commission v Greece (golden shares)*, paras 82-86; Case C-274/06 *Commission v Spain (golden shares)*, paras 50-52; Case C-207/07 *Commission v Spain (golden shares in the energy sector)*, paras 55-57; Case C-326/07 *Commission v Italy (golden shares)*, paras 66-72; Case C-463/00 *Commission v Spain (golden shares)*, paras 77-80; Case C-483/99 *Commission v France (golden shares – Sociéte Nationale Elf-Aquitaine)*, paras 50-52.
304 Case C-112/05 *Commission v Germany (golden shares – Volkswagen I)*, para 78.
305 Ibid, para 80.

Interestingly, the Court emphasised that 'it cannot be ruled out that, in certain special circumstances, the Federal and State authorities in question may use their position in order to defend general interests which might be contrary to the economic interests of the company concerned, and therefore, contrary to the interests of its other shareholders'.[306] This statement takes an ideological stance on perhaps the most controversial politico-economic question that a corporate governance system is supposed to resolve: whose interests should a corporation serve?

By ruling that the public interest objectives can be contrary to the economic objectives of the company and by equating the latter with the interests of its shareholders, the Court implicitly promoted a corporate governance system governed by *shareholders' primacy* and the *principle of proportionality between ownership and control* with a view to liberalising the market for corporate control. However, the choice of corporate governance model is a fundamental political question, which depends on various socio-economic factors that differ significantly among Member States. The salience of the issue becomes apparent if one considers that the regulation of corporate control affects the most important aspects of a capitalist economy, influencing a nation's employment level, the conditions of work and production, as well as the distribution of wealth.[307] Whether corporate governance should be dominated by the *shareholders' primacy norm* or by the *stakeholders' primacy norm* is a national political economy choice, which should be clearly distinguished from the objective of market integration pursued by the Treaties. Consequently, a judicially-driven convergence into a European corporate governance model governed by shareholders' primacy is legally and politically questionable. This relates to the broader discussion about the legal structure of the free movement provisions, which sometimes fails to respect the vertical balance of competence between the EU and the Member States and does not ensure that the normative values underpinning the socio-economic European space are articulated through a political process that can legitimise them in a democratic way.[308]

Drawing from the contextual reading of the case law in relation to the other fundamental freedoms, it is argued that, in light of the politically and economically contentious context of golden shares, the most appropriate adjudicative

---

306   Ibid, para 79.
307   Benjamin Werner, 'National responses to the European Court of Justice case law on Golden Shares: the role of protective equivalents' (2016) 24 *Journal of European Public Policy* 989, at p. 993.
308   Floris De Witte, 'The constitutional quality of the free movement provisions: looking for context in the case law on Article 56 TFEU' (2017) 42 European Law Review 313, p. 337–339.

approach is the 'procedural proportionality' or 'good governance model'. Through this approach the Court can be more deferential towards national policy objectives in the field of corporate governance, whilst at the same time disapplying discriminatory measures or special shareholding that derogate from ordinary company law and grant an undue advantage to the Member States to the detriment of private investors. The procedural proportionality or 'good governance model' is based upon the principle of legal certainty and includes the review of elements such as respect for the decision-making autonomy of the undertaking concerned, strict time limits, objective criteria, obligation to provide a formal statement of reasons when adopting certain decisions and availability of effective judicial remedies. The judicial review of these elements as conducted in the *Belgian* case has an important pedagogical value as it can be used as a guiding principle upon which Member States can structure their special shareholding in privatised undertakings in order to be compatible with the free movement of capital.

D The Definition of 'Capital Restrictions' in the Golden Shares Case Law

The analysis above showed that in the golden shares case law the Court has left very limited room for the Member States to justify their special rights in privatised undertakings. In light of the unsuccessful invocation of the aforementioned derogation grounds and the high standard of proof required in the proportionality assessment, it is essential to go a step back in the judicial reasoning and to explore the precise contours of the scope of 'capital restrictions'.[309] This is because a more appropriate delineation of the notion of 'capital restrictions' can allow a better drawing of the dividing line between the competence of the EU and the Member States in the field of corporate governance and can accordingly give Member States sufficient room to exercise their regulatory autonomy to protect public interest objectives, within the contours of the Internal Market.

In particular, the golden shares case law, the Court has adopted the 'deterrent effect test', which leads to a strikingly broad interpretation of the notion of 'capital restrictions' encompassing *all* measures liable to deter/discourage foreign investors. This over-inclusive definition is reminiscent of the broad

---

[309] This part further expands on ideas previously discussed in: Ilektra Antonaki, 'Keck in Capital? Redefining "Restrictions" in the "Golden Shares" Case Law' (2016) *Erasmus Law Review* 177; Ilektra Antonaki, 'Free movement of capital and protection of social objectives in the EU: Critical reflections on the case law regarding golden shares and privatisations' in Sacha Garben & Inge Govaere, The Internal Market 2.0. (Oxford: Hart Publishing, 2020).

Dassonville formula[310] in the area of free movement of goods. Although the Court is notoriously known for not easily retreating from its previous case law, the *Keck* ruling[311] in the area of free movement of goods constitutes the prime example where the Court explicitly reconsidered the broad interpretation of 'measures having equivalent effect to a quantitative restriction' (MEEQR) and introduced the concept of 'selling arrangements' in an attempt to restrict the scope of Article 34 TFEU.

The present section draws from the jurisprudential developments in the area of free movement of goods and investigates whether a concept similar to the *Keck* notion of 'selling arrangements' could or should be introduced in the free movement of capital in order to delimit the boundaries of Article 63 TFEU.[312] Such a concept could take the form of an 'investment arrangements' test,[313] whereby measures that do not derogate from ordinary company law and that respect equality between the State and private parties as market participants escape from the material scope of the free movement of capital and therefore cannot be regarded as 'capital restrictions'. The section is divided into four parts. The first part seeks to explore the evolution of the concept of restrictions in the free movement of goods through a brief overview of the relevant case law. The second part examines the transposition of the *Keck* ruling in the area of workers, services and establishment. The third part analyses the Court's negative reaction to the attempts of the Member States to invoke the *Keck* test in the golden shares case law. Finally, the fourth part introduces a legal test for the delimitation of the scope of 'capital restrictions' on the basis of which certain measures can escape from judicial scrutiny if they satisfy two conditions: first, they do not derogate from ordinary company law; and second,

---

310 Case 8-74 *Dassonville*, para 5: 'All trading rules enacted by Member States which are capable of hindering, directly or indirectly, actually or potentially, intra-Community trade are to be considered as measures having an effect equivalent to quantitative restrictions'.

311 Joined cases C-267/91 and C-268/91 *Criminal proceedings against Bernard Keck and Daniel Mithouard*, ECLI:EU:C:1993:905.

312 Wolf-Georg Ringe, 'Company Law and Free Movement of Capital' (2010) 69 Cambridge Law Journal 378, p. 402; Anne Looijestijn-Clearie, 'All that glitters is not gold: European Court of Justice strikes down golden shares in two Dutch companies' (2007) 8 *European Business Organization Law Review* 429, p. 452; Florian Sanders, 'Case C-112/05, European Commission v. Federal Rebulic of Germany: The Volkswagen Case and Art. 56 EC – A Proper Result, Yet Also a Missed Opportunity?' (2007–2008) 14 Columbia Journal of European Law 359, p. 368.

313 Andrea Biondi, 'When the State is the Owner – Some Further Comments on the Court of Justice 'Golden Shares' Strategy' in Bernitz and Ringe (eds), *Company Law and Economic Protectionism: New Challenges to European Integration* (Oxford University Press 2010), p. 96.

they respect the principle of equality between the State and private parties as market participants.

1 The Concept of 'Restrictions' in the Free Movement of Goods
a) *The Pre-Keck Case Law on MEEQRS*

The establishment and development of the EU's Internal Market has been to a large extent supported and promoted by the dynamics of negative integration. It was the Luxembourg Court that stepped in and took the lead in overcoming the political stagnation of the 1960s/1970s and facilitating the process of economic integration. With the two landmark decisions in *Dassonville*[314] and *Cassis de Dijon*,[315] the Court unleashed the powers of negative integration and inaugurated a new era, where any national rule capable of hindering, directly or indirectly, actually or potentially, intra-Community trade could be regarded as a 'measure having equivalent effect to a quantitative restriction'.[316]

The far-reaching consequences did not take too long to make themselves felt: in the aftermath of the two rulings, a wave of speculative national litigation mushroomed, calling for all sorts of indistinctly applicable national regulatory requirements to be disapplied as contrary to the free movement provisions.[317]

---

314 Case 8-74 *Dassonville*.
315 Case 120/78 *Cassis de Dijon*.
316 Case 8-74 *Dassonville*, p. 5.
317 Jukka Snell, 'The Notion of Market Access: A Concept or a Slogan?' (2010) 47 *Common Market Law Review* 437. See for example Case 286/81 *Oosthoek's Uitgeversmaatschappij BV*, ECLI:EU:C:1982:438 concerning a Dutch rule prohibiting the offering of free gifts for sales promotion purposes; Case 155/80 *Summary proceedings agains Sergius Oebel*, ECLI:EU:C:1981:177 regarding a German prohibition on night-work in bakeries; Opinion of Mr Advocate General Darmon in Case C-69/88 *H. Krantz GmbH & Co. v Ontvanger der Directe Belastingen and Netherlands State*, ECLI:EU:C:1989:627 on a Dutch rule granting tax authorities the power to seize goods sold on instalment terms with reservation of title in case the purchasers were not able to repay their tax debts; Case C-145/88 *Torfaen Borough Council v B & Q plc.*, ECLI:EU:C:1989:593 on the British prohibition of Sunday trading; Case C-23/89 *Quietlynn Limited and Brian James Richards v Southend Borough Council*, ECLI:EU:C:1990:300 regarding the British legislation prohibiting the sale of lawful sex articles from unlicensed sex establishments; Case 382/87, *R. Buet*, [1989] ECR - 01235 concerning a French prohibition on canvassing in connection with the sale of English-language teaching material; Case C-271/92 *Laboratoire de Prothèses Oculaires v Union Nationale des Syndicats d'Opticiens de France and Groupement d'Opticiens Lunetiers Détaillants and Syndicat des Opticiens Français Indépendants and Syndicat National des Adapteurs d'Optique de Contact*, ECLI:EU:C:1993:214 dealing with a provision in the French Code de la Santé Publique reserving solely to holders of an optician's certificate (Diplôme d' opticien-lunetier) the sale of optical appliances and corrective lenses; Case C-126/91 *Schutzverband gegen Unwesen in der Wirtschaft e.V. v Yves Rocher GmbH*,

These legal actions against national rules regulating marketing and selling conditions were perceived as an intrusion into the domain of national regulatory autonomy and it was increasingly suggested that the Court should clarify and delineate the boundaries of Article 34 TFEU.[318] In the same vein, Advocate General Tesauro in *Hünermund* admitted that he had changed his mind in relation to his views in previous case law[319] and he opined that the all-inclusive *Dassonville* formula could not be construed as meaning that a potential reduction in imports caused solely and exclusively by a more general (and hypothetical) contraction of sales, could constitute an MEEQR.[320] Accordingly, he considered that rules which regulated the manner in which a trading activity was carried out were in principle to be regarded as falling outside the scope of Article [34 TFEU], insofar as they did not intend to regulate trade itself and they were not liable to render market access less profitable (and thus indirectly more difficult) for importers.[321] He believed that this approach was in line with the principle of mutual recognition established in *Cassis de Dijon* and did not in any way undermine its truly integrationist inspiration.[322] A different (i.e. more intrusive) interpretation of Article [34 TFEU] 'would ultimately render nugatory the Treaty provisions ... or in any event devalue them'.[323]

b) *The Keck Ruling and the Introduction of the Concept of 'Selling Arrangements'*

In 1993, with the *Keck* ruling, the Court introduced the 'selling arrangements' test in an effort to clarify the boundaries of the broad definition of MEEQR.

ECLI:EU:C:1993:191 on a German rule prohibiting advertisements using price comparisons (displaying the new price and comparing it with the old one so as to catch the eye).

318 Eric L. White, 'In Search Of The Limits To Article 30 Of The EEC Treaty' (1989) 26 *Common Market Law Review* 235; L.W. Gormley, 'Case 145/88, Torfaen Borough Council v. B&Q PLC (formerly B&Q Retail Ltd.), Preliminary reference under Art. 177 EEC by the Cwmbran Magistrates' Court on the interpretation of Arts. 30 & 36 EEC. Judgment of the Court of Justice of the European Communities of 23 November 1989' (1990) 27 *Common Market Law Review* 141; Anthony Arnull, 'What shall we do on Sunday?' (1991) 16 *European Law Review* 112; Kamiel Mortelmans, 'Article 30 of the EEC Treaty and Legislation Relating to Market Circumstances: Time to Consider a New Definition?' (1991) 28 *Common Market Law Review* 115; J. Steiner, 'Drawing the line: Uses and abuses of Article 30 EEC' (1992) 29 *Common Market Law Review* 749.

319 *Opinion of Advocate General Tesauro in Case C-292/92 Ruth Hünermund*, ECLI:EU:C:1993:863, para 26.

320 Ibid, para 25.

321 Ibid.

322 Ibid.

323 Ibid, par 27.

The facts of the case are widely known. Mr Keck and Mr Mithouard, owners of a French supermarket, were prosecuted for reselling products in an unaltered state at prices lower than their actual purchase price ('resale at a loss') contrary to the pertinent French legislation. In their defence, they argued that a prohibition on resale at a loss was contrary to the free movement of goods under Article [34 TFEU]. The Court was faced with a dilemma: to continue the line of case law advocating a broad interpretation of Article 34 TFEU or to reconsider its position in view of the fact that the contested measure had arguably no effect on inter-State trade. It chose to do the latter.

In particular, it explicitly expressed its intention to re-examine and clarify its case law in view of the increasing tendency of traders to invoke Article 34 TFEU as a means of challenging any rules whose effect was to limit their commercial freedom even where such rules were not aimed at products from other Member States.[324] Thus, it introduced the concept of 'selling arrangements'. According to the Court's reasoning, rules that restricted or prohibited certain selling arrangements were not such as to hinder directly or indirectly, actually or potentially trade between Member States as long as two conditions were fulfilled: (i) they applied to all relevant traders operating within the national territory; and (ii) they affected in the same manner, in law and in fact, the marketing of domestic products and of those from other Member States.[325] These 'selling arrangements' were excluded from the scope of Article 34 TFEU, which meant that the national measure at issue was permissible without there being a need to examine possible justification grounds.

The exact content of the concept of 'selling arrangements' was revealed in subsequent case law: rules on shop opening hours,[326] rules requiring processed milk for infants be sold only in pharmacies[327] and certain restrictive rules on advertising[328] are some examples of the type of national regulatory provisions

---

324   Joined cases C-267/91 and C-268/91 *Keck and Mithouard*, para 14.
325   Ibid, para 16.
326   Joined cases C-401/92 and C-402/92 *Criminal proceedings against Tankstation 't Heukske vof and J. B. E. Boermans*, ECLI:EU:C:1994:220; Joined cases C-69/93 and C-258/93 *Punto Casa SpA v Sindaco del Comune di Capena and Comune di Capena and Promozioni Polivalenti Venete Soc. coop. arl (PPV) v Sindaco del Comune di Torri di Quartesolo and Comune di Torri di Quartesolo*, ECLI:EU:C:1994:226; Joined cases C 418/93 et al. *Semeraro Casa Uno Srl v Sindaco del Comune di Erbusco*, ECLI:EU:C:1996:242; Case C-483/12 *Pelckmans Turnhout NV v Walter Van Gastel Balen NV and Others*, ECLI:EU:C:2014:304.
327   Case C-391/92 *Commission v Greece (infant milk)*, ECLI:EU:C:1995:199.
328   Case C-292/92 *Ruth Hünermund and others v Landesapothekerkammer Baden-Württemberg*, ECLI:EU:C:1993:932; Case C-412/93 *Société d'Importation Edouard Leclerc-Siplec v TF1 Publicité SA and M6 Publicité SA*, ECLI:EU:C:1995:26; Joined cases C-34/95, C-35/95 and C-36/95 *Konsumentombudsmannen (KO) v De Agostini (Svenska) Förlag AB and*

that were captured by the concept of 'selling arrangements' and were thus excluded from the scope of Article 34 TFEU. In general terms, rules relating to the place and time of sales as well as to the marketing of specific products were in principle considered to be caught by the *Keck*-formula.[329]

However, the dichotomy between 'product requirement' and 'selling arrangements' rules proved rigid and artificial[330] and sparked an academic debate.[331] Lawrence Gormley noted that the exclusion of 'selling arrangements' from the scope of Article 34 TFEU would lead to a lack of judicial review of ostensibly innocent measures, which could however constitute disguised restrictions on inter-State trade.[332] Stephen Weatherill, while recognising that the ruling excluded from the scope of the Treaty certain regulatory choices that do not damage the realisation of economies of scale, nevertheless considered that it had a 'disturbingly formalistic tone' and it was 'flawed by the absence of an adequate articulation of just why it was possible to conclude that no sufficient impact on trade between States was shown'.[333] He thus proposed a refined *Keck*-test that would allow Member States to apply national regulatory measures to imported goods as long as they would apply equally in law and in fact to domestic and foreign goods and they would not impose

---

TV-Shop i Sverige AB, ECLI:EU:C:1997:344; Case C-405/98 *Konsumentombudsmannen (KO) v Gourmet International Products AB (GIP)*, ECLI:EU:C:2001:135.

[329] Case C-71/02 *Karner*, para 38.

[330] Stefaan Van den Bogaert and Pieter Van Cleynenbreugel, 'Free Movement of Goods' in Pieter Jan Kuijper, Fabian Amtenbrink, Deirdre Curtin, Bruno De Witte, Alison McDonnell and Stefaan Van den Bogaert (eds), *The Law of the European Union, Fifth Edition* (Wolters Kluwer 2018), pp. 485–537, at p. 519.

[331] Lawrence W. Gormley, 'Reasoning Renounced? The Remarkable Judgment in Keck & Mithouard?' (1994) 5 *European Business Law Review* 63; Miguel Poiares Maduro, 'Keck: The end? The beginning of the end? Or just the end of the beginning' (1994) 3 *Irish Journal of European Law* 30; Nicolas Bernard, 'Discrimination and Free Movement in E.C. Law' (1996) 45 *International and Comparative Law Quarterly* 82; Catherine Barnard, 'Fitting the remaining pieces into the goods and persons jigsaw?' (2001) 26 *European Law Review* 35; Alina Tryfonidou, 'Was Keck a Half-baked Solution After All?' (2007) 34 *Legal Issues of Economic Integration* 167; Ioannis Lianos, 'Shifting Narratives in the European Internal Market: Efficient Restrictions of Trade and the Nature of "Economic" Integration' (2010) 21 *European Business Law Review* 705; Catherine Barnard, 'What the Keck? Balancing the needs of the single market with state regulatory autonomy' (2012) 2 *European Journal of Consumer Law* 201; Stephen Weatherill, 'The Road to Ruin: 'Restrictions on Use' and the Circular Lifecycle of Article 34 TFEU' (2012) 2 *European Journal of Consumer Law* 359.

[332] Lawrence W. Gormley, 'Two Years After Keck' (1996) 19 *Fordham International Law Journal* 866.

[333] Stephen Weatherill, 'After *Keck*: Some Thoughts on How to Clarify the Clarification' (1996) 33 *Common Market Law Review* 885.

direct or *substantial* hindrance to market access.[334] The origin of this refined test can be traced back to the Advocate General Jacobs' opinion in *Leclerc-Siplec*,[335] where he expressed his famous objection to the *Keck*-inspired presumption of lawfulness of 'selling arrangements' and he proposed the adoption of a test based on '*substantial* restriction of market access' for determining whether non-discriminatory rules infringed Article 34 TFEU. In his highly cited and illustrative excerpt, he emphasised that 'If an obstacle to inter-State trade exists, it cannot cease to exist simply because an identical obstacle affects domestic trade. ... If a Member State imposes a *substantial barrier* on access to the market for certain products ... and a manufacturer of those products in another Member State suffers economic loss as a result, he will derive little consolation from the knowledge that a similar loss is sustained by his competitors in the Member State which imposes the restriction'.[336]

The *substantial barrier* test was also espoused by other Advocates General[337] and legal scholars as a criterion for establishing the existence of a 'measure having equivalent effect to a quantitative restriction'.[338] It was argued that the case law offered room for *de minimis* considerations in free movement law, in the sense that 'minimal restrictive effects' did not affect market access, while several trade restrictions hindered *significantly* market access and thus impinged

---

334 Ibid, p. 903.
335 *Opinion of Advocate General Jacobs in Case C-412/93 Leclerc-Siplec*, ECLI:EU:C:1994:393.
336 Ibid, para 39.
337 *Opinion of Advocate General Stix-Hackl in Case C-322/01 DocMorris NV*, ECLI:EU:C:2003:147, para 78, where he underlined that 'The decisive factor should therefore be whether or not a national measure *significantly* impedes access to the market'. See also *Opinion of Advocate General Van Gerven in Case C-145/88 Torfaen*, ECLI:EU:C:1989:279, para 24, where he argued that there was no room for a *de minimis* test, because Article 34 TFEU already presupposes a *serious*, and therefore a *more than appreciable*, obstruction to trade between Member States.
338 Max S. Jansson and Harri Kalimo, 'De Minimis Meets "Market Access": Transformations in the Substance – and the Syntax- of EU Free Movement Law?' (2014) 51 *Common Market Law Review* 523. It is interesting to note that the authors of this article distinguish three substantive groups of *de minimis* thresholds: the magnitude (severity) of the restrictive effect, the probability of the restrictive effect and the causality between the measure and the restrictive effect. See also J. Steiner, 'Drawing the line: Uses and abuses of Article 30 EEC' (1992) 29 Common Market Law Review 749; Catherine Barnard and Steve Peers (eds), *European Union Law* (Oxford University Press 2017), p. 352; Helen Toner, 'Non-discriminatory obstacles to the exercise of Treaty Rights – Articles 39, 43, 49, and 18 EC' (2004) 23 *Yearbook of European Law* 275, p. 285. Conversely c.f. Stephen Weatherill, 'After *Keck*: Some Thoughts on How to Clarify the Clarification' (1996) 33 Common Market Law Review 885, who refrains from describing the 'direct or substantial hindrance to market access' test as a *de minimis* threshold.

on Article 34 TFEU.[339] However, the position of the Court was less clear. Although it had ostensibly rejected the adoption of a *de minimis* test in the free movement assessment,[340] it effectively accepted a similar test by acknowledging that if the effect on market access was 'too uncertain or indirect'[341] or 'purely hypothetical'[342] then the contested measure did not infringe free movement provisions.[343] By contrast, measures which *significantly* impeded market access constitute 'measure having equivalent effect to a quantitative restriction' within the meaning of Article 34 TFEU.[344]

c) *The Post-Keck 'Market Access' Test*

Although the Court never overruled explicitly the *Keck*-test, progressively it clarified its content and its precise requirements. In particular, in subsequent case law the Court interpreted the two conditions contained in paragraph 16 of *Keck* as meaning that certain 'selling arrangements' could not escape the scrutiny of the free movement provisions if they were discriminatory or they imposed additional burdens on imported goods (in the sense of the 'dual burdens' that

---

339 Max S. Jansson and Harri Kalimo, 'De Minimis Meets "Market Access": Transformations in the Substance – and the Syntax- of EU Free Movement Law?' (2014) 51 Common Market Law Review 523, p. 526.

340 Joined cases 177 and 178/82 *Van de Haar*, at 13; Case C-67/97, *Ditlev Bluhme*, [1998] ECR I-08033, para 20; Joined cases C-1/90 and C-176/90 *Aragonesa de Publicidad and Publivía v Departamento de Sanidad*, ECLI:EU:C:1991:327, para 24; Joined cases C-277/91, C-318/91 and C-319/91 *Ligur Carni Srl and Genova Carni Srl v Unità Sanitaria Locale n. XV di Genova and Ponente SpA v Unità Sanitaria Locale n. XIX di La Spezia and CO.GE.SE.MA Coop a r l*, ECLI:EU:C:1993:927, para 37.

341 Case C-69/88 *H. Krantz GmbH & Co. tegen Ontvanger der Directe Belastingen en Staat der Nederlanden*, ECLI:EU:C:1990:97, para 11; Case C-190/98 *Volker Graf v Filzmoser Maschinenbau GmbH*, ECLI:EU:C:2000:49, para 25 (in the field of free movement for workers). Conversely, in Case C-415/93 *Bosman*, ECLI:EU:C:1995:463, para 103 the Court found that the transfer rules at issue *directly* affected players access to the employment market in other Member States and were thus capable of impeding the freedom of movement for workers. Similarly, in Case C-384/93 *Alpine Investments BV v Minister van Financiën*, ECLI:EU:C:1995:126, the Court ruled that the prohibition of cold calling by telephone for financial services *directly* affected access to the market in services in the other Member States and was thus capable of hindering intra-Community trade in services.

342 Case C-299/95 *Friedrich Kremzow v Republik Österreich*, ECLI:EU:C:1997:254, para 16.

343 Stephen Weatherill, 'After *Keck*: Some Thoughts on How to Clarify the Clarification' (1996) 33 Common Market Law Review 885, p. 900; Dimitrios Doukas, 'Untying the market access knot: Advertising restrictions and the free movement of goods and services' (2007) 9 *Cambridge Yearbook of European Legal Studies* 177.

344 Case C-108/09 *Ker-Optika bt v ÀNTSZ Dél-dunántúli Regionális Intézete*, ECLI:EU:C:2010:725, para 54 ; Case C-456/10 *Asociación Nacional de Expendedores de Tabaco y Timbre (ANETT) v Administración del Estado*, ECLI:EU:C:2012:241, paras 21, 43.

the principle of mutual recognition was intended to eliminate under the *Cassis de Dijon* judgment). Cases such as *Familiapress*,[345] *De Agostini*,[346] *Gourmet*[347] and *Alfa Vita*[348] signalled the transition from an approach based on a formalistic distinction between 'product rules' and 'selling arrangements' to a more straightforward test based on 'market access hindrance'.[349] In *Commission v Italy (trailers)*[350] and *Mickelsson and Roos*,[351] without departing from *Keck*, the Court seemed to focus more on a 'market access' test according to which rules restricting the *use* of products hinder the market access of foreign products and therefore constitute 'measures having equivalent effect to a quantitative restriction' prohibited under Article 34 TFEU.[352] Thus, the Italian prohibition on motorcycles towing trailers and the Swedish prohibition on the use of personal watercraft on waters other than general navigable waterways were regarded as trade restrictions, which could however be justified on road safety[353] and environmental protection grounds.[354]

---

345   Case C-368/95 *Vereinigte Familiapress Zeitungsverlags- und vertriebs GmbH v Heinrich Bauer Verlag*, ECLI:EU:C:1997:325.
346   Joined cases C-34/95, C-35/95 and C-36/95 *De Agostini*.
347   Case C-405/98 *Gourmet*.
348   Joined cases C-158 & 159/04 *Alfa Vita Vassilopoulos AE and Carrefour Marinopoulos AE v Elliniko Dimosio and Nomarchiaki Aftodioikisi Ioanninon*, ECLI:EU:C:2006:562, para 19.
349   For the notion of the market access, see Jukka Snell, 'The Notion of Market Access: A Concept or a Slogan?' (2010) 47 *Common Market Law Review* 437; Gareth Davies, 'Understanding Market Access: Exploring the Economic Rationality of Different Conceptions of Free Movement Law' (2010) 11 *German Law Journal* 671; Catherine Barnard, 'Restricting Restrictions: Lessons for the EU from the US?' (2009) 68 *Cambridge Law Journal* 575; Eleanor Spaventa, 'From Gebhard to Carpenter: Towards a (non-)economic European constitution' (2004) 41 *Common Market Law Review* 743; Peter Oliver and Stefan Enchelmaier, 'Free movement of goods: Recent developments in the case law' (2007) 44 *Common Market Law Review* 674.
350   Case C-110/05 *Commission v Italy (trailers)*, ECLI:EU:C:2009:66.
351   Case C-142/05 *Åklagaren v Percy Mickelsson and Joakim Roos*, ECLI:EU:C:2009:336.
352   For an academic discussion, see for instance Luca Prete, 'Of Motorcycle Trailers and Personal Watercrafts: the Battle over Keck' (2008) 35 *Legal Issues of Economic Integration* 133; Peter Pecho, 'Good-Bye Keck?: A Comment on the Remarkable Judgment in Commission v. Italy, C-110/05' (2009) 36 *Legal Issues of Economic Integration* 257; Pal Wenneras and Ketil Boe Moen, 'Selling Arrangements, Keeping Keck' (2010) 35 *European Law Review* 387; Peter Oliver, 'Of Trailers and Jet Skis: Is the Case Law on Article 34 TFEU Hurtling in a New Direction?' (2011) 33 *Fordhman International Law Journal* 1423; Gareth Davies, 'The Court's jurisprudence on free movement of goods: pragmatic presumptions, not philosophical principles' (2012) 2 *European Journal of Consumer Law* 25.
353   Case C-110/05 *Commission v Italy (trailers)*, para 69.
354   Case C-142/05 *Mickelsson and Roos*, para 36, provided that the competent national authorities designated within reasonable period waters other than general navigable waterways on which personal watercraft could be used.

2 The Application of *Keck* in the Other Freedoms (Workers, Services and Establishment)

Despite the change of terminology and the adoption of the broader 'market access' test, in the area of free movement of goods the Court has never officially abandoned the *Keck*-test. In the field of workers and services, although the Court has not ruled out the possibility of using a *Keck*-inspired approach, in practice it has refrained from doing so given the fact that most of the contested measures have been not found to be comparable to selling arrangements. In particular, in relation to the free movement of workers (Article 45 TFEU), in *Bosman*,[355] the Court ruled that:

> although the rules in issue in the main proceedings apply also to transfers between clubs belonging to different national associations within the same Member State and are similar to those governing transfers between clubs belonging to the same national association, they still directly affect players' access to the employment market in other Member States and are thus capable of impeding freedom of movement for workers. They cannot, thus, be deemed comparable to the rules on selling arrangements for goods which in Keck and Mithouard were held to fall outside the ambit of Article 30 of the Treaty.[356]

In relation to the freedom to provide services (Article 56 TFEU), in *Alpine Investments*,[357] the Court found that the *Keck*-test could not be applied by analogy *in casu*, because:

> a prohibition such as that at issue is imposed by the Member State in which the provider of services is established and affects not only offers made by him to addressees who are established in that State or move there in order to receive services but also offers made to potential recipients in another Member State. It therefore directly affects access to the market in services in the other Member States and is thus capable of hindering intra-Community trade in services.[358]

---

[355] Case C-415/93 *Bosman*.
[356] Ibid, para 103.
[357] Case C-384/93 *Alpine Investments*.
[358] Ibid, para 38.

However, in *Mobistar and Belgacom*,[359] the Court, without referring explicitly to the *Keck* test, seems to have implicitly accepted that certain measures might escape from the scope of services restrictions. In particular, it held that:

> measures, the only effect of which is to create additional costs in respect of the service in question and which affect in the same way the provision of services between Member States and that within one Member State, do not fall within the scope of Article 59 of the Treaty.[360]

In the same vein, it seems that the Court has indirectly and tacitly accepted the transposition of a *Keck*-like approach to the freedom of establishment. More precisely, in the *Kornhaas* case,[361] the Court implicitly distinguished between (innocent) *'business-related rules'* and *'establishment-related rules'* (requiring justification).[362] The case concerned a company incorporated under English law, which carried out most of its business (thus had its 'centre of main interests') in Germany through a branch. The dispute arose between the liquidator of the company and its director regarding an action for reimbursement of payments, which the latter had made as a managing director of the debtor company after it had become insolvent. The Court, after ruling that the law applicable to the insolvency proceedings was the German law pursuant to Article 4(1) of Regulation No 1346/2000, found that the pertinent German provision on the personal liability of the managing directors did not infringe the freedom of establishment under Article 49 TFEU, since such a provision:

> in no way concerns the formation of a company in a given Member State or its subsequent establishment in another Member State, to the extent that that provision of national law is applicable only after that company has been formed, in connection with its business [...].[363]

This ruling has been interpreted as departing from the liberal approach adopted in *Centros*[364] and introducing a distinction between company law

---

359   Joined cases C-544/03 and C-545/03 *Mobistar SA v Commune de Fléron and Belgacom Mobile SA v Commune de Schaerbeek*, ECLI:EU:C:2005:518.
360   Ibid, para 31.
361   Case C-594/14 *Simona Kornhaas v Thomas Dithmar als Insolvenzverwalter über das Vermögen der Kornhaas Montage und Dienstleistung Ltd*, ECLI:EU:C:2015:806.
362   Wolf-Georg Ringe, 'Case Comment: Kornhaas and the challenge of applying Keck in establishment' (2017) 42 *European Law Review* 270.
363   Case C-594/14 *Kornhaas*, para 28.
364   Case C-212/97 *Centros Ltd. v Erhvervs-og Selskabbsstyrelsen*, ECLI:EU:C:1999:126.

and insolvency law for the purposes of assessing their compatibility with EU free movement law.[365] In particular, in *Centros*, the Court had opened up the market for incorporations by ruling that provisions of national company law which prohibit the incorporation of a company in a Member State in which the company does not conduct business were contrary to the freedom of establishment.[366] In the light of this ruling, German (and other) companies registered their offices in England in order to benefit from the liberal English company law regime, while maintaining their economic activities exclusively in Germany or in the other Member States of origin. The *Kornhaas* case concerned the question whether such a company incorporated in England but operating exclusively in Germany was subject to German insolvency law and whether the latter constituted a restriction on the freedom of establishment. The Court ruled that the company was indeed subject to German insolvency law and that the national provision on the personal liability of the managing directors was not contrary to the freedom of establishment. The distinction between, on the one hand, rules of company concerning incorporation and establishment which can impose restrictions on the freedom of establishment and, on the other hand, rules of insolvency law concerning the business behaviour of the company which do not affect the freedom of establishment has been interpreted as reminiscent of the *Keck* doctrine.[367] Although the Court did not mention explicitly *Keck* in its judgment, it seems that the rationale behind this distinction was to create a category of 'business-related arrangements', which would fall outside the scope of the freedom of establishment.

The *Kornhaas* ruling received criticism from scholars arguing that:

> the scope of art. 49 TFEU (unlike art. 34 TFEU) does not differentiate but rather applies broadly to "the right to take up and pursue activities as self-employed persons and to set up and manage undertakings" without there being room for a differentiated interpretation.[368]

---

[365] Wolf-Georg Ringe, Kornhaas and the Limits of Corporate Establishment, https://www.law.ox.ac.uk/business-law-blog/blog/2016/05/kornhaas-and-limits-corporate-establishment.

[366] Case C-212/97 *Centros*, para 39.

[367] Wolf-Georg Ringe, 'Kornhaas and the Limits of Corporate Establishment' (*Oxfrod Business Law Blog*, 25 May 2016) <https://www.law.ox.ac.uk/business-law-blog/blog/2016/05/kornhaas-and-limits-corporate-establishment> accessed 31-01-2019.

[368] Wolf-Georg Ringe, 'Case Comment: Kornhaas and the challenge of applying Keck in establishment' (2017) 42 European Law Review 270, p. 276.

Although this criticism is certainly worthy of consideration, the Court, aware of the legal controversies of the case, tried to pre-empt the critiques by clarifying that the legal capacity of the debtor company is in no way called into question[369] and that the German provision is in fact applicable only from the time when the company must be considered to be insolvent or when its over-indebtedness is recognised in accordance with the applicable national law.[370] As the referring court rightly pointed out, the German provision in question does not govern the conditions in which a company established in accordance with the law of another EU State may install its administrative office in Germany, but only the legal consequences of such a decision and of wrongful conduct of its managing directors.[371] Therefore, the freedom of establishment is not affected.[372]

The refusal of the Court to qualify the German provision on the personal liability of the managing directors regarding payments that were made after the company became insolvent as a restriction on the freedom of establishment sends a strong signal that the Court is not willing to undertake a quality control of all company, insolvency, labour or tax law requirements of the Member States as this would be against not only the letter but also the spirit of the fundamental freedoms protected under the Treaties and the rationale of the whole project of market integration in the EU. The implicit transposition of the *Keck*-ruling in the area of establishment provides support and reinforces the argument that a similar approach should be adopted in the area of free movement of capital. As will be analysed below, the crucial factor that makes the transposition of *Keck* to the free movement of capital (and establishment) so imperative is that more often than not the national measures that are challenged as capital restrictions constitute regulatory requirements which *structure the market itself*, rather than imposing obstacles to the *market access* of foreign investors.

3   'Selling Arrangements' in the Golden Shares Case Law

In the golden shares case law, the Member States have consistently expressed their strong opposition to the strikingly broad interpretation of 'capital restrictions', arguing that it essentially deprives them of their right to choose and determine the corporate governance regime that suits best to the structure of their economy and corresponds to the needs of their industrial policy. Among

---

369   Case C-594/14 *Kornhaas*, para 26.
370   Ibid, para 28.
371   Ibid, para 10.
372   Ibid, para 10.

their various defences, some Member States attempted to draw a parallel between 'golden shares' and 'selling arrangements', arguing that a *Keck*-like approach should apply in relation to the special shareholding retained in privatised companies. They asked the Court to relativise its rigid legal reasoning in order to prevent a replication of the legal ramifications that we witnessed as a result of the over-extensive application of the free movement of goods in the aftermath of *Dassonville* and *Cassis de Dijon*. This argument has so far been invoked unsuccessfully five times: once by Spain,[373] once by the UK[374] and three times by Portugal.[375]

The first case where the argument that a *Keck*-like approach could be applied in the field of the free movement of capital concerned Britain's biggest airport operator, the British Airports Authority (BAA).[376] BAA was privatised in 1986 as part of the privatisation policy pursued by Margaret Thatcher. The privatisation process was governed by the Airports Act 1986. The UK Government retained control over the newly formed company that took over the functions of the previously state-owned enterprise by retaining a special shareholding. In particular, the Articles of Association of the privatised BAA provided for a rule that prevented the acquisition of more than 15 % of the voting shares in the company. Furthermore, they introduced a procedure, which empowered the UK Government to give consent to certain major operations of the company, such as disposal of assets, control of subsidiaries and winding-up. It is noteworthy that under the Airports Act 1986, the Articles of Association were approved by the Secretary of State and as such the rules at issue amounted to 'State measures', despite the fact that they were permitted by national company law.[377]

The Commission was of the opinion that although the provisions at issue applied without distinction, they could nevertheless *hinder* or *render less attractive* the exercise of the free movement rights of foreign investors.[378] In its response, the UK Government, after explaining that the existence of different classes of shares was consistent with national company law, put forward an inventive and eloquent argument: it invited the Court to interpret the

---

373 Case C-463/00 *Commission v Spain (golden shares)*.
374 Case C-98/01 *Commission v UK (golden shares)*.
375 Case C-171/08 *Commission v Portugal (golden shares – Portugal Telecom SGPS SA)*; Case C-543/08 *Commission v Portugal (golden shares – EDP)*; Case C-212/09 *Commission v Portugal (golden shares – GALP Energia SGPS SA)*.
376 Case C-98/01 *Commission v UK (golden shares)*.
377 Ibid, para 24.
378 Ibid, para 20.

contested special rights in the light of the ruling in *Keck and Mithouard*. The application of the *Keck*-formula would entail the exclusion of the contested special rights from the scope of capital restrictions under Article 63 TFEU. It reminded the Court of its own efforts to keep a tight rein on the speculative litigation that emerged in the field of goods after *Dassonville* and *Cassis de Dijon* by adopting a more moderate approach in *Keck and Mithouard*. It thus warned the Court that if the Commission's view prevailed, the negative implications of the broad definition of 'measures having equivalent effect to a quantitative restriction' would be replicated in the context of the free movement of capital.[379] It also added the criterion of *directness*, similar to the one that was used by the Court in the other freedoms, emphasising that the system of prior approval related to eventualities that were too *uncertain* or *indirect* to amount to a capital restriction.[380]

Furthermore, the UK Government contended that the measures at issue applied equally to foreign and domestic investors and did not restrict market access. Rules of private law such as the ones in the BAA's Articles of Association that *did not derogate from normal company law* and merely determined the characteristics of the special shareholding could not possibly amount to a restriction on market access.[381] It was persuasively argued that the Member States were entitled to engage in economic activities on the same basis as private market operators, within the framework of contracts governed by private law. As there was no secondary legislation on this particular matter, Community law could not impose on a company the obligation to be placed under market control or to attach to its shares the rights which all actual or potential investors might wish to see attached to them.[382] It was argued that if the UK special shareholding were open to challenge, this would mean that holders of ordinary shares could rely on the Treaty in order to renegotiate the rights attached to the shares they had bought.[383] In other words, ordinary shareholders would be allowed to convert their ordinary shares into special shares. However, this interpretation could not be accepted. Community law could not impose a specific model of corporate governance. This was – and still remains – a domain reserved for the national legislator.

In its reply, the Commission contended that the issue at hand was not the *manner* in which shares might be acquired or dealt with, but the *actual*

---

379 Ibid, para 28.
380 Ibid, para 36.
381 Ibid, para 29.
382 Ibid, para 31.
383 Ibid, para 35.

acquisition of shares and thus the negation of a fundamental aspect of the free movement of capital.[384] It underlined that in *Alpine Investments*[385] and *Bosman*[386] the Court had refused to transpose the doctrine of 'selling arrangements' to the free movement of services and workers.[387] However, a careful reading of the judgments in *Alpine Investments* and *Bosman* would reveal that the Court did not reject the argument that the doctrine of 'selling arrangements' could *in principle* apply by analogy to the other freedoms; rather it ruled that the national measures *at issue* (i.e. prohibition of cold calling by telephone for financial services and the sporting rules on the transfer of players) were not comparable to the rules on 'selling arrangements' of goods, as they directly affected access to the market (for service providers and players respectively) in other Member States and thus were capable of hindering intra-Community trade and impeding freedom of movement for workers. But the fact remained that *in principle* the *Keck*-test could be transposed to the other freedoms.

The Court was faced with an opportunity to reconsider anew the application of the *Keck*-test in the free movement of capital. However, it did not do so. By contrast, it sided with the Commission and followed the well-beaten path of 'direct hindrance of market access'. Although *in principle* it did not exclude the possibility of developing a concept of 'selling arrangements' in the free movement of capital, it nevertheless rejected it on the facts, by stating that the measures at issue were not comparable to the rules concerning 'selling arrangements'. It reiterated the famous paragraph 16 in *Keck*, and found that while the contested measures were not discriminatory, they nonetheless affected the position of a person acquiring a shareholding as such and were thus liable to deter investors from other Member States from making such investments and consequently affected their access to the market.[388]

In the same vein, the Court dismissed the *Keck*-argument in *Commission v Spain*.[389] The case concerned a Spanish privatisation law which granted special government control in five strategic undertakings: Respol (petroleum and energy), Telefónica (telecommunications), Argentaria (banking), Tabacalera (tobacco) and Endesa (electricity). More specifically, the Spanish legislation provided for a system of prior administrative approval with respect to major corporate decisions relating to voluntary winding-up, demerger or merger of

---

384 Ibid, para 34.
385 Case C-384/93 *Alpine Investments*, para 36-38.
386 Case C-415/93 *Bosman*, para 103.
387 Case C-98/01 *Commission v UK (golden shares)*, para 34.
388 Ibid, para 47.
389 Case C-463/00 *Commission v Spain (golden shares)*.

the undertaking, disposal of assets or shareholdings necessary for the attainment of the undertaking's object, a change in the undertaking's object etc. The Commission invoked the ruling in *Eglise de Scientologie*[390] where it was held that a provision of national law which makes a direct foreign investment subject to prior authorisation constitutes a restriction on the free movement of capital,[391] as it causes the exercise of the free movement of capital to be subject to the discretion of the administrative authorities and thus be such as to render that freedom illusory.[392]

The Spanish government counter-argued that the privatisation process was perfectly legal under national law,[393] that the system of prior approval applied without restriction on grounds of nationality[394] and that it should be regarded as compatible with EU law as a result of the application of the principle of neutrality with regard to the property ownership systems of the Member States under Article 345 TFEU.[395] In support of the Spanish Government, the UK – which had a particular interest in the outcome of the case as the ruling on its special shareholding in BAA was delivered on the same day – relied again on *Keck and Mithouard* and argued that the measure at issue did not restrict market access and thus did not infringe Article 63 TFEU.[396]

Using the same wording, the Court repeated its ruling in *Commission v UK*[397] and found that the measures at issue did not have comparable effects to those of the rules that according to the *Keck*-formula qualified as 'selling arrangements'. Although non-discriminatory, the system of prior approval had a deterrent effect on foreign capital inflows and was thus regarded as affecting the access of foreign investors to the relevant Spanish market.[398] Similarly, in *Commission v Portugal I*,[399] the Portuguese Republic invited the Court to apply the logic underlying the judgment in *Keck*, as the case concerned non-discriminatory rules regarding the *management* of shareholdings in the company and not rules regarding the *acquisition* of those shareholdings. However, the Court rejected once again the application of the concept of 'selling arrangements' in the golden shares case law.

---

390 Case C-54/99 *Association Eglise de scientologie de Paris*, para 14.
391 Case C-463/00 *Commission v Spain (golden shares)*, para 33.
392 Joined cases C-163/94, C-165/94 and C-250/94 *Sanz de Lera*, para 25.
393 Case C-463/00 *Commission v Spain (golden shares)*, para 39.
394 Ibid, para 55.
395 Ibid, para 41.
396 Ibid, para 58.
397 Case C-98/01 *Commission v UK (golden shares)*.
398 Ibid, para 61.
399 Case C-171/08 *Commission v Portugal (golden shares – Portugal Telecom SGPS SA)*.

4   In Search of a Refined Test for 'Capital Restrictions'

In order to develop an appropriate legal test for determining the scope of capital restrictions, it is first necessary to understand the logic behind the Court's rigorous interpretation of the free movement of capital in the golden shares case law. The underlying rationale of this interpretation is that golden shares, by their very nature, are inherently incompatible with EU law. This stems from the general ideological premise that State participation in the market should be limited and reflects a political choice favouring the model of *liberal market economy* as opposed to the model of *coordinated market economy* that allows the existence of corporate governance regimes with control enhancing mechanisms. In the field of corporate governance, this view finds more concrete expression in the embracement of two principles, namely the *principle of proportionality between ownership and control* and the *principle of shareholders' primacy*.

Indeed, in the golden shares case law, the Court seems to endorse the *principle of proportionality between corporate ownership and control*, implying that any shareholder should in principle own the same fraction of cash flow rights and voting rights. Its legal reasoning starts from the premise that the *principle of proportionality between ownership and control* should be respected, and thus any structure or mechanism that derogates from this principle should be disapplied as it discourages investors from acquiring shares in the undertaking concerned. According to this reasoning, the State's interference in the management of the company through the vehicle of golden shares is capable of *depressing the value of the shares*, thus *reducing the attractiveness* of an investment in that company.[400] The reason is that the State might exercise its special rights in order to pursue public interest objectives, 'which might be contrary to the economic interests of the company'.[401]

The concerns relating to the 'depression of the share value' and the protection of 'the economic interests of the company' reveal an implicit adherence to *shareholders' primacy value* as the principal normative foundation on the basis of which national corporate governance regimes should be structured.

---

400   Ibid, para 54.
401   Joined cases C-282/04 and C-283/04 *Commission v The Netherlands (golden shares)*, para 30. A similar view was expressed by Advocate General Maduro in *Federconsumatori*, where he argued that public ownership of shareholding does not reduce the attractiveness of investing in the company concerned, only insofar as the State respects the normal rules of operation of the market with a view to maximising its return on investment. See Opinion of *Advocate General Maduro in Joined cases C-463/04 and C-464/04 Federconsumatori and Others*, ECLI:EU:C:2006:524, paras 25-26.

State participation in preferred holding is regarded as having a deterrent effect on foreign investment on the grounds that it serves interests other than the interests of the shareholders.[402]

However, the maximisation of shareholders' profit is not the only consideration to be taken into account in the governance of a corporation.[403] In fact, it has rightly been pointed out that it is not a universal principle of company law that shareholders' powers must be exercised in the economic interest of the company and even when such principle operates it is not the competence of the EU to ensure that it is upheld.[404] It has been argued that this legal reasoning of the Court is based on three assumptions, whose acceptance though is far from evident: it implies that, first, the interests of the company are those of the shareholders, secondly, the shareholders' interests are embodied in the share value[405] and, thirdly, the existence of golden shares diminishes the value of the share.[406] All three assumptions raise highly controversial questions in

---

402 Carsten Gerner-Beuerle, 'Shareholders Between the Market and the State. The VW Law and other Interventions in the Market Economy' (2012) 49 *Common Market Law Review* 97. See also Martha O'Brien, 'Case C-326/07, Commission of the European Communities v. Italian Republic, Judgment of the Court of Justice (Third Chamber) of 26 March 2009' (2010) 47 *Common Market Law Review* 245, p. 260, who criticises the Court for being 'very strict in its refusal to allow Member States to exercise control over ownership of shares, voting rights and management decision-making in private companies through golden share mechanisms'.

403 Andrea Biondi, 'When the State is the Owner – Some Further Comments on the Court of Justice 'Golden Shares' Strategy' in Bernitz and Ringe (eds), *Company Law and Economic Protectionism: New Challenges to European Integration* (Oxford University Press 2010), p. 102.

404 Jonathan Rickford, 'Protectionism, Capital Freedom and the Internal Market' in Bernitz and Ringe (eds), *Company Law and Economic Protectionism – New Challenges to European Integration* (Oxford University Press 2010), p. 66.

405 Carsten Gerner-Beuerle, 'Shareholders Between the Market and the State. The VW Law and other Interventions in the Market Economy' (2012) 49 *Common Market Law Review* 97, p. 124.

406 However, this assumption is not empirically proven. In 2005, Oxera, authorised by the European Commission, provided an overview of the special rights retained by public authorities in privatised companies in the EU and an evaluation of their economic impact on the performance of affected companies. The Report examined six companies (Cimpor, Volkswagen, Repsol YPF, KPN, Portugal Telecom and BAA) and concluded that special rights held by public authorities tend to have a negative impact on the longer-term economic performance of EU privatised companies because four of the six companies examined tended to underperform relative to comparable companies not subject to special rights. However, the remaining two companies outperformed their comparators and, thus, this contradictory evidence was not consistent with the hypothesis that the impact of special rights is negative. Accordingly, Oxera concluded that: '… although there is some indication of a negative impact of special rights, the evidence obtained

the field of corporate governance and political economy regarding the role of a corporation in a society and the interests it should serve. It is in fact argued that the golden shares case law has advanced the rule that corporations should be governed with a view to maximise shareholders' profit to such an extent that it has turned Article 63 TFEU into a 'Charter of Shareholder Rights'.[407] It has managed to elevate the shareholders' primacy principle to a constitutional norm underpinning capital liberalisation.[408]

It is argued that the underlying rationale of the golden shares case law is based on a utopian nostalgia for the traditional forms of capitalism.[409] However, the transformations of modern economy have led to a high degree of 'financialisation', which is currently associated with economic stagnation, rising social inequalities and high levels of unemployment.[410] Furthermore, such a reading of the Treaty is open to question. Surely, the wording of Article 63 TFEU provides for the prohibition of 'all restrictions' on capital movements without any allusion to discrimination. However, this cannot be regarded as a *carte blanche* to abolish all national company law requirements that derogate from the *principle of proportionality between ownership and control* or that do not adhere completely to *shareholders' primacy* on the assumption that they render investment less attractive. The choice of corporate governance model is a fundamental political question, which depends on various socio-economic factors that differ significantly among Member States. Whether corporate governance should be dominated by the *shareholders' primacy norm* or by the *stakeholders' primacy norm* is a political question and should be clearly distinguished from the objective of market integration pursued by the Treaties.[411]

This by no means should be interpreted as leaving room for suspicious State interferences that could lead to serious market abuses and distortions of competition. The Court should not refrain from disapplying distinctly or indistinctly national measures that obstruct capital flows and undermine the process of financial integration. However, it should respect the division

---

from the benchmarking analysis is disparate and does not allow any strong conclusions to be drawn. However, the results do not imply that special rights have no negative impact on companies' long-term performance'. See Oxera, *Special rights of public authorities in privatised EU companies: the microeconomic impact* (2005), p. 68.

407 Harm Schepel, 'Of Capitalist Nostalgia and Financialisation: Shareholder Primacy in the Court of Justice' in Joerges and Glinski (eds), *The European Crisis and the Transformation of Transnational Governance* (Hart Publishing 2014).
408 Ibid, para 144.
409 Ibid, para 152.
410 Ibid, para 152.
411 Ibid, p. 126.

of competences between the EU and the Member States and the discretion of the Member States to determine the corporate governance regime of their national economy, and it should intervene only when the national choices seriously undermine the objectives of market integration either by *discriminating* against foreign investors or by *hindering the market access* of foreign investors *in derogation from ordinary company law*. The main objective of the free movement of capital is not the maximisation of shareholders' profit, but the establishment of a well-functioning and integrated market economy, which respects the national policy choices as expressed through various mechanisms of national company law.

In this respect, it should be noted that the question whether the contested measure *derogates from domestic company law* has been an important criterion determining the existence of a capital restriction.[412] The Court has used this criterion in the golden shares case law in order to delineate the scope of the free movement of capital. For instance, in *Commission* v. *Portugal (I) (Portugal Telecom SGPS SA)*,[413] the Court found that the contested special shareholding amounted to a State measure liable to restrict the free movement of capital. The special rights at issue included, among others, a right to elect at least one-third of the total number of directors, including the chairman of the board of directors, a right to elect one or two of the members of the executive committee and an approval procedure for important decisions, such as the appropriation of net income of the year, alterations to the articles of association and increases in share capital, and relocation of its registered office. Although the preferred shares were introduced in the Articles of Association, the Court noted that these Articles were adopted not only immediately after the adoption of the decree-law authorising the creation of golden shares within Portugal Telecom, but in particular at a time when the Portuguese Republic had a majority holding in the company's share capital and thus exercised control over that company.[414] More importantly, as underlined by Advocate

---

412 Ibid, p. 108. However, the author admits that company law is a highly complex field of law with many different variations, exceptions and special provisions, making the determination of what complies with or derogates from ordinary company law a rather intricate and challenging exercise (p. 138).

413 Case C-171/08 *Commission v Portugal (golden shares – Portugal Telecom SGPS SA)*.

414 Ibid, p. 53. Nevertheless, it should be noted that it is disputed whether the fact that a State makes use of its majority shareholding in order to introduce special rights in the Articles of Association – when this is allowed by national company law – is sufficient to qualify this act as a 'State measure'. Special rights are usually introduced by those in control, either in the initial phase of incorporation or after an amendment of the Articles in view of a planned divestiture. See Carsten Gerner-Beuerle, 'Shareholders Between the Market

General Mengozzi, the creation of the golden shares in question *was not the result of a normal application of company law*, as they were not transferable, in derogation from the Portuguese Commercial Companies Code.[415] Therefore, in those circumstances, the Court regarded the introduction of golden shares in Portugal Telecom as a 'State measure' liable to restrict the free movement of capital. The Portuguese Government had departed from the ordinary provisions of company law in order to avail itself of a privileged position in the privatised telecommunications company.

Similarly, in *Commission v Portugal (GALP Energia SGPS SA)*,[416] the Court held that the right of the State to appoint the chairman of the Board of Directors in GALP Energia SGPS SA was not stemming from a normal application of company law, since the Portuguese Commercial Companies Code expressly precluded the right to appoint certain directors being attached to certain categories of shares.[417] The national law at issue and GALP's Articles of Association *derogated from general company law* with the sole intention of benefitting the public authorities.[418] Consequently, the right of the State to appoint the chairman of GALP's Board of Directors was attributable to the Portuguese State and was thus falling within the scope of Article 63 TFEU.[419]

However, in the *Commission v UK (BAA)* case, the Court did not take into account the UK Government's claim that the contested provisions in the BAA's Articles of Association *did not derogate from normal company law* but merely determined the characteristics of the special shareholding and therefore they could not possibly amount to a restriction on market access of foreign investors.[420]

The application of the *derogation from ordinary company law criterion* was more complicated in *Commission v Germany (Volkswagen I)* case.[421] In particular, at stake were three provisions of the controversial Volkswagen Law: (1) the capping of the voting rights of every shareholder to 20% of Volkswagen's share capital; (2) the fixing of the blocking minority at 20% for the most important decisions of the general meeting of shareholders; and (3) the right of the

---

and the State. The VW Law and other Interventions in the Market Economy' (2012) 49 Common Market Law Review 97, p. 118.
415   *Opinion of Advocate General Mengozzi in Case C-171/08 Commission v. Portugal (I) (golden shares)*, ECLI:EU:C:2010:412, para. 62.
416   Case C-212/09 *Commission v Portugal (golden shares – GALP Energia SGPS SA)*.
417   Ibid, para 5.
418   Ibid, para 53.
419   Ibid, para 54.
420   Case C-98/01 *Commission v UK (golden shares)*, para 29.
421   Case C-112/05 *Commission v Germany (golden shares – Volkswagen I)*.

Federal State and the Land of Lower Saxony each to appoint two representatives to the company's supervisory board.

Regarding the third provision, the finding that it derogated from ordinary company law was a rather straightforward exercise. The entitlement of the Federal State and the Land of Lower Saxony to appoint a total of four persons in the supervisory board of Volkswagen constituted a derogation from general company law, as under the latter they would have been entitled to appoint a maximum of three representatives.[422]

The other two provisions were examined together and it was found that *the combination of the two* constituted a restriction on the free movement of capital. More precisely, the capping of the voting rights of every shareholder to 20 % of the company's share capital *derogated from general company law*, since Volkswagen was a listed company and for that reason a ceiling on the voting rights could not normally be inserted into its Articles of Association.[423] The fixing of the blocking minority at 20% (and thus the required majority at 80%) *derogated form ordinary company law* as the latter established a blocking minority of 25% (and thus required majority of 75%).[424] While it was true that general company law allowed the increase of the 75% percentage of required majority by the Articles of Association of a company,[425] the Court nevertheless emphasised that what was crucial was the *fact* that the Land of Lower Saxony held 20% of Volkswagen share capital.[426] In other words, the restriction came from a *combination* of *legislative provisions* granting certain privileges and the *factual situation* in which the Land of Lower Saxony was holding the required percentage of shareholding allowing it to benefit from those privileges.[427] Thus, the two provisions in question, *examined together* and *in combination with the factual situation*, enabled the Federal and State authorities to procure for themselves a blocking minority allowing them to oppose important resolutions on the basis of a reduced investment[428] and to limit the possibility for other shareholders to participate effectively in the management of the company.[429]

---

422   Ibid, para 60.
423   Ibid, para 41.
424   Ibid, para 44.
425   Ibid, para 45.
426   Ibid, para 48.
427   Wolf-Georg Ringe, 'Company Law and Free Movement of Capital' (2010) 69 Cambridge Law Journal 378, p. 401.
428   Case C-112/05 *Commission v Germany (golden shares – Volkswagen I)*, para 51.
429   Ibid, para 52.

It is interesting to note that following the 2007 judgment, Germany repealed the provisions regarding the appointment of the representatives and the capping of voting rights, but maintained the provision on the lower blocking minority. The Commission brought again infringement proceedings against Germany for failure to comply with the 2007 judgment.[430] However, the Court dismissed the action, holding that the restriction on the free movement of capital did not result from the lower blocking minority examined in isolation, but from the *combination* of the latter with the capping of voting rights. Therefore, by repealing the provision of the Volkswagen Law relating to the appointment of representatives to the supervisory board and the provision relating to the cap on voting rights, Germany did fulfil the obligations that followed from the 2007 judgment. This way, it could be argued that the Court implicitly confirmed the validity of the *derogation from ordinary law criterion*, since from the three contested provisions, the lower blocking minority was the only one that was allowed, albeit as an exception, under general company law.

On the basis of the aforementioned considerations and taking into account the evolution of the interpretation of restrictions in the field of free movement of goods, it is suggested here that a twofold test could be adopted in order to delineate in a more consistent manner the scope of capital restrictions:

Discrimination on grounds of nationality: Measures that discriminate between domestic and foreign investors (distinctly applicable measures) constitute restrictions on the free movement of capital, which can be justified only by the Treaty-based derogation grounds.

Derogation from ordinary company law: Measures that do not discriminate on grounds of nationality (indistinctly applicable measures) may be divided into two sub-categories:

(a) indistinctly applicable measures that (i) *do not derogate from ordinary company law* and (ii) *respect the principle of equality between the State and private parties as market participants without granting any privilege to the State* should be regarded as 'investment arrangements', which – just like the 'selling arrangements' in the field of free movement of goods – fall outside the scope of Article 63 TFEU. These rules merely *structure* the market and the corporate governance regime of a Member State, without hindering foreign investment.

---

430   Case C-95/12 *Commission v Germany* (*golden shares – Volkswagen II*). See also the annotation Florian Möslein, 'Compliance with ECJ judgments vs. compatibility with EU law – Free movement of capital issues unresolved after the second ruling on the Volkswagen law: Commission v. Germany' (2015) 52 *Common Market Law Review* 801.

(b) indistinctly applicable measures that (i) *derogate from ordinary company law* and (ii) *are available only to the State (to the exclusion of private investors)* constitute restrictions on the free movement of capital prohibited under Article 63 TFEU. It can then be examined whether they can be justified by the Treaty-based derogation grounds or overriding reasons in the public interest in accordance with the principle of proportionality.

As stated above, the first criterion, i.e. *derogation from ordinary company law*, stems from the golden shares case law and ensures that neither the State nor private parties depart from the normal application of national company law in order to avail themselves of undue advantages that infringe the national legislative framework and distort the market for corporate control. This way, both the principle of legal certainty and the discretion of Member States in organising their corporate governance systems are respected. Private market operators are expected to abide by the binding rules of national company law whilst at the same time they can exercise their private autonomy under certain optional choices allowed under the national legislative framework. In the same vein, the State, in its capacity as a shareholder, is expected to act in accordance with the binding rules of national company law, while at the same time it can make use of the options available under the national corporate governance regime.

However, it should be noted that although the *non-derogation from ordinary company law* might be a necessary condition for the exclusion of a certain measure from the scope of capital restrictions, it is nevertheless not a sufficient one. What is also needed is a guarantee that the rules of national company law from which the measure in question does not derogate, create a *level playing field* for all market participants, both public and private. In other words, it is necessary to ensure that the measure at stake respects *the principle of equality between the State and private parties as market participants* and does not grant an undue advantage to the State to the detriment of private operators.

This second criterion does not stem from the golden shares case law. To the contrary, it can be argued that the golden shares case law seems to start from the ideological premise that State participation in the market is not allowed and, therefore, golden shares are inherently incompatible with EU law regardless of whether they grant an undue advantage to the State. However, the view that golden shares are inherently incompatible with EU law reflects a political view which cannot be supported by the letter or the spirit of the Treaties, which merely demand the establishment and the proper functionning of a competitve internal market, without however prohibiting State participation in economic activity.

It has been argued that the political view that the State should be subject to more stringent conditions when acting as a market participant than those imposed on private operators view is supported by the legislative framework that governs EU public procurement law, whereby the State is treated with more suspicion than private market actors and is subject to more restrictive requirements when organising tenders for the purchase of goods, works or services.[431] However, the rationale underlying the strict requirements of transparency, equal treatment, open competition, and sound procedural management which bind the State in the field of public procurement is to ensure the non-discrimination between private actors. In other words, the purpose of EU public procurement law is to ensure that when contracting for the provision of goods or services, the State does not grant an unfair advantage to a private contractor as opposed to another private contractor.

Overall, it can be argued that indistinctly applicable measures should be regarded as restricting the free movement of capital only if the Member State is making use of its public regulatory powers to structure the market in its favour in derogation from ordinary company law. The mere assumption that State participation in a corporate structure hinders the market access of foreign investors – even if it is in accordance with national company law – is an overly broad interpretation of Article 63 TFEU, which oversteps the boundaries of the constitutional foundations of market integration. The European imperatives of economic and political integration do not openly demand such a dramatic retreat of the State from direct intervention in economic activity.[432] They merely demand a level playing field, whereby both the State and private operators abide by the rules of a competitive market.[433] The refined test on capital restrictions respects the competence of the Member States to determine their corporate governance systems and protect public interest objectives, whilst at the same time preventing protectionist measures which derogate from ordinary company law and hinder the market access of foreign investors.

---

431 Wolf-Georg Ringe, 'Company Law and Free Movement of Capital' (2010) 69 Cambridge Law Journal 378, p. 397.

432 Erika Szyszczak, 'Golden Shares and Market Governance' (2002) 29 Legal Issues of Economic Integration 255, p. 258.

433 Ibid.

Conclusion

Capital liberalisation has undoubtedly brought significant benefits to the global economy, by improving economic efficiency, allocating efficiently global resources, promoting foreign investment and supporting the transfer of technology and innovation around the globe. However, it is often associated with increased financial instability and rising levels of unemployment and income inequality. This is why international economic organisations such as the IMF and the OECD have concluded that capital liberalisation improves economic efficiency only if it is complemented by measures of prudential supervision and regulation, sound macroeconomic policies and transparency.

The negative social consequences of unfettered capital flows have caused a rising backlash against globalisation, which is often accompanied by measures of economic protectionism. In the field of trade, protectionist barriers on imports and exports of goods are counter-productive and they have a negative impact on growth and employment.[1] In the field of financial integration, however, defining what constitutes a protectionist measure and assessing its impact on economic growth and employment is a more difficult exercise.

In the EU, golden shares and forms of public ownership have been are regarded as protectionist measures aiming at protecting national industries against hostile takeovers, from foreign or even domestic competitors. However, while it is true that measures which prohibit the acquisition of shares by foreign investors constitute discriminatory restrictions on the free movement of capital, other measures affecting the voting rights of shareholders, the composition of the board of directors or the decision making process within an undertaking without discriminating between foreign and domestic investors might actually not restrict the free movement of capital.

In this context, this book has attempted to explore how the EU free movement of capital provisions can be interpreted in order allow room for State participation in the market for the purposes of protecting public interest objectives in the context of privatisations and golden shares. In order to do so, it has firstly discussed the international theoretical debate regarding the question whether capital liberalisation actually contributes to economic growth or rather exacerbates income inequality. Secondly, it has analysed the CJEU case

---

[1] Christine Lagarde, 'Fix the Roof While the Window of Opportunity is Open: Three Priorities for the Global Economy, Speech at University of Hong Kong' (*IMF,* 2018) <https://www.imf.org/en/News/Articles/2018/04/09/spring-meetings-curtain-raiser-speech> accessed 31-01-2019.

law on privatisations and golden shares and has concluded that the judicial endorsement of a very broad interpretation of capital restrictions limits the competence of the Member States to determine their corporate governance and property ownership systems and to protect societal values.

In particular, this broad interpretation deprives Member States of their right to prohibit the privatisation of public undertakings or to maintain golden shares in privatised companies, which are of strategic importance for the national industrial policy and often serve public interest objectives. The golden shares case law seems to be based on the ideological premise that golden shares are inherently incompatible with the fundamental freedoms. The rigorous interpretation of the free movement of capital under Article 63 TFEU implicitly favours the constitutional foundations of liberal market economies (as opposed to coordinated market economies) and promotes, through negative integration, a corporate governance system, which endorses the principle of proportionality between ownership and control and the principle of shareholders' primacy.

Golden shares deviate from the principle of proportionality between ownership and control, as they grant to public authorities voting rights, which do not correspond to their percentage of ownership. Furthermore, they do not adhere to shareholders' primacy, as the State's interference with the management of an undertaking for the purposes of protecting public interest objectives is allegedly capable of depressing the value of shares, thus reducing the attractiveness of investing in the undertaking concerned and thus undermining shareholders' interests. As such, they are considered to be restrictions on capital movements.

However, the prohibition on restrictions on capital movements under Article 63 TFEU should not be regarded as a blank check to abolish all national company law requirements, which derogate from the principle of proportionality between ownership and control or do not adhere completely to shareholders' primacy on the assumption that they render investment less attractive. While it is true that Member States should refrain from adopting measures that obstruct the functioning of the Internal Market, the choice of the market economy model remains a national competence. Member States are in principle entitled to define their market economy model, to participate in the market and to protect societal values. A judicially driven convergence into the model of liberal market economies can be barely squared with the wording and the spirit of the Treaties, let alone with the international debate about the possible contributory effect of capital liberalisation to the rising levels of income inequality. Such a convergence raises concerns regarding the division of competences between the EU and the Member States in the fields of corporate governance and property ownership systems and the protection of public interest objectives. In this respect, the book has put forward two proposals: firstly, the rediscovery of the principle of neutrality under Article 345 TFEU as a legal provision shielding national decisions to maintain public ownership in undertakings from Internal Market scrutiny; and, secondly, the recalibration of the capital restrictions test in the golden shares case law by reference to a Keck-inspired notion of investment arrangements.

In relation to the first proposal regarding Article 345 TFEU, it is suggested that the right to opt for a private or public property ownership system of undertakings should be covered by the principle of neutrality enshrined in Article 345 TFEU. EU law is neutral with respect to privatisations and nationalisations. If a prohibition of privatisation is regarded as a restriction on the free movement of capital, this is liable to render Article 345 TFEU devoid of any legal meaning whatsoever. Measures intrinsically linked with the national property ownership system, such as a prohibition on privatisation, should in principle be excluded from the scope of the free movement provisions by virtue of Article 345 TFEU. However, it is acknowledged that the ruling in *Essent*, where the Court held that the reasons underlying the choice of a public ownership system under Article 345 TFEU could be used as a justification for the capital restriction imposed by the prohibition of privatisation, aims to achieve a reconciliation between capital liberalisation and public interest objectives.

In relation to the second proposal regarding the recalibration of the 'capital restrictions' test, the analysis draws inspiration from the concept of 'selling arrangements' as developed in the field of free movement of goods and proposes the transposition of a similar concept in the field of free movement of capital. According to this test, if the contested measure discriminates between domestic and foreign investors, it constitutes a discriminatory measure, which can only be justified on the Treaty-based derogation grounds. If the contested measure does not discriminate on the basis of nationality, it constitutes a capital restriction only if it (i) derogates from ordinary company law and (ii) is available only to the State (to the exclusion of private investors). If, however, the non-discriminatory measure (i) does not derogate from ordinary company law and (ii) respects the principle of equality between the State and private parties as market participants without granting any privilege to the State, it should then be regarded as 'investment arrangement', falling outside the scope of Article 63 TFEU, since it merely structures the market and the national corporate governance regime, without hindering foreign investment. Such a test can offer room for State participation in the market for the purposes of pursuing public interest objectives, whist at the same time ensuring that the State participates in the market under equal conditions with private market operators and that protectionist measures which derogate from ordinary company law and grant privileges to the State are prohibited.

Seen from a broader perspective, the two main proposals of this book follow the contemporary economic school of thought advocating a more restrictive approach regarding international capital flows in order to prevent the risks of financial instability and social inequality and seek to reinforce the social dimension of the European integration project. They also attempt to bridge the gap between the State and the Market and to create sufficient room for the State to engage in economic activities as a market participant. Beyond the social considerations, such as the protection of workers and the provision of services of general interest, there are also economic arguments supporting certain forms of public ownership, as recent evidence shows that the State's contribution to the achievement of an innovation-led economic growth is much greater than usually thought.[2] It is therefore not surprising that, despite ambitious privatisation programmes undertaken in recent decades, many governments still maintain public ownership in commercial enterprises in strategically sensitive sectors such as electricity and gas, transportation and finance in order to protect public interest objectives.[3]

---

2 Jukka Snell, 'Economic Justifications and the Role of the State' in Koutrakos, Nic Shuibhne and Syrpis (eds), *Exceptions from EU Free Movement Law: Derogation, Justification and Proportionality* (Hart Publishing 2016), p. 25; Mariana Mazzucato, *The Entrepreneurial State: debunking public vs. private sector myths* (Anthem 2013).

3 OECD, *The Size and Sectoral Distribution of SOEs in OECD and Partner Countries* (OECD Publishing 2014), p. 7. See also Hans Christiansen, *The Size and Composition of the SOE Sector in OECD Countries* (2011). According to the OECD report, the largest State-owned enterprises sectors in the OECD are found in four European countries: Norway, France, Slovenia and Finland.

Bibliography

EU Secondary Legislation

Directives

First Council Directive for the implementation of Article 67 of the Treaty (1960) *OJ* 43, 12.7.1960, p. 921–932

Second Council 63/21/EEC Directive of 18 December 1962 adding to and amending the First Directive for the implementation of Article 67 of the Treaty (1963) *OJ* 9, 22.1.1963, p. 62–74

Council Directive 77/799/EEC of 19 December 1977 concerning mutual assistance by the competent authorities of the Member States in the field of direct taxation (1977) *OJ* L 336, 27.12.1977, p. 15–20

Sixth Council Directive 82/891/EEC of 17 December 1982 based on Article 54 (3) (g) of the Treaty, concerning the division of public limited liability companies (1982) *OJ* L 378, 31.12.1982, p. 47–54

Council Regulation (EEC) No 2137/85 of 25 July 1985 on the European Economic Interest Grouping (EEIG) (1985) *OJ* L 199, 31.7.1985, p. 1–9

Council Directive 88/361/EEC of 24 June 1988 for the implementation of Article 67 of the Treaty (1988) *OJ* L 178, 8.7.1988, p. 5–18

Eleventh Council Directive 89/666/EEC of 21 December 1989 concerning disclosure requirements in respect of branches opened in a Member State by certain types of company governed by the law of another State (1989) *OJ* L 395, 30.12.1989, p. 36–39

Council Directive 98/59/EC of 20 July 1998 on the approximation of the laws of the Member States relating to collective redundancies (1998) *OJ* L 225, 12.8.1998, p. 16–21

Directive 2003/54/EC concerning common rules for the internal market in electricity and repealing Directive 96/92/EC (2003) *OJ* L 176, 15/07/2003, pp. 37–56

Directive 2003/55/EC concerning common rules for the internal market in natural gas and repealing Directive 98/30/EC (2003) *OJ* L 176, 15/07/2003, pp. 57–78

Directive 2004/25/EC of the European Parliament and of the Council of 21 april 2004 on takeover bids (2004) *OJ* L 142, 30.4.2004, p. 12–23

Directive 2005/56/EC of the European Parliament and of the Council of 26 October 2005 on cross-border mergers of limited liability companies (2005) *OJ* L 310, 25.11.2005, p. 1–9

Directive 2006/43/EC of the European Parliament and of the Council of 17 May 2006 on statutory audits of annual accounts and consolidated accounts, amending

Council Directives 78/660/EEC and 83/349/EEC and repealing Council Directive 84/253/EEC (2006) *OJ L 157, 9.6.2006, p. 87–107*

Directive 2006/123/EC of the European Parliament and of the Council of 12 December 2006 on services in the internal market (2006) *OJ L 376, 27.12.2006, p. 36–68*

Directive 2009/72/EC concerning common rules for the internal market in electricity and repealing Directive 2003/54/EC (2009) *OJ L 211, 14/08/2009, pp. 55–93*

Directive 2009/73/EC concerning common rules for the internal market in natural gas and repealing Directive 2003/55/EC (2009) *OJ L 211, 14/08/2009, pp. 94–136*

Directive 2009/101/EC of the European Parliament and of the Council of 16 September 2009 on coordination of safeguards which, for the protection of the interests of members and third parties, are required by Member States of companies within the meaning of the second paragraph of Article 48 of the Treaty, with a view to making such safeguards equivalent (2009) *OJ L 258, 1.10.2009, p. 11–19*

Directive 2011/35/EU of the European Parliament and of the Council of 5 April 2011 concerning mergers of public limited liability companies (2011) *OJ L 110, 29.4.2011, p. 1–11*

Directive 2012/17/EU of the European Parliament and of the Council of 13 June 2012 amending Council Directive 89/666/EEC and Directives 2005/56/EC and 2009/101/EC of the European Parliament and of the Council as regards the interconnection of central, commercial and companies registers (2012) *OJ L 156, 16.6.2012, p. 1–9*

Directive 2012/30/EU of the European Parliament and of the Council of 25 October 2012 on coordination of safeguards which, for the protection of the interests of members and others, are required by Member States of companies within the meaning of the second paragraph of Article 54 of the Treaty on the Functioning of the European Union, in respect of the formation of public limited liability companies and the maintenance and alteration of their capital, with a view to making such safeguards equivalent (2012) *OJ L 315, 14.11.2012, p. 74–97*

Directive 2013/34/EU of the European Parliament and of the Council of 26 June 2013 on the annual financial statements, consolidated financial statements and related reports of certain types of undertakings, amending Directive 2006/43/EC of the European Parliament and of the Council and repealing Council Directives 78/660/EEC and 83/349/EEC (2013) *OJ L 182, 29.6.2013, p. 19–76*

Directive (EU) 2017/1132 of the European Parliament and of the Council of 14 June 2017 relating to certain aspects of company law (2017) *OJ L 169, 30.6.2017, p. 46–127*

Regulations

Council Regulation (EC) No 2157/2001 of 8 October 2001 on the Statute for a European company (SE) (2001) *OJ L 294, 10.11.2001, p. 1–21*

Council Regulation (EC) No 1435/2003 of 22 July 2003 on the Statute for a European Cooperative Society (SCE) (2003) *OJ L 207, 18.8.2003, p. 1–24*
Regulation (EC) No 1228/2003 on conditions for access to the network for cross-border exchanges in electricity (2003) *OJ L 176, 15/07/2003, pp. 1–10*
Regulation (EC) No 1775/2005 on conditions for access to the natural gas transmission networks (2005) *OJ L 289, 03/11/2005, pp. 1–13*
Council Regulation (EU) No 1286/2009 of 22 December 2009 amending Regulation (EC) No 881/2002 imposing certain specific restrictive measures directed against certain persons and entities associated with Usama bin Laden, the Al-Qaeda network and the Taliban (2009) *OJ L 346, 23.12.2009, p. 42–46*
Regulation (EC) No 713/2009 establishing an Agency for the Cooperation of Energy Regulators (2009) *OJ L 211, 14/08/2009, pp. 1–14*
Regulation (EC) No 714/2009 on conditions for access to the network for cross-border exchanges in electricity and repealing Regulation (EC) No 1228/2003 (2009) *OJ L 211, 14/08/2009, pp. 15–35*
Regulation (EC) No 715/2009 on conditions for access to the natural gas transmission networks and repealing Regulation (EC) No 1775/2005 (2009) *OJ L 211, 14/08/2009, pp. 36–54*
Regulation (EU) 2019/452 of the European Parliament and of the Council of 19 March 2019 establishing a framework for the screening of foreign direct investments into the Union (2019) *OJ L 79I, 21.3.2019, p. 1–14*.

International law

Articles of Agreement of the International Monetary Fund (signed and entered into force 27 December 1945) 2 UNTS 39
Legal Department of the IMF, Decision No 8648-[87/104], Multiple Currency Practices Applicable Solely to Capital Transactions (1987)
1994 North American Free Trade Agreement, 32 ILM 289, 605 (1993)
1998 Energy Charter Treaty, 34 ILM 360 (1995)
2012 U.S. Model Bilateral Investment Treaty
General Agreement on Trade in Services (adopted 15 April 1994, entered into force 1 January 1995) 1869 UNTS 183
OECD, Code of Liberalisation of Capital Movements (12 December 1961) OECD/C(61)96

Case Law

Court of Justice
Case 7-61 *Commission v Italy*, ECLI:EU:C:1961:31

Case 7-61 *Commission v Italy (pork)*, ECLI:EU:C:1961:31
Case 6-64 *Flaminio Costa v E.N.E.L.*, ECLI:EU:C:1964:66
Joined cases 56 and 58-64 *Établissements Consten S.à.R.L. and Grundig-Verkaufs-GmbH v Commission*, ECLI:EU:C:1966:41
Case 36-74 *B.N.O. Walrave and L.J.N. Koch v Association Union cycliste internationale*, ECLI:EU:C:1974:140
Case 8-74 *Procureur du Roi v Benoît and Gustave Dassonville*, ECLI:EU:C:1974:82
Case 43-75 *Gabrielle Defrenne v Société anonyme belge de navigation aérienne Sabena*, ECLI:EU:C:1976:56
Case 7/78 *Regina v Ernest George Thompson, Brian Albert Johnson and Colin Alex Norman Woodiwiss*, ECLI:EU:C:1978:209
Case 120/78 *Rewe-Zentral AG v Bundesmonopolverwaltung für Branntwein (Cassis de Dijon)*, ECLI:EU:C:1979:42
Case 823/79 *Criminal proceedings against Giovanni Carciati*, ECLI:EU:C:1980:230
Case 169/80 *Administration des douanes v Société anonyme Gondrand Frères and Société anonyme Garancini*, ECLI:EU:C:1981:171
Case 279/80 *Criminal proceedings against Alfred John Webb*, ECLI:EU:C:1981:314
Case 203/80 *Criminal Proceedings Against Guerrino Casati*, ECLI:EU:C:1981:261
Case 58/80 *Dansk Supermarked A/S v A/S Imerco*, ECLI:EU:C:1981:17
Case 155/80 *Summary proceedings agains Sergius Oebel*, ECLI:EU:C:1981:177
Case 286/81 *Oosthoek's Uitgeversmaatschappij BV*, ECLI:EU:C:1982:438
Case 72/83 *Campus Oil Limited and others v Minister for Industry and Energy and others*, ECLI:EU:C:1984:256
Joined cases 177 and 178/82 *Criminal proceedings against Jan van de Haar and Kaveka de Meern BV*, ECLI:EU:C:1984:144
Joined cases 286/82 and 26/83 *Graziana Luisi and Giuseppe Carbone v Ministero del Tesoro* ECLI:EU:C:1984:35
Case 182/83 *Robert Fearon & Company Limited v Irish Land Commission*, ECLI:EU:C:1984:335
Case 152/84 *M. H. Marshall v Southampton and South-West Hampshire Area Health Authority (Teaching)*, ECLI:EU:C:1986:84
Case 311/85 *ASBL Vereniging van Vlaamse Reisbureaus v ASBL Sociale Dienst van de Plaatselijke en Gewestelijke Overheidsdiensten*, ECLI:EU:C:1987:418
Case 178/84 *Commission v Germany (Beer Purity)*, ECLI:EU:C:1987:126
Case 352/85 *Bond van Adverteerders and others v The Netherlands State*, ECLI:EU:C:1988:196
Case 308/86 *Criminal proceedings against R. Lambert*, ECLI:EU:C:1988:405
Case 81/87 *The Queen v H. M. Treasury and Commissioners of Inland Revenue, ex parte Daily Mail and General Trust plc.*, ECLI:EU:C:1988:456
Case C-145/88 *Torfaen Borough Council v B & Q plc.*, ECLI:EU:C:1989:593

BIBLIOGRAPHY

Case C-188/89 *A. Foster and others v British Gas plc.*, ECLI:EU:C:1990:313

Case C-69/88 *H. Krantz GmbH & Co. tegen Ontvanger der Directe Belastingen en Staat der Nederlanden*, ECLI:EU:C:1990:97

Case C-23/89 *Quietlynn Limited and Brian James Richards v Southend Borough Council*, ECLI:EU:C:1990:300

Case C-367/89 *Aimé Richardt and Les Accessoires Scientifiques SNC*, ECLI:EU:C:1991:376

Joined cases C-1/90 and C-176/90 *Aragonesa de Publicidad and Publivía v Departamento de Sanidad*, ECLI:EU:C:1991:327

Case C-288/89 *Gouda and Others*, ECLI:EU:C:1991:323

Case C-288/89 *Stichting Collectieve Antennevoorziening Gouda and others v Commissariaat voor de Media*, ECLI:EU:C:1991:323

Case C-300/90 *Commission v Belgium*, ECLI:EU:C:1992:37

Case C-30/90 *Commission v UK*, ECLI:EU:C:1992:74

Case C-204/90 *Hanns-Martin Bachmann v Belgian State*, ECLI:EU:C:1992:35

Joined cases C-267/91 and C-268/91 *Criminal proceedings against Bernard Keck and Daniel Mithouard*, ECLI:EU:C:1993:905

Case C-271/92 *Laboratoire de Prothèses Oculaires v Union Nationale des Syndicats d'Opticiens de France and Groupement d'Opticiens Lunetiers Détaillants and Syndicat des Opticiens Français Indépendants and Syndicat National des Adapteurs d'Optique de Contact*, ECLI:EU:C:1993:214

Joined cases C-277/91, C-318/91 and C-319/91 *Ligur Carni Srl and Genova Carni Srl v Unità Sanitaria Locale n. XV di Genova and Ponente SpA v Unità Sanitaria Locale n. XIX di La Spezia and CO.GE.SE.MA Coop a r l*, ECLI:EU:C:1993:927

Case C-292/92 *Ruth Hünermund and others v Landesapothekerkammer Baden-Württemberg*, ECLI:EU:C:1993:932

Case C-126/91 *Schutzverband gegen Unwesen in der Wirtschaft e.V. v Yves Rocher GmbH*, ECLI:EU:C:1993:191

Joined cases C-401/92 and C-402/92 *Criminal proceedings against Tankstation 't Heukske vof and J. B. E. Boermans*, ECLI:EU:C:1994:220

Case C-275/92 *Her Majesty's Customs and Excise tegen Gerhart Schindler en Jörg Schindler*, ECLI:EU:C:1994:119

Joined cases C-69/93 and C-258/93 *Punto Casa SpA v Sindaco del Comune di Capena and Comune di Capena and Promozioni Polivalenti Venete Soc. coop. arl (PPV) v Sindaco del Comune di Torri di Quartesolo and Comune di Torri di Quartesolo*, ECLI:EU:C:1994:226

Case C-384/93 *Alpine Investments BV v Minister van Financiën*, ECLI:EU:C:1995:126

Case C-415/93 *Bosman*, ECLI:EU:C:1995:463

Case C-391/92 *Commission v Greece (infant milk)*, ECLI:EU:C:1995:199

Joined cases C-358/93 and C-416/93 *Criminal proceedings against Aldo Bordessa and Vicente Marí Mellado and Concepción Barbero Maestre*, ECLI:EU:C:1995:54

Joined cases C-163/94, C-165/94 and C-250/94 *Criminal proceedings against Lucas Emilio Sanz de Lera, Raimundo Díaz Jiménez and Figen Kapanoglu*, ECLI:EU:C:1995:451

Case C-279/93 *Finanzamt Köln-Altstadt v Roland Schumacker*, ECLI:EU:C:1995:31

Case C-484/93 *Peter Svensson and Lena Gustavsson v Ministre du Logement et de l'Urbanisme*, ECLI:EU:C:1995:379

Case C-412/93 *Société d'Importation Edouard Leclerc-Siplec v TF1 Publicité SA and M6 Publicité SA*, ECLI:EU:C:1995:26

Case C-415/93 *Union royale belge des sociétés de football association ASBL v Jean-Marc Bosman*, ECLI:EU:C:1995:463

Case C-143/93 *Gebroeders van Es Douane Agenten BV v Inspecteur der Invoerrechten en Accijnzen*, ECLI:EU:C:1996:45

Case C-237/94 *John O'Flynn tegen Adjudication Officer*, ECLI:EU:C:1996:206

Joined cases C 418/93 et al. *Semeraro Casa Uno Srl v Sindaco del Comune di Erbusco*, ECLI:EU:C:1996:242

Case C-299/95 *Friedrich Kremzow v Republik Österreich*, ECLI:EU:C:1997:254

Case C-250/95 *Futura Participations SA and Singer v Administration des contributions*, ECLI:EU:C:1997:239

Joined cases C-34/95, C-35/95 and C-36/95 *Konsumentombudsmannen (KO) v De Agostini (Svenska) Förlag AB and TV-Shop i Sverige AB*, ECLI:EU:C:1997:344

Case C-28/95 *Leur-Bloem v Inspecteur der Belastingsdienst/Ondernemingen Amsterdam 2*, ECLI:EU:C:1997:369

Case C-57/96 *Meints v Minister van Landbouw, Natuurbeheer en Visserij*, ECLI:EU:C:1997:564

Case C-29/95 *Pastoors and Trans-Cap v Belgian State*, ECLI:EU:C:1997:28

Case C-222/95 *Société civile immobilière Parodi v Banque H. Albert de Bary et Cie*, ECLI:EU:C:1997:345

Case C-398/95 *Syndesmos ton en Elladi Touristikon kai Taxidiotikon Grafeion v Ypourgos Ergasias*, ECLI:EU:C:1997:282

Case C-368/95 *Vereinigte Familiapress Zeitungsverlags- und vertriebs GmbH v Heinrich Bauer Verlag*, ECLI:EU:C:1997:325

Case C-187/96 *Commission v Greece*, ECLI:EU:C:1998:101

Case C-410/96 *Criminal proceedings against André Ambry*, ECLI:EU:C:1998:578

Case C-120/95 *Nicolas Decker v Caisse de maladie des employés privés*, ECLI:EU:C:1998:167

Case C-158/96 *Raymond Kohll v Union des caisses de maladie*, ECLI:EU:C:1998:171

Case C-212/97 *Centros Ltd. v Erhvervs-og Selskabbsstyrelsen*, ECLI:EU:C:1999:126

Joined cases C-369/96 and C-376/96 *Criminal proceedings against Jean-Claude Arblade and Arblade & Fils SARL and Bernard Leloup, Serge Leloup and Sofrage SARL*, ECLI:EU:C:1999:575

Case C-302/97 *Klaus Konle v Republik Österreich*, ECLI:EU:C:1999:271
Case C-222/97 *Manfred Trummer and Peter Mayer*, ECLI:EU:C:1999:143
Case C-124/97 *Markku Juhani Läärä, Cotswold Microsystems Ltd and Oy Transatlantic Software Ltd v Kihlakunnansyyttäjä (Jyväskylä) and Suomen valtio (Finnish State)*, ECLI:EU:C:1999:435
Case C-67/98 *Questore di Verona v Diego Zenatti*, ECLI:EU:C:1999:514
Case C-439/97 *Sandoz GmbH v Finanzlandesdirektion für Wien*, ECLI:EU:C:1999:499
Case C-55/98 *Skatteministeriet v Bent Vestergaard*, ECLI:EU:C:1999:533
Case C-423/98 *Alfredo Albore*, ECLI:EU:C:2000:401
Case C-54/99 *Association Eglise de scientologie de Paris*, ECLI:EU:C:2000:124
Case C-251/98 *C. Baars v Inspecteur der Belastingen Particulieren/Ondernemingen Gorinchem*, ECLI:EU:C:2000:205
Joined cases C-51/96 and C-191/97 *Christelle Deliège v Ligue francophone de judo et disciplines associées ASBL*, ECLI:EU:C:2000:199
Case C-478/98 *Commission v Belgium (Eurobond)*, ECLI:EU:C:2000:497
Case C-58/99 *Commission v Italy (golden shares – ENI/Telecom Italia)*, ECLI:EU:C:2000:280
Case C-281/98 *Roman Angonese v Cassa di Risparmio di Bolzano SpA*, ECLI:EU:C:2000:296
Case C-35/98 *Staatssecretaris van Financiën v B.G.M. Verkooijen*, ECLI:EU:C:2000:294
Case C-190/98 *Volker Graf v Filzmoser Maschinenbau GmbH*, ECLI:EU:C:2000:49
Case C-157/99 *B.S.M. Geraets-Smits v Stichting Ziekenfonds VGZ and H.T.M. Peerbooms v Stichting CZ Groep Zorgverzekeringen*, ECLI:EU:C:2001:404
Case C-405/98 *Konsumentombudsmannen (KO) v Gourmet International Products AB (GIP)*, ECLI:EU:C:2001:135
Case C-390/99 *Canal Satélite Digital*, ECLI:EU:C:2002:34
Case C-503/99 *Commission v Belgium (golden shares)*, ECLI:EU:C:2002:328
Case C-483/99 *Commission v France (golden shares – Société Nationale Elf-Aquitaine)*, ECLI:EU:C:2002:327
Case C-279/00 *Commission v Italy*, ECLI:EU:C:2002:89
Case C-367/98 *Commission v Portugal (golden shares)*, ECLI:EU:C:2002:326
Case C-367/98 *Commission v Portugal (golden shares)*, ECLI:EU:C:2002:326
Joined cases C-515/99, C-519/99 to C-524/99 and C-526/99 to C-540/99 *Hans Reisch and Others*, ECLI:EU:C:2002:135
Case C-309/99 *J. C. J. Wouters, J. W. Savelbergh en Price Waterhouse Belastingadviseurs BV tegen Algemene Raad van de Nederlandse Orde van Advocaten, in tegenwoordigheid van: Raad van de Balies van de Europese Gemeenschap*, ECLI:EU:C:2002:98
Joined cases C388/00 and C429/00 *Radiosistemi Srl v Prefetto di Genova*, ECLI:EU:C:2002:390

Case C-208/00 *Überseering BV v Nordic Construction Company Baumanagement GmbH (NCC)*, ECLI:EU:C:2002:632

Case C-436/00 *X and Y*, ECLI:EU:C:2002:704

Case C-6/01 *Associação Nacional de Operadores de Máquinas Recreativas (Anomar) and Others v Estado português*, ECLI:EU:C:2003:446

Joined cases C-261/01 and C-262/01 *Belgische Staat v Eugène van Calster and Others*, ECLI:EU:C:2003:571

Case C-168/01 *Bosal*, ECLI:EU:C:2003:479

Case C-388/01 *Commission v Italy (golden shares)*, ECLI:EU:C:2003:30

Case C-463/00 *Commission v Spain (golden shares)*, ECLI:EU:C:2003:272

Case C-98/01 *Commission v UK (golden shares)*, ECLI:EU:C:2003:273

Case C-243/01 *Criminal proceedings against Piergiorgio Gambelli and Others*, ECLI:EU:C:2003:597

Case C-300/01 *Doris Salzmann*, ECLI:EU:C:2003:283

Case C-112/00 *Eugen Schmidberger, Internationale Transporte und Planzüge v Republik Österreich*, ECLI:EU:C:2003:333

Case C-364/01 *The heirs of H. Barbier v Inspecteur van de Belastingdienst Particulieren/Ondernemingen buitenland te Heerlen*, ECLI:EU:C:2003:665

Case C-452/01 *Margarethe Ospelt and Schlössle Weissenberg Familienstiftung*, ECLI:EU:C:2003:493

Case C-385/99 *V.G. Müller-Fauré v Onderlinge Waarborgmaatschappij OZ Zorgverzekeringen UA and E.E.M. van Riet v Onderlinge Waarborgmaatschappij ZAO Zorgverzekeringen*, ECLI:EU:C:2003:270

Case C-315/02 *Anneliese Lenz v Finanzlandesdirektion für Tirol*, ECLI:EU:C:2004:446

Case C-71/02 *Herbert Karner Industrie-Auktionen GmbH v Troostwijk GmbH*, ECLI:EU:C:2004:181

Case C-242/03 *Ministre des Finances v Jean-Claude Weidert and Élisabeth Paulus*, ECLI:EU:C:2004:465

Case C-36/02 *Omega Spielhallen- und Automatenaufstellungs-GmbH v Oberbürgermeisterin der Bundesstadt Bonn*, ECLI:EU:C:2004:614

Case C-319/02 *Petri Manninen*, ECLI:EU:C:2004:484

Case C-110/03 *Belgium v Commission*, ECLI:EU:C:2005:223

Case C-174/04 *Commission v Italy (golden shares)*, ECLI:EU:C:2005:350

Case C-20/03 *Criminal proceedings against Marcel Burmanjer, René Alexander Van Der Linden and Anthony De Jong*, ECLI:EU:C:2005:307

Case C-376/03 *D. v Inspecteur van de Belastingdienst/Particulieren/Ondernemingen buitenland te Heerlen*, ECLI:EU:C:2005:424

Case C-512/03 *J.E.J. Blanckaert v Inspecteur van de Belastingdienst/Particulieren/Ondernemingen buitenland te Heerlen*, ECLI:EU:C:2005:516

Joined cases C-544/03 and C-545/03 *Mobistar SA v Commune de Fléron and Belgacom Mobile SA v Commune de Schaerbeek*, ECLI:EU:C:2005:518

Case C-109/04 *Karl Robert Kranemann v Land Nordrhein-Westfalen*, ECLI:EU:C:2005:187

Case C-39/04 *Laboratoires Fournier*, ECLI:EU:C:2005:161

Case C-209/03 *The Queen, on the application of Dany Bidar v London Borough of Ealing and Secretary of State for Education and Skills*, ECLI:EU:C:2005:169

Case C-411/03 *SEVIC Systems AG*, ECLI:EU:C:2005:762

Case C-329/03 *Trapeza tis Ellados AE v Banque Artesia*, ECLI:EU:C:2005:645

Case C-144/04 *Werner Mangold v Rüdiger Helm*, ECLI:EU:C:2005:709

Joined cases C-158 & 159/04 *Alfa Vita Vassilopoulos AE and Carrefour Marinopoulos AE v Elliniko Dimosio and Nomarchiaki Aftodioikisi Ioanninon*, ECLI:EU:C:2006:562

Case C-196/04 *Cadbury Schweppes plc*, ECLI:EU:C:2006:544

Joined cases C-282/04 and C-283/04 *Commission v The Netherlands (golden shares)*, ECLI:EU:C:2006:608

Case C-452/04 *Fidium Finanz AG v Bundesanstalt für Finanzdienstleistungsaufsicht*, ECLI:EU:C:2006:631

Case C-471/04 *Finanzamt Offenbach am Main-Land v Keller Holding GmbH*, ECLI:EU:C:2006:143

Case C-513/03 *Heirs of M. E. A. van Hilten-van der Heijden*, ECLI:EU:C:2006:131

Case C-513/04 *Mark Kerckhaert and Bernadette Morres v Belgische Staat*, ECLI:EU:C:2006:713

Opinion of Advocate General Maduro in Joined Cases C-158 & 159/04 *Alfa Vita Vassilopoulos AE*, ECLI:EU:C:2006:212

Case C-344/04 *The Queen, on the application of International Air Transport Association and European Low Fares Airline Association v Department for Transport*, ECLI:EU:C:2006:10

Case C-374/04 *Test Claimants in Class IV of the ACT Group Litigation*, ECLI:EU:C:2006:773

Case C-446/04 *Test Claimants in the FII Group Litigation*, ECLI:EU:C:2006:774

Case C-368/04 *Transalpine Ölleitung in Österreich GmbH*, ECLI:EU:C:2006:644

Case C-379/05 *Amurta SGPS v Inspecteur van de Belastingdienst/Amsterdam*, ECLI:EU:C:2007:655

Case C-150/04 *Commission v Denmark*, ECLI:EU:C:2007:69

Case C-112/05 *Commission v Germany (golden shares – Volkswagen I)*, ECLI:EU:C:2007:623

Case C-385/05 *Confédération générale du travail and Others*, ECLI:EU:C:2007:37

Case C-338/04 *Criminal proceedings against Massimiliano Placanica, Christian Palazzese and Angelo Sorricchio*, ECLI:EU:C:2007:133

Case C-370/05 *Criminal proceedings against Uwe Kay Festersen*, ECLI:EU:C:2007:59

Case C-443/06 *Erika Waltraud Ilse Hollmann v Fazenda Pública*, ECLI:EU:C:2007:600

Case C-451/05 *Européenne et Luxembourgeoise d'investissements SA (ELISA) v Directeur général des impôts and Ministère public*, ECLI:EU:C:2007:594

Joined cases C-463/04 and C-464/04 *Federconsumatori and Others and Associazione Azionariato Diffuso dell'AEM SpA and Others v Comune di Milano (AEM/Edison)*, ECLI:EU:C:2007:752

Case C-438/05 *International Transport Workers' Federation and Finnish Seamen's Union v Viking Line ABP and OÜ Viking Line Eesti*, ECLI:EU:C:2007:772

Case C-208/05 *ITC Innovative Technology Center GmbH v Bundesagentur für Arbeit*, ECLI:EU:C:2007:16

Case C-492/04 *Lasertec Gesellschaft für Stanzformen mbH v Finanzamt Emmendingen*, ECLI:EU:C:2007:273

Case C-341/05 *Laval un Partneri Ltd v Svenska Byggnadsarbetareförbundet, Svenska Byggnadsarbetareförbundets avdelning 1, Byggettan and Svenska Elektrikerförbundet*, ECLI:EU:C:2007:809

Case C-231/05 *Oy AA*, ECLI:EU:C:2007:439

Case C-436/06 *Per Grønfeldt and Tatiana Grønfeldt v Finanzamt Hamburg-Am Tierpark*, ECLI:EU:C:2007:820

Case C-101/05 *Skatteverket v A*, ECLI:EU:C:2007:804

Case C-158/06 *Stichting ROM-projecten v Staatssecretaris van Economische Zaken*, ECLI:EU:C:2007:370

Case C-524/04 *Test Claimants in the Thin Cap Group Litigation*, ECLI:EU:C:2007:161

Case C-157/05 *Winfried L. Holböck v Finanzamt Salzburg-Land*, ECLI:EU:C:2007:297

Case C-207/07 *Commission v Spain (golden shares in the energy sector)*, ECLI:EU:C:2008:428

Case C-274/06 *Commission v Spain (golden shares)*, ECLI:EU:C:2008:86

Case C-346/06 *Dirk Rüffert v Land Niedersachsen*, ECLI:EU:C:2008:189

Case C-11/07 *Hans Eckelkamp and Others v Belgische Staat*, ECLI:EU:C:2008:489

Case C-308/06 *The Queen, on the application of International Association of Independent Tanker Owners (Intertanko) and Others v Secretary of State for Transport*, ECLI:EU:C:2008:312

Case C-194/06 *Staatssecretaris van Financiën v Orange European Smallcap Fund NV*, ECLI:EU:C:2008:289

Case C-256/06 *Theodor Jäger v Finanzamt Kusel-Landstuhl*, ECLI:EU:C:2008:20

Joined cases C-402/05 P and C-415/05 P *Yassin Abdullah Kadi and Al Barakaat International Foundation v Council and Commission*, ECLI:EU:C:2008:461

Case C-142/05 *Åklagaren v Percy Mickelsson and Joakim Roos*, ECLI:EU:C:2009:336

Case C-101/08 *Audiolux SA e.a v Groupe Bruxelles Lambert SA (GBL) and Others and Bertelsmann AG and Others*, ECLI:EU:C:2009:626

Case C-326/07 *Commission v Italy (golden shares)*, ECLI:EU:C:2009:193

Case C-531/06 *Commission v Italy (pharmacies)*, ECLI:EU:C:2009:315
Case C-110/05 *Commission v Italy (trailers)*, ECLI:EU:C:2009:66
Case C-521/07 *Commission v Netherlands*, ECLI:EU:C:2009:360
Case C-377/07 *Finanzamt Speyer-Germersheim v STEKO Industriemontage GmbH*, ECLI:EU:C:2009:29
Case C-182/08 *Glaxo Wellcome GmbH & Co. KG v Finanzamt München II*, ECLI:EU:C:2009:559
Case C-35/08 *Grundstücksgemeinschaft Busley and Cibrian Fernandez v Finanzamt Stuttgart-Körperschaften*, ECLI:EU:C:2009:625
Case C-169/07 *Hartlauer Handelsgesellschaft mbH v Wiener Landesregierung and Oberösterreichische Landesregierung*, ECLI:EU:C:2009:141
Case C-318/07 *Hein Persche v Finanzamt Lüdenscheid*, ECLI:EU:C:2009:33
Case C-42/07 *Liga Portuguesa*, ECLI:EU:C:2009:519
Case C-42/07 *Liga Portuguesa de Futebol Profissional and Bwin International*, ECLI:EU:C:2009:519
Case C-567/07 *Minister voor Wonen, Wijken en Integratie v Woningstichting Sint Servatius*, ECLI:EU:C:2009:593
Case C-201/08 *Plantanol GmbH & Co KG v Hauptzollamt Darmstadt*, ECLI:EU:C:2009:539
Joined cases C-155/08 and C-157/08 *X and E. H. A. Passenheim-van Schoot v Staatssecretaris van Financiën*, ECLI:EU:C:2009:368
Case C-46/08 *Carmen Media Group Ltd v Land Schleswig-Holstein and Innenminister des Landes Schleswig-Holstein*, ECLI:EU:C:2010:505
Case C-512/08 *Commission v France (medical equipment)*, ECLI:EU:C:2010:579
Case C-543/08 *Commission v Portugal (golden shares – EDP)*, ECLI:EU:C:2010:669
Case C-171/08 *Commission v Portugal (golden shares – Portugal Telecom SGPS SA)*, ECLI:EU:C:2010:412
Case C-64/08 *Criminal proceedings against Ernst Engelmann*, ECLI:EU:C:2010:506
Case C-447/08 *Criminal proceedings against Otto Sjöberg and Anders Gerdin* ECLI:EU:C:2010:415
Case C-72/09 *Établissements Rimbaud SA v Directeur général des impôts and Directeur des services fiscaux d'Aix-en-Provence*, ECLI:EU:C:2010:645
Case C-541/08 *Fokus Invest AG v Finanzierungsberatung-Immobilientreuhand und Anlageberatung GmbH (FIAG)*, ECLI:EU:C:2010:74
Case C-233/09 *Gerhard Dijkman and Maria Dijkman-Lavaleije v Belgische Staat*, ECLI:EU:C:2010:397
Case C81/09 *Idryma Typou AE v Ypourgos Typou kai Meson Mazikis Enimerosis*, ECLI:EU:C:2010:622
Case C-108/09 *Ker-Optika bt v ÀNTSZ Dél-dunántúli Regionális Intézete*, ECLI:EU:C:2010:725

Case C-258/08 *Ladbrokes Betting & Gaming and Ladbrokes International*, ECLI:EU:C:2010:308

Case C-316/07 *Markus Stoß, Avalon Service-Online-Dienste GmbH and Olaf Amadeus Wilhelm Happel*, ECLI:EU:C:2010:504

Case C-555/07 *Seda Kücükdeveci v Swedex GmbH & Co. KG.*, ECLI:EU:C:2010:21

Case C-203/08 *Sporting Exchange Ltd v Minister van Justitie*, ECLI:EU:C:2010:307

Case C-510/08 *Vera Mattner v Finanzamt Velbert*, ECLI:EU:C:2010:216

Case C-409/06 *Winner Wetten GmbH v Bürgermeisterin der Stadt Bergheim*, ECLI:EU:C:2010:503

Case C-10/10 *Commission v Austria (Gifts for Teaching and Research Institutions)*, ECLI:EU:C:2011:399

Case C-250/08 *Commission v Belgium (purchase of immovable property)*, ECLI:EU:C:2011:793

Case C-271/09 *Commission v Poland (pension funds)*, ECLI:EU:C:2011:855

Case C-212/09 *Commission v Portugal (golden shares – GALP Energia SGPS SA)*, ECLI:EU:C:2011:717

Case C-347/09 *Criminal proceedings against Jochen Dickinger and Franz Ömer*, ECLI:EU:C:2011:582

Joined cases C-436/08 and C-437/08 *Haribo Lakritzen Hans Riegel BetriebsgmbH and Österreichische Salinen AG v Finanzamt Linz*, ECLI:EU:C:2011:61

Case C-310/09 *Ministre du Budget, des Comptes publics et de la Fonction publique v Accor SA*, ECLI:EU:C:2011:581

Case C-132/10 *Olivier Halley, Julie Halley and Marie Halley v Belgische Staat*, ECLI:EU:C:2011:586

Case C-450/09 *Ulrich Schröder v Finanzamt Hameln*, ECLI:EU:C:2011:198

Case C-262/09 *Wienand Meilicke and Others v Finanzamt Bonn-Innenstadt*, ECLI:EU:C:2011:438

Case C-456/10 *Asociación Nacional de Expendedores de Tabaco y Timbre (ANETT) v Administración del Estado*, ECLI:EU:C:2012:241

Case C-379/11 *Caves Krier Frères Sàrl v Directeur de l'Administration de l'emploi*, ECLI:EU:C:2012:798

Case C-387/11 *Commission v Belgium (tax on income from capital and movable property)*, ECLI:EU:C:2012:670

Case C-342/10 *Commission v Finland*, ECLI:EU:C:2012:688

Case C-244/11 *Commission v Greece (golden shares)*, ECLI:EU:C:2012:694

Case C-542/09 *Commission v Netherlands (access to education)*, ECLI:EU:C:2012:346

Case C-171/11 *Fra.bo SpA v Deutsche Vereinigung des Gas- und Wasserfaches eV (DVGW) – Technisch-Wissenschaftlicher Verein*, ECLI:EU:C:2012:453

Case C31/11 *Marianne Scheunemann v Finanzamt Bremerhaven*, ECLI:EU:C:2012:481

Case C-130/10 *Parliament v Council*, ECLI:EU:C:2012:472

Case C-318/10 *Société d'investissement pour l'agriculture tropicale SA (SIAT) v État belge*, ECLI:EU:C:2012:415

Case C-35/11 *Test Claimants in the FII Group Litigation*, ECLI:EU:C:2012:707

Case C-39/11 *VBV – Vorsorgekasse AG v Finanzmarktaufsichtsbehörde (FMA)*, ECLI:EU:C:2012:327

Case C-498/10 *X NV v Staatssecretaris van Financiën*, ECLI:EU:C:2012:635

Joined cases C-584/10 P, C-593/10 P and C-595/10 P *Commission and Others v Yassin Abdullah Kadi*, ECLI:EU:C:2013:518

Case C-383/10 *Commission v Belgium*, ECLI:EU:C:2013:364

Case C-95/12 *Commission v Germany (golden shares – Volkswagen II)*, ECLI:EU:C:2013:676

Case C-284/12 *Deutsche Lufthansa AG v Flughafen Frankfurt-Hahn GmbH*, ECLI:EU:C:2013:755

Case C-20/12 *Elodie Giersch and Others v État du Grand-Duché de Luxembourg*, ECLI:EU:C:2013:411

Case C-197/11 *Eric Libert and Others v Gouvernement flamand and All Projects & Developments NV and Others v Vlaamse Regering*, ECLI:EU:C:2013:288

Case C-282/12 *Itelcar – Automóveis de Aluguer Lda v Fazenda Pública*, ECLI:EU:C:2013:629

Case C-322/11 *K*, ECLI:EU:C:2013:716

Case C-168/11 *Manfred Beker and Christa Beker v Finanzamt Heilbronn*, ECLI:EU:C:2013:117

Joined cases C-105/12 to C-107/12 *Staat der Nederlanden v Essent NV, Essent Nederland BV, Eneco Holding NV and Delta NV*, ECLI:EU:C:2013:677

Case C-186/11 *Stanleybet International Ltd, William Hill Organization Ltd, William Hill plc, Sportingbet plc v Ipourgos Oikonomias kai Oikonomikon Ipourgos Politismou*, ECLI:EU:C:2013:33

Case C-181/12 *Yvon Welte v Finanzamt Velbert*, ECLI:EU:C:2013:662

Case C-176/12 *Association de médiation sociale v Union locale des syndicats CGT and Others*, ECLI:EU:C:2014:2

Case C-190/12 *Emerging Markets Series of DFA Investment Trust Company*, ECLI:EU:C:2014:249

Case C-47/12 *Kronos International Inc. v Finanzamt Leverkusen*, ECLI:EU:C:2014:2200

Case C-483/12 *Pelckmans Turnhout NV v Walter Van Gastel Balen NV and Others*, ECLI:EU:C:2014:304

Case C-326/12 *Rita van Caster and Patrick van Caster v Finanzamt Essen-Süd*, ECLI:EU:C:2014:2269

Joined cases C53/13 and C80/13 *Strojírny Prostějov et ACO Industries Tábor*, ECLI:EU:C:2014:2011

Case C-98/14 *Berlington Hungary Tanácsadó és Szolgáltató kft and Others v Magyar Állam*, ECLI:EU:C:2015:386

Case C-559/13 *Finanzamt Dortmund-Unna v Josef Grünewald*, ECLI:EU:C:2015:109

Case C-560/13 *Finanzamt Ulm v Ingeborg Wagner-Raith*, ECLI:EU:C:2015:347

Case C-594/14 *Simona Kornhaas v Thomas Dithmar als Insolvenzverwalter über das Vermögen der Kornhaas Montage und Dienstleistung Ltd*, ECLI:EU:C:2015:806

Case C-463/13 *Stanley International Betting and Stanleybet Malta*, ECLI:EU:C:2015:25

Case C-201/15 *Anonymi Geniki Etairia Tsimenton Iraklis (AGET Iraklis) v Ypourgos Ergasias, Koinonikis Asfalisis kai Koinonikis Allilengyis*, ECLI:EU:C:2016:972

Case C-375/14 *Criminal proceedings against Rosanna Laezza*, ECLI:EU:C:2016:60

Case C-336/14 *Criminal proceedings against Sebat Ince*, ECLI:EU:C:2016:72

Case C-479/14 *Sabine Hünnebeck v Finanzamt Krefeld*, ECLI:EU:C:2016:412

Case C-580/15 *Maria Eugenia Van der Weegen and Others v Belgische Staat*, ECLI:EU:C:2017:429

Case C-106/16 *Polbud – Wykonawstwo sp. z o.o.*, ECLI:EU:C:2017:804

Case C-317/15 *X v Staatssecretaris van Financiën*, ECLI:EU:C:2017:119

Case C-110/17 *Commission v Belgium (tax on income from immovable property)*, ECLI:EU:C:2018:250

Case C-171/17 *Commission v Hungary*, ECLI:EU:C:2018:881

Case C-45/17 *Frédéric Jahin v Ministre de l'Économie et des Finances and Ministre des Affaires sociales et de la Santé*, ECLI:EU:C:2018:18

Case C-68/17 *IR v JQ*, ECLI:EU:C:2018:696

Case C-190/17 *Lu Zheng v Ministerio de Economía y Competitividad*, ECLI:EU:C:2018:357

Joined cases C-52/16 and C-113/16 *'SEGRO' Kft. v Vas Megyei Kormányhivatal Sárvári Járási Földhivatala and Günther Horváth v Vas Megyei Kormányhivatal*, ECLI:EU:C:2018:157

Case C-3/17 *Sporting Odds Limited v Nemzeti Adó- és Vámhivatal Központi Irányítása*, ECLI:EU:C:2018:130 (Court of Justice)

Case C-569/16 *Stadt Wuppertal v Maria Elisabeth Bauer and Volker Willmeroth v Martina Broßonn*, ECLI:EU:C:2018:871

Case C-414/16 *Vera Egenberger v Evangelisches Werk für Diakonie und Entwicklung e.V.*, ECLI:EU:C:2018:257

Opinions of Advocates General

Opinion of Advocate General Van Gerven in Case C-145/88 Torfaen, ECLI:EU:C:1989:279

Opinion of Mr Advocate General Darmon in Case C-69/88 H. Krantz GmbH & Co. v Ontvanger der Directe Belastingen and Netherlands State, ECLI:EU:C:1989:627

Opinion of Advocate General Tesauro in Case C-292/92 Ruth Hünermund, ECLI:EU:C:1993:863

Opinion of Advocate General Jacobs in Case C-412/93 Leclerc-Siplec, ECLI:EU:C:1994:393

Opinion of Advocate General Alber in Case C-251/98 Baars, ECLI:EU:C:1999:502

Opinion of Advocate General Colomer in Cases C-367/98, C-483/99 and C-503/99 Commission v Belgium, Commission v France and Commission v Portugal, ECLI:EU:C:2001:369

Opinion of Advocate General Stix- Hackl in Case C-322/01 DocMorris NV, ECLI:EU:C:2003:147

Opinion of Advocate General Maduro in Case C-446/03 Marks & Spencer, ECLI:EU:C:2005:201

Opinion of Advocate General Jacobs in Case C-147/03 Commission v Austria (conditions of access to university education), ECLI:EU:C:2005:40

Opinion of Advocate General Maduro in Joined cases C-463/04 and C-464/04 Federconsumatori and Others, ECLI:EU:C:2006:524

Opinion of Advocate General Maduro in Joined Cases C-94/04 and C-202/04 Federico Cipolla v Rosaria Fazari, ECLI:EU:C:2006:76

Opinion of Advocate General Maduro in Joined Cases C-158/04 and C-159/04 Alfa Vita Vassilopoulos AE, ECLI:EU:C:2006:212

Opinion of Advocate General Maduro in Joined cases C-282/04 and C-283/04 Commission v The Netherlands (golden shares), ECLI:EU:C:2006:234

Opinion of Advocate General Bot in Case C-101/05 Skatteverket v A, ECLI:EU:C:2007:493

Opinion of Advocate General Mengozzi in Case C-341/05 Laval un Partneri Ltd v Svenska Byggnadsarbetareförbundet and Others, ECLI:EU:C:2007:291

Opinion of Advocate General Poiares Maduro in Case C-438/05 The International Transport Workers' Federation and The Finnish Seamen's Union v Viking Line ABP and OÜ Viking Line Eesti, ECLI:EU:C:2007:292

Opinion of Advocate General Kokott in Case C-311/08 Société de Gestion Industrielle, ECLI:EU:C:2009:545

Opinion of Advocate General Mengozzi in Case C-171/08 Commission v. Portugal (I) (golden shares), ECLI:EU:C:2010:412

Opinion of Advocate General Trstenjak in Case C-282/10 Maribel Dominguez v Centre informatique du Centre Ouest Atlantique and Préfet de la région Centre ECLI:EU:C:2011:559

Opinion of Advocate General Jääskinen in Joined cases C-105/12 to C-107/12 Staat der Nederlanden v Essent NV, ECLI:EU:C:2013:242

Opinion of Advocate General Wahl in Case C-201/15 AGET Iraklis, ECLI:EU:C:2016:429

Opinion of Advocate General Bot in Joined Cases C569/16 and C570/16 Stadt Wuppertal v Maria Elisabeth Bauer and Volker Willmeroth ECLI:EU:C:2018:337

Opinion of Advocate General Campos Sánchez-Bordona in Case C-563/17 Associação Peço a Palavra, ECLI:EU:C:2018:937

General Court

Case T-315/01 *Yassin Abdullah Kadi v Council and Commission*, ECLI:EU:T:2005:332

Case T-306/01 *Yusuf and Al Barakaat International Foundation v Council and Commission*, ECLI:EU:T:2005:331

Case T-228/02 *Organisation des Modjahedines du peuple d'Iran v Council*, ECLI:EU:T:2006:384

Case T-85/09 *Yassin Abdullah Kadi v Commission*, ECLI:EU:T:2010:418

Case T-565/08 *Corsica Ferries France v Commission*, ECLI:EU:T:2012:415

Case T-57/11 *Castelnou Energía v Commission*, ECLI:EU:T:2014:1021

EFTA Court

Case E-1/00 *State Debt Management Agency*, (EFTA Court)

International Courts

Case Concerning the Payment of Various Serbian Loans Issued in France, Ser A, No 20, 1929 (Permanent Court of International Justice)

Judgment of 23 May 2002, *Segi and Others and Gestoras pro Amnistía v The 15 Member States of the European Union*, Nos 6422/02 and 9916/02 (ECtHR)

Judgment of 30 June 2005, *Bosphorus v Ireland*, No 45036/98 (ECtHR)

National Courts

Shelley v. Kraemer, 334 US 1 (1948) (United States Supreme Court)

Lüth, BVerfGE 7, 198 (1958) (Bundesverfassungsgericht)

Décision n° 86-207 DC du 26 juin 1986 *Loi autorisant le Gouvernement à prendre diverses mesures d'ordre économique et social*, ECLI:FR:CC:1986:86207DC (Conseil Constitutionnel)

Décision n° 2002-460 DC du 22 août 2002 *Loi d'orientation et de programmation pour la sécurité intérieure*, ECLI:FR:CC:2002:2002460DC (Conseil Constitutionnel)

Décision n° 2003-480 DC du 31 juillet 2003 *Loi relative à l'archéologie préventive*, ECLI:FR:CC:2003:2003480DC (Conseil Constitutionnel)

De Staat der Nederlanden/Eneco Horlding N.V., ECLI:NL:HR:2015:1728 (Hoge Raad)

Opinion 2/13 Accession of the European Union to the European Convention for the Protection of Human Rights and Fundamental Freedoms, ECLI:EU:C:2014:2454

Opinion 2/15 on the Free Trade Agreement between the European Union and the Republic of Singapore, 16 May 2017

Books

Abdelal, R. *Capital Rules: The Construction of Global Finance* (Harvard University Press 2009).

Allais, M. *La crise mondiale d'aujourd'hui: Pour de profondes réformes des institutions financières et monétaires* (Clément Juglar 1999).

Andenas, M., .Gormley, L., Hadjiemmanuil, C. and Harden, I. *European Economic and Monetary Union: The Institutional Framework* (Kluwer Law International 1997).

Arteta, C., Eichengreen, B. and Wyplosz, C. *On the Growth Effects of Capital Account Liberalization* (University of California 2001).

Badie, B., Berg-Schlosser, D. and Morlino, L. *International Encyclopedia of Political Science* (SAGE Publications 2011).

Balassa, B. *The Theory of Economic Integration* (Irwin Homewood 2011).

Baldwin, R., Cohen, D., Sapir, A. and Venables, A. *Market Integration, Regionalism and the Global Economy* (Cambridge University Press 1999).

Baldwin, R. and Wyplosz, C. *The Economics of European Integration* (MacGraw-Hill Education 2006).

Baldwin, R. and Wyplosz, C. *The Economics of European Integration* (McGraw-Hill 2012).

Bank, W. *Global Economic Prospects and the Developing Countries* (The World Bank 1998/1999).

Barnard, C. *The Substantive Law of the EU: The Four Freedoms* (Oxford University Press 2016).

Barry, FG. *The internationalisation of production in Europe: case studies of foreign direct investment in old and new EU member states* (European Investment Bank 2004).

Benyon, FS. *Direct Investment, National Champions and EU Treaty Freedoms From Maastricht to Lisbon* (Hart Publishing 2010).

Bork, R. *Antitrust Paradox* (Simon & Schuster 1993).

Bouin, O. *The Privatisation in Developing Countries: Reflections on a Panacea* (OECD 1992).

Braconnier, S. *Droit des services publics* (Paris: PUF 2007).

Bungenberg, M., and Griebel, Jr. *International investment law and EU law* (Springer 2011).

Cadeau, E., Linotte, D. and Romi, R. *Droit du service public* (LexisNexis 2014).

Carayon, B. *Patriotisme économique, de la guerre à la paix économique* (Editions du Rocher 2006).

Cerny, P. *Rethinking World Politics: A Theory of Transnational Neopluralism* (Oxford University Press 2010).

Chang, H-J. *Economics:The User's Guide* (Penguin 2014).

Chari, R. *Life After Privatization* (Oxford University Press 2015).

Chevallier, J. *Le service public* (Paris: PUF [1987] 2008).

Chwieroth, J. *Capital Ideas: The IMF and the Rise of Financial Liberalisation* (Princeton University Press 2010).

Clapham, A. *Human Rights in the Private Sphere* (Clarendon Press, Oxford 1996).

Colson, J-P. and Idoux, P. *Droit Public Économique* (L.G.D.J. 2008).

Craig, P. *EU Administrative Law* (Oxford University Press 2012).

Craig, P. and De Búrca, G. *EU Law: Text, Cases and Materials* (Oxford University Press 2011).

Dahlberg, M. *Direct Taxation in Relation to the Freedom of Establishment and the Free Movement of Capital* (Kluwer Law International 2005).

Dashwood, A., Dougan, M., Rodger, B., Spaventa, E. and Wyatt, D. *Wyatt and Dashwood's European Union Law* (Hart Publishing 2011).

De Luca, N. *European Company Law: Text, Cases and Materials* (Cambridge University Press 2017).

Dean, H. *Social Policy* (Polity Press 2012).

Dimopoulos, A. *EU Foreign Investment Law* (Oxford University Press 2011).

Dore, R. *British Factory, Japanese Factory: The Origins of National Diversity in Industrial Relations* (University of California Press 1973).

Douma, S. *Optimization of Tax Sovereignty and Free Movement* (IBFD 2011).

Duguit, L. *L'État, le droit objectif et la loi positive* (Paris: Dalloz [1901] 2003).

Duguit, L. *Les transformations du droit public* (Hachette Livre BNF [1913] 2014).

Duguit, Lo. *Souveraineté et liberté, Leçons faites à l'Université Columbia (New-York) en 1920–1921* (Librairie F. Alcan 1921).

Duguit, Lo. *Traité de droit constitutionnel* (Paris: De Boccard [1911] 1930).

Dunne, N. *Competition Law and Economic Regulation – Making and Managing Markets* (Cambridge University Press 2015).

Dyson, K. *European States and the Euro: Europeanization, Variation, and Convergence* (Oxford University Press 2002).

Dyson, K. and Featherstone, K. *The Road To Maastricht: Negotiating Economic and Monetary Union* (Oxford University Press 1999).

Eichengreen, B. *Toward a New International Financial Architecture: A Practical Post-Asia Agenda* (Peterson Institute for International Economics 1999).

Farmer, P. and Lyal, R. *EC Tax Law* (Oxford University Press 1995).

Ferrera, M., Hemmerijck, A. and Rhodes, M. *The Future of Social Europe: Recasting Work and Welfare in the New Economy – Report prepared for the Portuguese Presidency of the EU* (Celta Editoria 2000).

Foucault, M. *The Birth of Biopolitics: Lectures at the Collège de France 1978–1979* (Basingstoke: Palgrave-Macmillan 2008).

Ganghof, S. *The Politics of Income Taxation* (ECPR Press 2006).

Gormley, L. *EU Taxation Law* (2005).

Grant, J. *European Takeovers: The Art of Acquisition* (Euromoney Institutional Investor 2018).

Grundmann, S. *European Company Law – Organization, Finance and Capital Markets* (Intersentia 2012).

Hall, P. and Soskice, D. *Varieties of Capitalism: The Institutional Foundations of Comparative Advantage* (Oxford University Press 2001).

Hallerberg, M., Strauch, RR. and Hagen, Jv. *Fiscal Governance in Europe* (Cambridge University Press 2009).

Harrod, RF. *The Life of John Maynard Keynes* (New York: Harcourt, Brace and Company 1951, repr. 1963, 1969).

Hart, J. *Rival Capitalists: International Competitiveness in the United States, Japan, and Western Europe* (Cornell University Press 1994).

Hartkamp, A., Sieburgh, C. and Devroe, W. *Cases, Materials and Text on European Law and Private Law* (Hart Publishing 2017).

Hayek, FAv. *Der Wettbewerb als Entdeckungsverfahren* (Kiel 1968).

Hien, J. and Joerges, C. *Ordoliberalism, Law and the Rule of Economics* (Hart Publishing 2017).

Hinarejos, A. *The Euro Area Crisis in Constitutional Perspective* (Oxford University Press 2015).

Hindelang, S. *The Free Movement of Capital and Foreign Direct Investment: The Scope of Protection in EU Law* (Oxford University Press 2009).

Hodson, D. *Governing the Euro Area in Good Times and Bad* (Oxford University Press 2011).

Houet, J. *Les Golden Shares en droit de l'Union Européenne* (Larcier 2015).

Issing, O. *The Birth of the Euro* (Cambridge University Press 2001).

Jeanne, O., Subramanian, A and Williamson, J. *Who Needs to Open the Capital Account?* (Peterson Institute for International Economics 2012).

Keegan, W. *Mrs. Thatcher's Economic Experiment* (Penguin 1984).

Kenen, P. *Economic and Monetary Union in Europe: Moving beyond Maastricht* (Cambridge University Press 1995).

Keohane, R. *After Hegemony: Cooperation and Discord in the World Political Economy* (Princeton University Press 1984).

Keynes, JM. *The General Theory of Employment, Interest and Money* (Palgrave Macmillan 1936).

Keynes, JM. *The Collected Writings of John Maynard Keynes, XXV: Activities 1940–1944 Shaping the Post-War World – The Clearing Union* (CUP 1980).

Kraakman, R. and others, *The Anatomy of Corporate Law – A Comparative and Functional Approach* (Oxford University Press 2009).

Kraay, A. *In Search of the Macroeconomic Effect of Capital Account Liberalization* (World Bank 1998).

Kurzer, P. *Markets and Moral Regulation: Cultural Changes in the European Union* (Cambridge University Press 2001).

Law, J. *A Dictionary of Finance and Banking* (Oxford University Press 2014).

Leeson, R. *Ideology and the International Economy: The Decline and Fall of Bretton Woods* (Palgrave Macmillan UK 2003).

Lincoln, JR. and Kalleberg, AL. *Culture, Control, and Commitment: A Study of Work Organization in the United States and Japan* (Cambridge University Press 1990).

Linotte, D. and Romi, R. *Services publics et droit public économique* (LexisNexis 2001).

Linotte, D. and Romi, R. *Droit public économique* (LexisNexis 2012).

Littler, A. *Member States versus the European Union – The Regulation of Gambling* (Brill Academic Publishers 2011).

Loeffler, E., Sobczak, D. and Hine-Hughes, F. *Liberalisation and privatisation in the EU – Services of general interest and the roles of the public sector* (Multi-Science Publishing, European Union 2012).

Lowenfeld, A. *Bretton Woods Conference (1944)* (Oxford University Press 2013).

Lowenfeld, AF. *International Economic Law* (Oxford University Press 2008).

Mallin, C. *Corporate Governance* (Oxford University Press 2004).

Masouros, P. *Corporate Law and Economic Stagnation: How Shareholder Value and Short-Termism Contribute to the Decline of the Western Economies* (Eleven International Publishing 2013).

Masson, P. and Taylor, M. *Policy Issues in the Operation of Currency Unions* (Cambridge University Press 1993).

Mazower, M. *Dark Continent, Europe's twentieth century* (USA: Vintage 2000).

Mazzucato, M. *The Entrepreneurial State: debunking public vs. private sector myths* (Anthem 2013).

McNamara, K. *The Currency of Ideas: Monetary Politics in the European Union* (Cornell University Press 1998).

Molle, W. *The Economics of European Integration: Theory, Practice, Policy* (Ashgate 2006).

Nic Shuibhne, N. *Coherence of EU Free Movement Law: Constitutional Responsibility and the Court of Justice* (Oxford University Press 2013).

Ocampo, JA. and Stiglitz, JE. *Capital Market Liberalization and Development* (Oxford University Press 2008).

OECD, *The Size and Sectoral Distribution of SOEs in OECD and Partner Countries* (OECD Publishing 2014).

OECD, *G20/OECD Principles of Corporate Governance* (OECD Publishing 2015).

Olaerts, M and Schwarz, CA. *Shareholder democracy: an analysis of shareholder involvement in corporate policies* (Eleven international publishing 2012).

Padoa-Schioppa, T. *The Road to Monetary Union in Europe: The Emperor, the Kings, and the Genies* (Oxford University Press 2000).

Papadopoulos, T. *EU Law and Harmonization of Takeovers in the Internal Market* (Kluwer Law International 2010).

Parkinson, JE. *Corporate Power and Responsibility: Issues in the Theory of Company Law* (Oxford University Press 1995).

Piketty, T. *Capital in the Twenty-First Century* (The Belknap Press of Harvard University Press 2014).

Polanyi, K. *The Great Transformation* (Beacon Press 1944, 1957, 2001).

Porter, ME. *The Competitive Advantage of Nations* (Free Press, New York 1990).

Posner, R. *Antitrust Law* (The University of Chicago Press 2001).

Prosser, T. *The limits of competition law: markets and public services* (Oxford University Press 2005).

Rolland, L. *Précis de droit administratif* (Dalloz 1933).

Sauter, W. and Schepel, H. *State and Market in European Union Law – The Public and Private Spheres of the Internal Market before the EU Courts* (Cambridge University Press 2009).

Schweiger, C. *The EU and the Global Financial Crisis, New Varieties of Capitalism* (Edward Elgar Publishing 2014).

Smith, A. *The Wealth of Nations* (W. Strahan and T. Cadell, London 1776).

Stiglitz, J. *The Economic Role of the State* (Blackwell 1989).

Stiglitz, J. *The Euro: How a Common Currency Threatens the Future of Europe* (W. W. Norton Company 2016).

Stiglitz, J. *Globalization and its Discontents* (W.W. Norton & Company 2002).

Stiglitz, J. *The Roaring Nineties: A New History of the World's Most Prosperous Decade* (W.W. Norton & Company 2003).

Stiglitz, J., Ocampo, JA., Spiegel, S., Ffrench-Davis, R. and Nayyar, D. *Stability with Growth: Macroeconomics, Liberalization and Development* (Oxford University Press 2006).

Sustein, CR. *The Partial Constitution* (Harvard University Press 1998).

Szyszczak, E. *The Regulation of the State in Competitive Markets in the EU* (Hart Publishing 2007).

Tridimas, T. *The General Principles of EU law* (Oxford University Press 2006).

Tudor, I. *The Fair and Equitable Treatment Standard in the International Law of Foreign Investment* (Oxford University Press 2008).

Valette, J-P, *Le service public à la française* (Paris: Ellipses 2000).

Van den Bogaert, S. *Practical Regulation of the Mobility of Sportsmen in the EU Post Bosman* (Kluwer Law International 2005).

Van Vooren, B. and Wessel, RA. *EU External Relations Law: Text, Cases and Materials* (Cambridge University Press 2014).

Vigneron, P., Steinfeld, P., Defalque, L. and Pertek, J. *Libre circulation des personnes et des capitaux. Rapprochement des legislations* (Les éditions de l' Université de Bruxelles 2006).

Vogel, L. *Traité de droit économique, Tome 4: Droit européen des affaires* (Bruylant 2015).

Whish, R. and Bailey, D. *Competition Law* (Oxford University Press 2012).

Edited Books

Barnard, C. and Peers, S. (eds), *European Union Law* (Oxford University Press 2017).

Bücker, A. and Warneck, W. (eds), *Reconciling Fundamental Social Rights and Economic Freedoms After Viking, Laval and Rüffert* (Nomos 2011).

Busch, D and Ferrarini, G. (eds), *European Banking Union* (Oxford University Press 2015).

Calhoun, C. (ed), *Dictionary of the Social Sciences* (Oxford University Press 2002).

Eichengreen, BJ. and Flandreau, M. (eds), *The Gold Standard in Theory and History* (Routledge 1997).

Fox, D. and Ernst, W. (eds), *Money in the Western Legal Tradition: Middle Ages to Bretton Woods* (Oxford University Press 2016).

Freedland, M. and Prassl, J. (eds), *Viking, Laval and Beyond* (Hart Publishing 2014).

Horsefield, JK. (ed), *The International Monetary Fund, 1945–1965: Twenty Years of International Monetary Cooperation, Volume III: Documents* (IMF 1969).

Krieger, J. (ed), *The Oxford Companion to Politics of the World* (Oxford University Press 2001).

Lang, M. and Pistone, P. (eds), *The EU and Third Countries: Direct Taxation* (Kluwer Law International 2008).

Moran, M. and Prosser, T. (eds), *Privatization and Regulatory Change in Europe* (Open University Press 1994).

Roland, G. (ed), *Privatization: Successes and Failures* (Columbia University Press 2008).

Sajó, As. and Uitz, Rt. (eds), *The Constitution in Private Relations: Expanding Constitutionalism* (Eleven International Publishing 2005).

Vickers, J. and Wright, V. (eds), *The Politics of Privatisation in Western Europe* (Routledge 2005).

Book Chapters

Alesina, A., Grilli, V. and Milesi-Ferretti, GM. 'The Political Economy of Capital Controls' in Leiderman L and Razin A (eds), *Capital Mobility: The Impact on Consumption, Investment, and Growth* (Cambridge University Press 1994).

Baldwin, R. and Venables, A. 'Regional economic integration' in Grossman G and Rogoff K (eds), *Handbook of International Economics* (Elsevier 1995).

Barnard, C. 'Derogations, Justifications and the Four Freedoms: Is State Interest Really Protected?' in Barnard C and Odudu O (eds), *The Outer Limits of European Union Law* (Hart Publishing 2009).

Barnard, C. 'The Worker Protection Justification: Lessons from Consumer Law' in Koutrakos P, Nic Shuibhne N and Syrpis P (eds), *Exceptions from EU Free Movement Law: Derogation, Justification and Proportionality* (Hart Publishing 2016).

Bartman, S. 'The EC Directive on Takeover Bids: Opting in as a Token of Good Corporate Governance' in Bartman S (ed) *European Company Law In Accelerated Progress* (Kluwer Law International 2006).

Biondi, A. 'When the State is the Owner – Some Further Comments on the Court of Justice 'Golden Shares' Strategy' in Bernitz U and Ringe W-G (eds), *Company Law and Economic Protectionism: New Challenges to European Integration* (Oxford University Press 2010).

Blin, O. 'Capitaux' in Simon D and Poillot Peruzzetto S (eds), *Répertoire de Droit Européen* (Dalloz 2016).

Böhm, F. Eucken, W. and Großmann-Dörth, H. 'Palgrave Macmillan UK' in Peacock A and Willgerodt H (eds), *Germany's Social Market Economy: Origins and Evolution* (1989).

Bortolotti, B. and Milella, V. 'Privatization in Western Europe: Stylized Facts, Outcomes, and Open Issues' in Roland G (ed) *Privatization: Successes and Failures* (Columbia University Press 2008).

Boulogne-Yang-Ting, C. 'Patriotisme économique et mécanismes du droit des sociétés et boursier' in Virassamy G (ed) *Entreprise et patriotisme économique* (L'Harmattan 2008).

Brewster, C., Goergen, M. and Wood, G. 'Corporate Governance Systems and Industrial Relations' in Wilkinson A and Townsend K (eds), *The Future of Employment Relations: New Paradigms, New Developments* (Palgrave Macmillan 2011).

Charlton, A. 'Capital Market Liberalization and Poverty' in Ocampo JA and Stiglitz J (eds), *Capital Market Liberalization and Development* (Oxford University Press 2008).

Cremona, M. 'The External Dimension of the Internal Market' in (eds), (Oxford:)' in Barnard C and Scott J (eds), *The Law of the Single European Market* (Hart Publishing 2002).

De Witte, F. 'The architecture of the EU's social market economy' in Koutrakos P and Snell J (eds), *Research Handbook on the Law of the EU's Internal Market* (Edward Elgal Publishing 2017).

Dyson, K. 'Economic and Monetary Union' in Jones E, Menon A and Weatherill S (eds), *The Oxford Handbook of the European Union* (Oxford Univrsity Press 2012).

Easterly, W., Islam, R. and Stiglitz, J. 'Volatility and Macroeconomic Paradigms for Rich and Poor' in Drèze J (ed) *Advances in Macroeconomic Theory* (Palgrave Macmillan UK 2001).

Enchelmaier, S. 'Horizontality: the application of the four freedoms to restrictions imposed by private parties' in Koutrakos P and Snell J (eds), *Research Handbook on the Law of the EU's Internal Market* (Edward Elgal Publishing 2017).

Flynn, L. 'Freedom to Fund?: The Effects of the Internal Market Rules, With Particular Emphasis on Free Movement of Capital' in Neergaard U, Szyszczak E, van de Gronden JW and Krajewski M (eds), *Social services of general interest in the EU* (Spinger 2013).

Flynn, L. 'Free movement of capital' in Barnard C and Peers S (eds), *European Union Law* (Oxford University Press 2017).

Forbes, KJ. 'The Microeconomic Evidence on Capital Controls: No Free Lunch' in Edwards S (ed) *Capital Controls and Capital Flows in Emerging Economies: Policies, Practices, and Consequences* (University of Chicago Press 2007).

Gardbaum, S. 'The Place Of Constitutional Law in the Legal System' in Rosenfeld M and Sajó As (eds), *The Oxford Handbook of Comparative Constitutional Law* (Oxford University Press 2012).

Gilson, RJ. 'From Corporate Law to Corporate Governance' in Gordon JN and Ringe W-G (eds), *The Oxford Handbook of Corporate Law and Governance* (Oxford University Press 2018).

Hall, P. and Gingerich, D. 'Varieties of Capitalism and Institutional Complementarities in the Political Economy: An Empirical Analysis' in Hancké B (ed) *Debating Varieties of Capitalism: A Reader* (Oxford University Press 2009).

Hansen, JL. 'Full Circle: Is there a Difference Between the Freedom of Establishment and the Freedom to Provide Services?' in Andenas M and Roth W-H (eds), *Services and Free Movement in EU Law* (Oxford University Press 2002).

Horsley, T. 'The Concept of an Obstacle to intra-EU Capital Movements in EU Law' in Nic Shuibhne N and Gormley LW (eds), *From Single Market to Economic Union: Essays in Memory of John A Usher* (Oxford Univesrity Press 2012).

Horsley, T. 'Death, Taxes, and (Targeted) Judicial Dynamism – The Free Movement of Capital in EU Law' in Arnull A and Chalmers D (eds), *The Oxford Handbook of European Union Law* (Oxford University Press 2015).

Ikenberry, J. 'The Political Origins of Brettion Woods' in D. Bordo M and Eichengreen B (eds), *A Retrospective on the Bretton Woods System: Lessons for International Monetary Reform* (University of Chicago Press 1993).

Joerges, C. 'The European Economic Constitution and its Transformation Through the Financial Crisis' in Patterson D and Södersten A (eds), *A Companion to European Union law and International Law* (Wiley & Sons 2013).

Keynes, JM. 'Proposals for an International Clearing Union' in Horsefield JK (ed) *The International Monetary Fund, 1945–1965: Twenty Years of International Monetary Cooperation, Volume III: Documents* (IMF 1969).

Kosta, V. 'The principle of proportionality in EU law: an interest-based taxonomy' in Mendes J (ed) *EU Executive Discretion and the Limits of Law* (Oxford University Press forthcoming 2019).

Kovar, R. 'Nationalisations – privatisations et droit communautaire' in Schwarze J (ed) *Discretionary Powers of the Member States in the Field of Economic Policies and their Limits under the EEC Treaty: Contributions to an International Colloquium of the European University Institute held in Florence on 14–15 May 1987* (Nomos 1988).

Kwame Sundaram, J. 'A Critical Review of the Evolving Privatization Debate' in Roland G (ed) *Privatization: Successes and Failures* (Columbia University Press 2008).

Lane, C. 'Institutional Transformation and System Change: Changes in Corporate Governance of German Corporations' in Morgan G, Whitley R and Moen E (eds), *Changing Capitalisms? Internationalization, Institutional Change and Systems of Economic Organisation* (Oxford University Press 2006).

Levine, R. 'Finance and Growth: Theory and Evidence' in Aghion P and Durlauf SN (eds), *Handbook of Economic Growth* (Elsevier 2005).

Louis, J-V. 'The New Monetary Law of the European Union and its Scope of Application' in Giovanoli M (ed) *International Monetary Law: Issues for the New Millennium* (Oxford University Press 2000).

Maduro, MP. 'The Chameleon State – EU Law and the blurring of the private/public distinction in the market' in Nickel R (ed) *Conflict of Laws and Laws of Conflict in Europe and Beyond – Patterns of Supranational and Transnational Juridification* (Intersentia 2010).

Maitrot de la Motte, A. 'Les spécificités de la libre circulation des capitaux: l'exemple de la contestation des entraves fiscales' in Dubout Ed and Maitrot de la Motte A (eds), *L'unité des libertés de circulation – In varietate concordia* (Bruylant 2013).

Mülbert, PO. 'Make It or Break It: The Break-Through Rule as a Break-Through for the European Takeover Directive?' in Ferrarini G, Hopt KJ, Winter J and Wymeersch E (eds), *Reforming Company and Takeover Law in Europe* (Oxford University Press 2004).

Müller-Armack, A. 'The Meaning of the Social Market Economy' in Peacock AT and Willgerodt H (eds), *Germany's Social Market Economy: Origins and Evolution* (Macmillan 1989).

Nestor, S. and Mahboodi, L. 'Privatisation of public utilities: the OECD experience' in OECD (ed) *Privatisation, competition and regulation* (OECD 2000).

Keefle, D O and Bavasso, A. 'Four freedoms, one market and national competence: In search of a dividing line' in O Keeffe D (ed) *Judicial Review in European Union Law: Essays in Honour of Lord Slynn* (Springer Netherlands 2000).

Ocampo, JA. 'Capital-Account and Counter-Cyclical Prudential Regulations in Developing Countries' in Ffrench-Davis R and Griffith-Jones S (eds), *From Capital Surges to Drought: Seeking Stability for Emerging Economies* (Palgrave/MacMillan 2003).

Ocampo, JA. 'A Broad view of Macroeconomic Stability' in Serra N and Stiglitz JE (eds), *The Washington Consensus Reconsidered* (Oxford University Press 2008).

Partsch, P. 'Articles 56-60 CE' in Pingel I (ed) *Rome à Lisbonne: Commentaire article par article des traités UE et CE* (Dalloz 2010).

Peers, S. 'Free Movement of Capital: Learning lessons or slipping on spilt milk?' in Barnard C and Scott J (eds), *The Law of the Single European Market: Unpacking the Premises* (Hart Publishing 2002).

Prechal, S. 'Direct Effect Reconsidered, Redefined and Rejected' in Prinssen JM and Schrauwen A (eds), *Direct Effect-Rethinking: A Classic of EC Legal Doctrine* (Europa Law Publishing 2002).

Preuß, U. 'The German Drittwirkung Doctrine and Its Socio-Political Background' in Sajó A and Uitz R (eds), *The Constitution in Private Relations: Expanding Constitutionalism* (Eleven International Publishing 2005).

Prosser, T. and Moran, M. 'Privatization and Regulatory Change: The Case of Great Britain' in Moran M and Prosser T (eds), *Privatization and Regulatory Change in Europe* (Open University Press 1994).

Rhodes, M. 'Defending the Social Contract: The EU Between Global Constraints and Domestic Imperatives' in Hine D and Kassim H (eds), *Beyond the Market: The EU and National Social Policy* (Routledge 1998).

Rickford, J. 'Free movement of capital and protectionism after Volkswagen and Viking Line' in Tison M and Wymeersch E (eds), *Perspectives in Company Law and Financial Regulation – Essays in Honour of Eddy Wymeersch* (Cambridge University Press 2009).

Rickford, J. 'Protectionism, Capital Freedom and the Internal Market' in Bernitz U and Ringe W-G (eds), *Company Law and Economic Protectionism – New Challenges to European Integration* (Oxford University Press 2010).

Ringe, W-G. 'Is Volkswagen the New Centros? Free movement of Capital's Impact on Company Law' in Prentice D and Reisberg A (eds), *Corporate Finance Law in the UK and EU* (Oxford University Press 2011).

Rodríguez, F. and Rodrik, D. 'Trade Policy and Economic Growth: A Skeptic's Guide to the Cross-National Evidence' in Bernanke B and Rogoff K (eds), *NBER Macroeconomics Annual 2000* (MIT Press 2001).

Rodrik, D. 'Who Needs Capital-Account Convertibility?' in Fischer S, Cooper RN, Dornbusch R, Garber PM, Massad C, Polak JJ, Rodrik D and Tarapore SS (eds), *Should the IMF Pursue Capital-Account Convertibility? (Essays in International Finance No*

207, May 1998) (International Finance Section, Department of Economics, Princeton University 1998).

Schepel, H. 'Of Capitalist Nostalgia and Financialisation: Shareholder Primacy in the Court of Justice' in Joerges C and Glinski C (eds), *The European Crisis and the Transformation of Transnational Governance* (Hart Publishing 2014).

Schmukler, S. 'The Benefits and Risks of Financial Globalization' in Ocampo JA and Stiglitz J (eds), *Capital Market Liberalization and Development* (Oxford University Press 2008).

Shelton, D. and Gould, A. 'Positive and Negative Obligations' in Shelton D (ed) *The Oxford Handbook of International Human Rights Law* (Oxford University Press 2013).

Snell, J. 'And then there were two: Products and Citizens in Community Law' in Tridimas T and Nebbia P (eds), *European Union Law for the Twenty-First Century* (Hart Publishing 2005).

Snell, J. 'Free movement of capital: Evolution as a non-linear process' in Craig P and De Búrca G (eds), *The Evolution of EU Law* (Oxford University Press 2011).

Snell, J. 'Economic Justifications and the Role of the State' in Koutrakos P, Nic Shuibhne N and Syrpis P (eds), *Exceptions from EU Free Movement Law: Derogation, Justification and Proportionality* (Hart Publishing 2016).

Sommeregger, G. 'The Horizontalization of Equality: The German Attempt to Promote Non-Discrimination in the Private Sphere via Legislation' in Sajó A and Uitz R (eds), *The Constitution in Private Relations: Expanding Constitutionalism* (Eleven International Publishing 2005).

Stiglitz, J. 'Foreword' in Roland G (ed) *Privatization: Successes and Failures* (Columbia University Press 2008).

Tridimas, T. 'The principle of proportionality' in Schütze R and Tridimas T (eds), *Oxford principles of European Union law Volume I, The European Union legal order* (Oxford University Press 2018).

Van Apeldoorn, B. 'The Contradictions of 'Embedded Neoliberalism' and Europe's Multi-level Legitimacy Crisis: The European Project and its Limits' in Drahokoupil J, Van Apeldoorn B and Horn L (eds), *Contradictions and Limits of Neoliberal European Governance: From Lisbon to Lisbon* (Palgrave 2009).

Van den Bogaert, S. 'Horizontality: The Court Attacks?' in Barnard C and Scott J (eds), *The Law of the Single European Market – Unpacking the Premises* (Hart Publishing 2002).

Van den Bogaert, S. 'Bosman: The Genesis of European Sports Law' in Maduro MP and Azoulai L (eds), *The Past and Future of EU Law: The Classics of EU Law Revisited on the 50th Anniversary of the Rome Treaty* (Hart Publishing 2010).

Van den Bogaert, S., Cuyvers, A. and Antonaki, I. 'Free movement of services, establishment and capital' in Kuijper PJ, Amtenbrink F, Curtin D, De Witte B, McDonnell A and Van den Bogaert S (eds), *The Law of the European Union, Fifth Edition* (Wolters Kluwer 2018).

Van den Bogaert, S. and Van Cleynenbreugel, P. 'Free Movement of Goods' in Kuijper PJ, Amtenbrink F, Curtin D, De Witte B, McDonnell A and Van den Bogaert S (eds), *The Law of the European Union, Fifth Edition* (Wolters Kluwer 2018).

Weir, C. 'The Market for Corporate Control' in Wright DM, Siegel DS, Keasey K and Filatotchev I (eds), *The Oxford Handbook of Corporate Governance* (Oxford University Press 2013).

Journal Articles

Adolff, J. 'Turn of the Tide?: The "Golden Share" Judgments of the European Court of Justice and the Liberalization of the European Capital Markets' (2002) 3 *German Law Journal* 20.

Aizenman, J. and Glick, R. 'Sterilization, monetary policy, and global financial integration' (2008) 17 *Review of International Economics* 777.

Akkermans, B. and Ramaekers, E. 'Article 345 TFEU (ex Article 295 EC), Its Meanings and Interpretations' (2010) 16 *European Law Journal* 292.

Alexander, L. 'The Public/Private Distinction and Constitutional Limits on Private Power' (1993) 10 *Constitutional Commentary* 361.

Allen, M. 'The Varieties of Capitalism Paradigm: Not Enough Variety?' (2004) 2 *Socio-economic Review* 87.

Amin, S. and Luckin, D. 'The Challenge of Globalization' (1996) 3 *Review of International Political Economy* p. 216.

Amoako-Adu, B., Baulkaran, V. and Smith, BF. 'Executive compensation in firms with concentrated control: The impact of dual class structure and family management' (2011) 17 *Journal of Corporate Finance* 1580.

Andenas, M. Gütt, T. and Pannier, M. 'Free Movement of Capital and National Company Law' (2005) 16 *European Business Law Review* 757.

Antonaki, I. 'Keck in Capital? Redefining "Restrictions" in the "Golden Shares" Case Law' (2016) *Erasmus Law Review* 177.

Antonaki,, I. 'Collective redundancies in Greece: AGET Iraklis' (2017) 54 *Common Market Law Review* 1513.

Arnull, A. 'What shall we do on Sunday?' (1991) 16 *European Law Review* 112.

Arrowsmith, S. 'Rethinking the approach to economic justifications under the EU's free movement rules' (2015) 68 *Current Legal Problems* 307.

Artés, A. 'Advancing Harmonization: Should the ECJ Apply Golden Shares' Standards to National Company Law?' (2009) 20 *European Business Law Review* 457.

Ashiagbor, D. 'Unravelling the Embedded Liberal Bargain: Labour and Social Welfare Law in the Context of EU Market Integration' (2013) 19 *European Law Journal* 303.

Azoulai, L. 'The Court of Justice and the social market economy: The emergence of an ideal and the conditions for its realization' (2008) 45 *Common Market Law Review* 1335.

Babayev, R. 'Contractual Discretion and the Limits of Free Movement Law' (2015) 23 *European Review of Private Law* 875.

Babayev, R. 'Private Autonomy at Union Level: On Article 16 CFREU and Free Movement Rights' (2016) 53 *Common Market Law Review* 979.

Barnard, C. 'Fitting the remaining pieces into the goods and persons jigsaw?' (2001) 26 *European Law Review* 35.

Barnard, C. 'Viking and Laval: An Introduction' (2007–2008) 10 *Cambridge Yearbook of European Legal Studies* 463.

Barnard, C. 'Social dumping or dumping socialism?' (2008) 67 *The Cambridge Law Journal* 262.

Barnard, C. 'Restricting Restrictions: Lessons for the EU from the US?' (2009) 68 *Cambridge Law Journal* 575.

Barnard, C. 'What the Keck? Balancing the needs of the single market with state regulatory autonomy' (2012) 2 *European Journal of Consumer Law* 201.

Bartel, AP. and Harrison, AE. 'Ownership versus Environment: Disentangling the Sources of Public-Sector Inefficiency' (2005) 87 *The Review of Economics and Statistics* 135.

Bartman, S. 'Shareholder Democracy à la Dworkin' (2010) 7 *European Company Law* 5.

Bazex, M. 'L'appréhension des services publics par le droit communautaire' (1995) *Revue française de droit administratif* (RFDA) 295.

Belloubet-Frier, N. 'Service public et droit communautaire' (1994) *Actualité juridique du droit administratif* (AJDA) 270.

Bercusson, B. 'The Trade Union Movement and the European Union: Judgment Day' (2007) 13 *European Law Journal* 279.

Bernard, N. 'Discrimination and Free Movement in E.C. Law' (1996) 45 *International and Comparative Law Quarterly* 82.

Bernitz, U. 'The Attack on the Nordic Multiple Voting Rights Model: The Legal Limits under EU Law' (2004) 15 *European Business Law Review* 1423.

Bernitz, U. and Reich, N. 'Case No. A 268/04, The Labour Court, Sweden (Arbetsdomstolen) Judgment No. 89/09 of 2 December 2009, Laval un Partneri Ltd. v. Svenska Bygggnadsarbetareförbundet et al'. (2011) 48 *Common Market Law Review* 603.

Besson, S. 'European Legal Pluralism after Kadi' (2009) 5 *European Constitutional Law Review* 237.

Beukers, T. 'Case C-409/06, Winner Wetten GmbH v. Bürgermeisterin der Stadt Bergheim, Judgment of the Court (Grand Chamber) of 8 September 2010, not yet reported' (2011) 48 *Common Market Law Review* 1985.

Beyleveld, D. and Pattinson, SD. 'Horizontal applicability and horizontal effect' (2002) 118 *Law Quarterly Review* 623.

Bezborodov, S. 'Freedom of Establishment in the EC Economic Partnership Agreements: in Search of its Direct Effect on Direct Taxation' (2007) 35 *Intertax* 658.

Birch, K. and Mykhnenko, V. 'Varieties of neoliberalism? Restructuring in large industrially dependent regions across Western and Eastern Europe' (2009) 9 *Journal of Economic Geography* 355.

Boer, SD. 'Freedom of Establishment versus Free Movement of Capital: Ongoing Confusion at the ECJ and in the National Courts?' (2010) 50 *European Taxation* 250.

Bortolotti, B. Fantini, M. and Siniscalco, D. 'Privatization around the world: evidence from panel data' (2004) 88 *Journal of Public Economics Journal of Public Economics* 305.

Breakey, H. 'Positive Duties and Human Rights: Challenges, Opportunities and Conceptual Necessities' (2015) 63 *Political Studies* 1198.

Bulterman, M. 'Fundamental Rights and the United Nations Financial Sanction Regime: The Kadi and Yusuf Judgments of the Court of First Instance of the European Communities' (2006) 19 *Leiden Journal of International Law* 753.

Butler, AS. 'Constitutional Rights in Private Litigation: A Critique and Comparative Analysis' (1993) 22 *Anglo-American Law Review* 1.

Cabral, P. and Neves, R. 'General Principles of EU Law and Horizontal Direct Effect' (2011) 17 *European Public Law* 437.

Caporaso, JA and Tarrow, S. 'Polanyi in Brussels: Supranational Institutions and the Transnational Embedding of Markets' (2009) 63 *International Organization* 593.

Catá Backer, L. 'The Private Law of Public Law: Public Authorities as Shareholders, Golden Shares, Sovereign Wealth Funds, and the Public Law Element in Private Choice of Law' (2008) 82 *Tulane Law Review* 1.

Chanda, A. 'The Influence of Capital Controls on Long Run Growth: Where and How Much?' (2005) 77 *Journal of Development Economics* 441.

Chemerinsky, E. 'Rethinking State Action' (1985) 80 *Northwestern University Law Review* 503.

Cherevach, V. and Megens, B. 'Commission of the European Communities v Federal Republic of Germany Case C-112/05 – The VW Law Case; Some Critical Comments' (2009) 16 *Maastricht Journal of European and Comparative Law* 370.

Choudhury, B. 'Evolution or Devolution? – Defining Fair and Equitable Treatment in International Investment Law' (2005) 6 *Journal of World Investment and Trade* 297.

E Comments, 'The Rule of Law in the Union, the Rule of Union Law and the Rule of Law by the Union: Three interrelated problems' (2016) 53 *Common Market Law Review* 597.

Constantinesco, L-J. 'La constitution économique de la C.E.E' (1977) 13 *Revue Trimestrielle de Droit Européen* 244.

Cordewener, A. Kofler, G. and Van Thiel, S. 'The Clash Between European Freedoms and National Direct Tax Law: Public Interest Defences Available to the Member States' (2009) 46 *Common Market Law Review* 1951.

Cordewener, A. Kofler, GW. and Schindler, CP. 'Free Movement of Capital and Third Countries: Exploring the Outer Boundaries with Lasertec, A and B and Holböck' (2007) 47 *European Taxation* 371.

Cordewener, A. Kofler, GW. and Schindler, CP. 'Free Movement of Capital, Third Country Relationships and National Tax Law: An Emerging Issue before the ECJ' (2007) 47 *European Taxation* 107.

Cremona, M. 'EC Competence, 'Smart Sanctions', and the Kadi Case' (2009) 28 *Yearbook of European Law* 559.

Cuyvers, A. 'Joined Cases C-338/04, C-359/04 and C-360/04, Massimiliano Placanica, Christian Palazzese and Angelo Sorricchio (Placanica)' (2008) 45 *Common Market Law Review* 515.

Cuyvers, A. 'The Kadi II Judgment of the General Court: The ECJ's Predicament and the Consequences for Member States' (2011) 7 *European Constitutional Law Review* 481.

Cuyvers, A. ' "Give me one good reason": The unified standard of review for sanctions after Kadi II' (2014) 51 *Common Market Law Review* 1759.

Damjanovic, D. 'The EU market rules as social market rules: Why the EU can be a social market economy' (2013) 50 *Common Market Law Review* 1685.

Dashwood, A. 'Viking and Laval: Issues of Horizontal Direct Effect' (2007) 10 *Cambridge Yearbook of European Legal Studies* 525.

Dashwood, A. 'Viking and Laval: Issues of Horizontal Direct Effect' (2007–2008) 10 *Cambridge Yearbook of European Legal Studies* 525.

Davies, A. 'One Step Forward, Two Steps Back? The Viking and Laval Cases in the ECJ' (2008) 37 *Industrial Law Journal* 126.

Davies, G. 'Freedom of Movement, Horizontal Effect, and Freedom of Contract' (2010) 20 *European Review of Private Law* 805.

Davies, G. 'Understanding Market Access: Exploring the Economic Rationality of Different Conceptions of Free Movement Law' (2010) 11 *German Law Journal* 671.

Davies, G. 'The Court's jurisprudence on free movement of goods: pragmatic presumptions, not philosophical principles' (2012) 2 *European Journal of Consumer Law* 25.

De Luca, N. 'Unequal Treatment and Shareholders' Welfare Growth: Fairness v. Precise Equality' (2009) 34 *Delaware Journal of Corporate Law* 853.

De Witte, B. and Kilpatrick, C. 'A comparative framing of fundamental rights challenges to social crisis measures in the Eurozone' (2014) 1 *European Journal of Social Law* 2.

De Witte, F. 'Sex, Drugs & EU Law: The Recognition of Moral and Ethical Diversity in EU Law' (2013) 50 *Common Market Law Review* 1545.

De Witte, F. 'The constitutional quality of the free movement provisions: looking for context in the case law on Article 56 TFEU' (2017) 42 *European Law Review* 313.

Deakin, S. 'Regulatory Competition after Laval' (2007–2008) 10 *Cambridge Yearbook of European Legal Studies* 581.

Deeg, R. and Jackson, G. 'Comparing Capitalisms: The Implications of National Diversity for the Study of International Business' (2008) 39 *Journal of International Business Studies* 540.

Desrieux, C. 'La gestion contractuelle des services publics: Une critique de l'approche par les droits de propriété' (2007) 59 *Revue économique* 451.

Devroe, W. 'Privatizations and Community Law: Neutrality Versus Policy' (1997) 34 *Common Market Law Review* 267.

Dewenter, KL and Malatesta, PH. 'State-owned and privately-owned firms: an empirical analysis of profitability, leverage, and labor intensity' (2001) 91 *American Economic Review* 320.

Díaz-Alejandro, CF. 'Goodbye Financial Repression, Hello Financial Crash' (1985) 19 *Journal of Development Economics* 1.

Dierckx, S. 'After the Crisis and Beyond the New Constitutionalism? The Case of the Free Movement of Capital' (2013) 10 *Globalizations* 803.

Djankov, S. and Murrell, P. 'Enterprise Restructuring: A Qualitative Survey' (2002) 40 *Journal of Economic Literature* 739.

Dolzer, R. 'Fair and Equitable Treatment – A Key Standard in Investment Treaties' (2005) 39 *The International Lawyer* 87.

Dougan, M. 'When worlds collide! Competing visions of the relationship between direct effect and supremacy' (2007) 44 *Common Market Law Review* 931.

Doukas, D. 'Untying the market access knot: Advertising restrictions and the free movement of goods and services' (2007) 9 *Cambridge Yearbook of European Legal Studies* 177.

Duguit, Lo. 'Des fonctions de l'Etat moderne: étude de sociologie juridique ' (1894) *Revue internationale de sociologie* 161.

Dyzenhaus, D. 'The New Positivists' (1989) 39 *University of Toronto Law Journal* 361.

Edison, H., Levine, R., Ricci, L and T Sløk, T. 'International Financial Integration and Economic Growth' (2002) 21 *Journal of International Money and Finance* 749.

Edwards, V. 'The Directive on Takeover Bids – Not Worth the Paper It's Written On?' (2004) 1 *European Company and Financial Law Review* 416.

Enchelmaier, S. 'Always at your service (within limits): the ECJ's case law on article 56 TFEU (2006–11)' (2011) 36 *European Law Review* 615.

Faist, T. 'Social Citizenship in the European Union: Nested Membership' (2001) 39 *Journal of Common Market Studies* 37.

Falcao, T. 'Third-Country Relations with the European Community: A Growing Snowball' (2009) 37 *Intertax* 307.

Ferrarini, G. 'One Share – One Vote: A European Rule?' (2006) 3 *European Company and Financial Law Review* 147.

Ferrera, M. 'European Integration and National Social Citizenship: Changing Boundaries, New Structuring?' (2003) 36 *Comparative Political Studies* 611.

Ferri, D. and Marquis, M. 'Inroads to Social Inclusion in Europe's Social Market Economy: The Case of State Aid Supporting Employment of Workers with Disabilities' (2011) 4 *European Journal of Legal Studies* 38.

Fischer, S. 'Globalization and Its Challenges' (2003) 93 *American Economic Review* 1.

Fleming, M. 'Domestic Financial Policies under Fixed and Floating Exchange Rate' (1962) 9 *IMF Staff Papers* 369.

Flynn, L. 'Coming of Age: The Free Movement of Capital Case Law 1993–2002' (2002) 39 *Common Market Law Review* 773.

Fontanelli, F. 'General Principles of the EU and a Glimpse of Solidarity in the Aftermath of Mangold and Kücükdeveci' (2011) 17 *European Public Law* 225.

Forbes, KJ 'Capital controls: mud in the wheels of market efficiency' (2005) 25 *Cato Journal* 153.

Forbes, KJ. 'One Cost of the Chilean Capital Controls: Increased Financial Constraints for Smaller Traded Firms' (2007) 71 *Journal of International Economics* 294.

Frantziou, E. 'Case C-176/12 Association de Médiation Sociale: Some Reflections on the Horizontal Effect of the Charter and the Reach of Fundamental Employment Rights in the European Union' (2014) 10 *European Constitutional Law Review* 332.

Frantziou, E. 'The Horizontal Effect of the Charter of Fundamental Rights of the EU: Rediscovering the Reasons for Horizontality' (2015) 21 *European Law Journal* 657.

Gallagher, KP. and Ocampo, JA. 'IMF's New View on Capital Controls' (2013) XLVIII *Economy & Political Weekly* 10.

Ganghof, S. and Genschel, P. 'Taxation and Democracy in the EU' (2008) 15 *Journal of European Public Policy* 58.

Garben, S. 'The European Pillar of Social Rights: Effectively Addressing Displacement?' (2018) 14 *European Constitutional Law Review* 210.

Gardbaum, S. 'Where the (state) action is' (2006) 4 *International Journal of Constitutional Law* 760.

Gardbaum, S. 'The "Horizontal Effect" of Constitutional Rights' (2003) 102 *Michigan Law Journal* 387.

Gaydarska, N and Rammeloo, S. 'The legality of the "golden share" under EC law' (2009) 5 *Maastricht Working Papers Faculty of Law*.

Gearty, C. 'In Praise of Awkwardness: Kadi in the CJEU' (2014) 10 *European Constitutional Law Review* 15.

Gerner-Beuerle, C. 'Shareholders Between the Market and the State. The VW Law and other Interventions in the Market Economy' (2012) 49 *Common Market Law Review* 97.

Gerner-Beuerle, C., Kershaw, D. and Solinas, M. 'Is the Board Neutrality Rule Trivial? Amnesia about Corporate Law in European Takeover Regulation' (2011) 22 *European Business Law Review* 559.

Ghosh, A. Ostry, J and Qureshi, M. 'When Do Capital Inflow Surges End in Tears?' (2016) 106 *American Economic Review* 581.

Ghosh, M. and Whalley, J. 'State Owned Enterprises, Shirking and Trade Liberalization' (2008) 25 *Economic Modelling* 1206.

Gold, J.'Unauthorized Changes of Par Value and Fluctuating Exchange Rates in the Bretton Woods System' (1971) 65 *American Journal of International Law* 113.

Gold, J.'The Legal Structure of the Par Value System' (1973) 5 *Law and Policy of International Business* 155.

Gordon, B. 'Tax competition and harmonisation under EU law: economic realities and legal rules' (2014) 39 *European Law Review* pp. 790.

Gormley, LW. 'Case 145/88, Torfaen Borough Council v. B&Q PLC (formerly B&Q Retail Ltd.), Preliminary reference under Art. 177 EEC by the Cwmbran Magistrates' Court on the interpretation of Arts. 30 & 36 EEC. Judgment of the Court of Justice of the European Communities of 23 November 1989' (1990) 27 *Common Market Law Review* 141.

Gormley, LW. 'Reasoning Renounced? The Remarkable Judgment in Keck & Mithouard?' (1994) 5 *European Business Law Review* 63.

Gormley, LW. 'Two Years After Keck' (1996) 19 *Fordham International Law Journal* 866.

Gormley, LW. 'Private Parties and the Free Movement of Goods: Responsible, Irresponsible, or a Lack of Principles?' (2015) 38 *Fordham International Law Journal* 993.

Greenwald, B. and Stiglitz, J. 'Externalities in Economies with Imperfect Information and Incomplete Markets' (1986) 101 *The Quarterly Journal of Economics* 229.

Greenwood, J. 'The costs and implications of PBC sterilization' (2008) 28 *The Cato Journal* 205.

Grilli, V. and Milesi-Ferretti, GM. 'Economic Effects and Structural Determinants of Capital Controls' (1995) 42 *IMF Staff Papers* 517.

Grundmann, S. 'The Banking Union Translated into (Private Law) Duties: Infrastructure and Rulebook' (2015) 16 *European Business Organization Law Review* 357.

Grundmann, S. and Möslein, F. 'Golden Shares – State Control in Privatised Companies: Comparative Law, European Law and Policy Aspects' (2001–2002) 4 *EUREDIA* 623.

Grundmann, S and Möslein, F. 'The Golden Share – State Control in Privatised Companies: Comparative Law, European Law and Policy Aspects' (2001–2002) 4 *European Banking and Financial Law Journal – Euredia* 623.

Hagelina, N., Holménb, M. and Pramborgc, B. 'Family ownership, dual-class shares, and risk management' (2006) 16 *Global Finance Journal* 283.

Hardin, G. 'The Tragedy of the Commons' (1968) 162 *Science* 1243.

Hartkamp, A. 'The Effect of the EC Treaty in Private Law: On Direct and Indirect Horizontal Effects of Primary Community Law' (2010) 3 *European Review of Private Law* 529.

Haslehner, W. '"Consistency" and Fundamental Freesoms: The Case of Direct Taxation' (2013) 50 *Common Market Law Review* 737.

Hatzopoulos, V. 'Case C-275/92, Her Majesty's Customs and Excise v. Gerhart and Jorg Schindler, [1994] ECR 1-1039' (1995) 32 *Common Market Law Review* 841.

Hatzopoulos, V. 'The Court's approach to services (2006–2012): From case law to case load?' (2013) 50 *Common Market Law Review* 459.

Hay, C. 'The normalizing role of rationalist assumptions in the institutional embedding of neoliberalism' (2004) 33 *Economy and Society* 500.

Hemels, S. and others, 'Freedom of establishment or free movement of capital: Is there an order of priority? Conflicting visions of national courts and the ECJ' (2010) 19 *EC Tax Review* 19.

Henry, PB. 'Capital Account Liberalization: Theory, Evidence, and Speculation' (2007) XLV *Journal of Economic Literature* 887.

Hinarejos, A. 'Laval and Viking: The Right to Collective Action versus EU Fundamental Freedoms' (2008) 8 *Human Rights Law Review* 714.

Hinarejos, A. 'Changes to Economic and Monetary Union and Their Effects on Social Policy' (2016) 32 *The International Journal of Comparative Labour Law and Industrial Relations* 231.

Hirte, H. 'The Takeover Directive – A Mini-Directive on the Structure of the Corporation: Is it a Trojan Horse?' (2005) 2 *European Company and Financial Law Review* 1.

Hjipanayi, C. 'The Fundamental Freedoms and Third Countries: Recent Perspectives' (2008) 48 *European Taxation* 571.

Höpner, M. and Schäfer, A. 'Embeddedness and Regional Integration. Waiting for Polanyi in a Hayekian Setting' (2012) 66 *International Organization* 429.

Horowitz, HW. 'The Misleading Search for State Action under the Fourteenth Amendment' (1957) 30 *Southern California Law Review* 208.

Howard, E. 'ECJ Advances Equality in Europe by Giving Horizontal Direct Effect to Directives' (2011) 17 *European Public Law* 729.

Hunt, M. 'The "horizontal effect" of the Human Rights Act' (1998) *Public Law* 423.

IMF, 'Capital Account Liberalization: Theoretical and Practical Aspects' (1998).

Isenbaert, M. 'The Contemporary Meaning of 'Sovereignty' in the Supranational Context of the EC as Applied to the Income Tax Case Law of the ECJ' (2009) 18 *EC Tax Review* 264.

Isiksel, NT. 'Fundamental rights in the EU after Kadi and Al Barakaat' (2010) 16 *European Law Journal* 551.

Jansson, MS. and Kalimo, H. 'De Minimis Meets "Market Access": Transformations in the Substance – and the Syntax- of EU Free Movement Law?' (2014) 51 *Common Market Law Review* 523.

Jeronimo, V., Pagán, J. and Soydemir, G. 'Privatization and European Economic and Monetary Union' (2000) 26 *Eastern Economic Journal* 321.

Joerges, C. and Rödl, F. 'Informal Politics, Formalised Law and the 'Social Deficit' of European Integration: Reflections after the Judgments of the ECJ in Viking and Laval' (2009) 15 *European Law Journal* 1.

Johnston, A. 'Frozen in Time? The ECJ Finally Rules on the Kadi Appeal' (2009) 68 *The Cambridge Law Journal* 1.

Jourdan, P. 'La formation du concept de service public' (1987) *Revue du droit public et de la science politique en France et à l'étranger* 99.

Kay, RS. 'The State Action Doctrine, the Public-Private Distinction, and the Independence of Constitutional Law' (1993) 10 *Constitutional Commentary* 329.

Kilpatrick, C. 'Laval's regulatory conundrum: collective standard-setting and the Court's new approach to posted workers' (2009) 34 *European Law Review* 844.

Kilpatrick, C. 'Are the bailout measures immune to EU Social challenge because they are not EU Law?' (2014) 10 *European Constitutional Law Review* 393.

Kilpatrick, C. 'Has Polycentric Strike Law Arrived in the UK? After Laval, After Viking, After Demir?' (2014) 30 *International Journal of Comparative Labour Law and Industrial Relations* 293.

Korinek, A. 'The New Economics of Prudential Capital Controls: A Research Agenda' (2011) 59 *IMF Economic Review* 523.

Kose, MA. and Prasad, E. 'Liberalizing Capital Account Restrictions' (2004) 41 *IMF Finance and Development* 50.

Kose, MA. Prasad, E. Rogoff, K and Wei, S-J. 'Financial Globalization: A Reappraisal' (2009) 56 *IMF Staff Papers*.

Kovar, R. 'Droit communautaire et service public' (1996) *Revue trimestrielle de Droit Européen* (RTD Eur) 215.

Krenn, C. 'A missing piece in the horizontal effect "jigsaw": Horizontal direct effect and the free movement of goods' (2012) 49 *Common Market Law Review* 177.

Krüger Andersen, P. 'The Takeover Directive and Corporate Governance: The Danish Experience' (2004) 15 *European Business Law Review* 1461.

Krugman, P. 'Saving Asia: It's Time to Get Radical' (1998) 138 *Fortune* 74.

Kukovec, D. 'Law and the Periphery' (2015) 21 *European Law Journal* 406.

Laffey, D., Della Sala, V. and Laffey, K. 'Patriot games: the regulation of online gambling in the European Union' (2016) 23 *Journal of European Public Policy* 1425.

Landsmeer, A. 'Movement of Capital and Other Freedoms' (2001) 28 *Legal Issues of Economic Integration* 57.

Larik, J. 'The Kadi Saga as a Tale of 'Strict Observance' of International Law: Obligations Under the UN Charter, Targeted Sanctions and Judicial Review in the European Union' (2014) 61 *Netherlands International Law Review* 23.

Larner, W. 'Neo-liberalism: policy, ideology, governmentality' (2000) 63 *Studies in Political Economy* 5.

Lavranos, N. 'The Impact of the Kadi Judgment on the International Obligations of the EC Member States and the EC' (2009) 28 *Yearbook of European Law* 616.

Lazzerini, N. 'Case C-176/12, Association de Médiation Sociale v. Union Locale des Syndicats CGT and Others, Judgment of the Court of Justice (Grand Chamber) of 15 January 2014' (2014) 51 *Common Market Law Review* 907.

Leczykiewicz, D. 'Horizontal application of the Charter of Fundamental Rights' (2013) 38 *European Law Review* 479.

Lenaerts, K. 'Exploring the Limits of the EU Charter of Fundamental Rights' (2012) 8 *European Constitutional Law Review* 375.

Lenaerts, K. and Foubert, P. 'Social Rights in the Case-Law of the European Court of Justice: The Impact of the Charter of Fundamental Rights of the European Union on Standing Case-Law' (2001) 28 *Legal Issues of Economic Integration* 267.

Lengauer, A. 'Case C-302/97, Klaus Konle v. Republic of Austria, Judgment of the Full Court of 1 June 1999' (2000) 37 *Common Market Law Review* 177.

Lianos, I. 'Shifting Narratives in the European Internal Market: Efficient Restrictions of Trade and the Nature of "Economic" Integration' (2010) 21 *European Business Law Review* 705.

Liddle, R. 'The European Social Model and the ECJ' (2008) 4 *Social Europe Journal* 27.

Littler, A. 'Regulatory perspectives on the future of interactive gambling in the internal market' (2008) 33 *European Law Review* 211.

Lohse, EJ. 'Fundamental Freedoms and Private Actors – towards an 'Indirect Horizontal Effect' (2007) 13 *European Public Law* 159.

Long, M. 'Service public, services publics: déclin ou renouveau?' (1995) *Revue française de droit administratif* (RFDA) 497.

Long, M. 'Service public et réalités économiques du XIXe siècle au droit communautaire' (2001) *Revue française de droit administratif* (RFDA) 1161.

Looijestijn-Clearie, A. 'All that glitters is not gold: European Court of Justice strikes down golden shares in two Dutch companies' (2007) 8 *European Business Organization Law Review* 429.

Losada Fraga, F. Juutilainen, T. Havu, K. and Vesala, J. 'Property and European Integration: Dimensions of Article 345 TFEU' (2012) 148 *Tidskrift utgiven av Juridiska föreningen i Finland* 203.

Lovén Seldén, K. 'Laval and Trade Union Cooperation: Views on the Mobilizing Potential of the Case' (2014) 30 *International Journal of Comparative Labour Law and Industrial Relations* 87.

MacCarthaigh, M. 'Managing state-owned enterprises in an age of crisis: an analysis of Irish experience' (2011) 32 *Policy Studies* 215.

Maduro, MP. 'Keck: The end? The beginning of the end? Or just the end of the beginning' (1994) 3 *Irish Journal of European Law* 30.

Maduro, MP. 'Harmony and Dissonance in Free Movement' (2001) 4 *Cambridge Yearbook of European Legal Studies* 315.

Maitrot de la Motte, A. 'Les exceptions à la liberté européenne de circulation des capitaux: réflexions sur le champ d'application de l'article 64 TFUE' (2011) 24 *Revue de Droit Fiscal* 26.

Malmberg, J. and Sigeman, T. 'Industrial actions and EU economic freedoms: The autonomous collective bargaining model curtailed by the European Court of Justice' (2008) 45 *Common Market Law Review* 1115.

Markakis, M. 'Can Governments Control Mass Layoffs by Employers? Economic Freedoms vs Labour Rights in Case C-201/15 AGET Iraklis' (2017) 13 *European Constitutional Law Review* 724.

Markesinis, BS. 'Privacy, freedom of expression, and the horizontal effect of the Human Rights Bill: lessons from Germany' (1999) 115 *Law Quarterly Review* 47.

Marshall, WP. 'Diluting Constitutional Rights: Rethinking State Action' (1985) 80 *Northwestern University Law Review* 558.

Martin, A. and Mercurio, B. 'The IMF and Its Shifting Mandate Towards Capital Movements and Capital Controls: A Legal Perspective' (2017) 44 *Legal Issues of Economic Integration* 211.

Mathisen, G. 'Consistency and Coherence as Conditions for Justification of Member State Measures Restricting Free Movement' (2010) 47 *Common Market Law Review* 1021.

Mayer-Schonberger, V. and Strasser, M. 'Closer look at telecom deregulation: The european advantage' (1998) 12 *Harvard Journal of Law and Technology* 561.

McCahery, JA. and Vermeulen, EPM. 'The Case Against Reform of the Takeover Bids Directive' (2011) 22 *European Business Law Review* 541.

Megginson ,WL and Netter, JM. 'From State to Market: A Survey of Empirical Studies on Privatisation' (2001) 39 *Journal of Economic Literature* pp. 321.

Megginson, WL. and Netter, JM. 'From State to Market: A Survey of Empirical Studies on Privatization' (2001) 39 *Journal of Economic Literature* 321.

Mishkin, FS. 'Why We Shouldn't Turn Our Backs on Financial Globalization' (2009) 56 *IMF Staff Papers* 139.

Mitroyanni, J. 'Exploring the Scope of the Free Movement of Capital in Direct Taxation' (2005) 8 *EC Tax Journal* 1.

Moloney, N. 'European Banking Union: assessing its risks and resilience' (2014) 51 *Common Market Law Review* 1609.

Moloney, N. 'Capital markets union: "ever closer union" for the EU financial system?' (2016) 41 *European Law Review* 307.

Moloney, N. ' Institutional governance and capital markets union: incrementalism or a 'big bang'?' (2016) 13 *European Company and Financial Law Review* 376.

Monks, J. 'European Court of Justice (ECJ) and Social Europe: A Divorce Based on Irreconcilable Differences?' (2008) 4 *Social Europe Journal* 22.

Morgan, J. 'Questioning the True Effect of the Human Rights Act' (2002) 22 *Legal Studies* 259.

Morgenthau, H. 'Bretton Woods and International Cooperation' (1945) 23 *Foreign Affairs* 182.

Mortelmans, K. 'Article 30 of the EEC Treaty and Legislation Relating to Market Circumstances: Time to Consider a New Definition?' (1991) 28 *Common Market Law Review* 115.

Möslein, F. 'Compliance with ECJ judgments vs. compatibility with EU law – Free movement of capital issues unresolved after the second ruling on the Volkswagen law: Commission v. Germany' (2015) 52 *Common Market Law Review* 801.

Möslein, F. 'Compliance with ECJ judgments vs. compatibility with EU law – Free movement of capital issues unresolved after the second ruling on the Volkswagen law: Commission v. Germany' (2015) 52 *Common Market Law Review* 801.

Mukwiri, J. 'Free movement of capital and takeovers: a case-study of the tension between primary and secondary EU legislation' (2013) 38 *European Law Review* 829.

Mukwiri, J. 'Reforming EU Takeover Law Remains on Hold' (2015) 12 *European Company Law* 186.

Mulder, J. 'Responsive Adjudication and the 'Social Legitimacy' of the Internal Market' (2016) 22 *European Law Journal* 597.

Mundell, R. 'Capital Mobility and Stabilization Policy Under Fixed and Flexible Exchange Rates' (1963) 29 *The Canadian Journal of Economics and Political Science* 475.

Murphy, CC. 'Using the EU Charter of Fundamental Rights Against Private Parties after Association De Médiation Sociale' (2014) *European Human Rights Law Review* 170.

Murphy, CC. 'Why does tax have to be so taxing? The court revisits the Franked Investment Income litigation' (2013) 38 *European Law Review* 695.

Murphy, R. 'Why does tax have to be so taxing? The court revisits the Franked Investment Income litigation (Case Comment)' (2013) 38 *European Law Review* 695.

Neely, CJ. 'An Introduction to Capital Controls' (1999) 81 *Federal Reserve Bank of St Louis Review* 13.

Nic Shuibhne, N. 'Margins of appreciation: national values, fundamental rights and EC free movement law' (2009) 34 *European Law Review* 230.

Nic Shuibhne, N. 'Settling Dust? Reflections on the Judgments in Viking and Laval' (2010) 21 *European Business Law Review* 681.

Nic Shuibhne, N. and Maci, M. 'Proving Public Interest: The Growing Impact of Evidence in Free Movement Case Law' (2015) 50 *Common Market Law Review* 965.

Nogarede, J. 'Levelling the (Football) Field: Should Individuals Play by Free Movement Rules?' (2012) 39 *Legal Issues of Economic Integration* 381.

Novitz, T. 'A Human Rights Analysis of the Viking and Laval Judgments' (2007–2008) 10 *Cambridge Yearbook of European Legal Studies* 541.

Novitz, T. 'The Internationally Recognized Right to Strike: A Past, Present and Future Basis upon Which to Evaluate Remedies for Unlawful Collective Action?' (2014) 30 *International Journal of Comparative Labour Law and Industrial Relations* 357.

O'Brien, M. 'Taxation and the Third Country Dimension of Free Movement of Capital in EU Law: The ECJ's Rulings and Unresolved Issues' (2008) 6 *British Tax Review* 628.

O'Brien, M. 'Case C-452/04, Fidium Finanz AG v. Bundesanstalt für Finanzdienstleistungsaufsicht, judgment of the Court of Justice (Grand Chamber) of 3 October 2006' (2007) 44 *Common Market Law Review* 1483.

O'Brien, M. 'Case C-326/07, Commission of the European Communities v. Italian Republic, Judgment of the Court of Justice (Third Chamber) of 26 March 2009' (2010) 47 *Common Market Law Review* 245.

O'Brien, M. 'Free movement of capital between EU Member States and third countries and the Euro-Mediterranean Agreements: SECIL' (2018) 55 *Common Market Law Review* 243.

Obstfeld, M. 'The Global Capital Market: Benefactor or Menace?' (1998) 12 *Journal of Economic Perspectives* 9.

Obstfeld, M. 'International Finance and Growth in Developing Countries: What Have We Learned?' (2009) 56 *IMF Staff Papers* 63.

Ocampo, JA. 'Latin America's Growth and Equity Frustrations During Structural Reforms' 18 *Journal of Economic Perspectives* 67.

OECD, 'International Capital Mobility: Structural Policies to Reduce Financial Fragility?' (2012) No. 13 *OECD Economics Department Policy Notes*.

Oliver, P. 'Of Trailers and Jet Skis: Is the Case Law on Article 34 TFEU Hurtling in a New Direction?' (2011) 33 *Fordhman International Law Journal* 1423.

Oliver, P. 'When, if ever, can restrictions on free movement be justified on economic grounds' (2016) 41 *European Law Review* 147.

Oliver, P. and Enchelmaier, S. 'Free movement of goods: Recent developments in the case law' (2007) 44 *Common Market Law Review* 674.

Oliver, P. and Roth, W-H. 'The internal market and the four freedoms' (2004) 41 *Common Market Law Review* 407.

Ostry, J. Loungani, P. and Furceri, D. 'Neoliberalism: Oversold?' (2016) 53 *Finance & Development* 38.

Pagoulatos, G. 'The Politics of Privatisation: Redrawing the Publi-Private Boundary' (2005) 28 *Western European Politics* 358.

Panayi, CH. 'Thin Capitalization Glo et al. – A Thinly Concealed Agenda?' (2007) 35 *Intertax* 298.

Papadopoulos, T. 'Infringements of Fundamental Freedoms within the EU Market for Corporate Control' (2012) 9 *European Company and Financial Law Review* 221.

Papadopoulos, T. 'Privatized Companies, Golden Shares and Property Ownership in the Euro Crisis Era: A Discussion after Commission v. Greece' (2015) 12 *European Company and Financial Law Review* 1.

Pecho, P. 'Good-Bye Keck?: A Comment on the Remarkable Judgment in Commission v. Italy, C-110/05' (2009) 36 *Legal Issues of Economic Integration* 257.

Peijpe, Tv. 'Collective Labour Law after Viking, Laval, Rüffert, and Commission v. Luxembourg' (2009) 25 *International Journal of Comparative Labour Law and Industrial Relations* 81.

Peters, C. and Gooijer, J. 'The free movement of capital and third countries' (2005) 45 *European Taxation* 475.

Phillipson, G. and Williams, A. 'Horizontal Effect and the Constitutional Constraint' (2011) 74 *Modern Law Review* 878.

Pistone, P. 'Kirchberg 3 October 2006: Three Decisions that Did ... Not Change the Future of European Taxes' (2006) 34 *Intertax* 582.

Pontier, J-M. 'Sur la conception française du service public' (1996) *Recueil Dalloz Sirey* 9.

Poulou, A. 'Financial assistance conditionality and human rights protection: What is the role of the EU Charter of Fundamental Rights?' (2017) 54 *Common Market Law Review* 991.

Prechal, S. and De Vries, S. 'Seamless web of judicial protection in the internal market?' (2009) 34 *European Law Review* 5.

Preedy, K. 'Fundamental Rights and Private Acts – Horizontal Direct or Indirect Effect? – A Comment' (2000) 8 *European Review of Private Law* 125.

Prete, L. 'Of Motorcycle Trailers and Personal Watercrafts: the Battle over Keck' (2008) 35 *Legal Issues of Economic Integration* 133.

Psarakis, G. 'One Share – One Vote and the Case for a Harmonised Capital Structure' (2008) 19 *European Business Law Review* 709.

Rammeloo, S. 'Past, Present (and Future?) of the German Volkswagengesetz under the EC Treaty' (2007) 4 *European Company Law* 118.

Reisen, H. and Soto, M. 'Which Types of Capital Inflows Foster Developing-Country Growth?' (2001) 4 *International Finance* 1.

Reynolds, S. 'Explaining the constitutional drivers behind a perceived judicial preference for free movement over fundamental rights' (2016) 53 *Common Market Law Review* 643.

Ringe, W-G. 'Case C-112/05, Commission v. Germany ("VW law"), Judgment of the Grand Chamber of 23 October 2007, nyr'. (2008) 45 *Common Market Law Review* 37.

Ringe, W-G. 'Company Law and Free Movement of Capital' (2010) 69 *Cambridge Law Journal* 378.

Ringe, W-G. 'Case Comment: Kornhaas and the challenge of applying Keck in establishment' (2017) 42 *European Law Review* 270.

Robin-Olivier, S. 'Bargaining in the shadow of free movement of capital' (2012) 8 *European Review of Contract Law* 167.

Rogoff, K. 'International Institutions for Reducing Global Financial Instability' (1999) 13 *Journal of Economic Perspectives* 21.

Rönnmar, M. 'Free Movement of Services versus National Labour Law and Industrial Relations Systems: Understanding the Laval Case from a Swedish and Nordic Perspective' (2007–2008) 10 *Cambridge Yearbook of European Legal Studies* 493.

Ruccia, N. 'The New and Shy Approach of the Court of Justice Concerning Golden Shares' (2013) 24 *European Business Law Review* 275.

Ruggie, J. 'International Regimes, Transactions, and Change: Embedded Liberalism in the Postwar Economic Order' (1982) 36 *International Organizations* 379.

Sachs, J and Warner, A. 'Economic reform and the process of global integration' (1995) 1 *Brooking Papers on Economic Activity* pp. 1.

Sachs, JD. and Warner, AM. 'The Curse of Natural Resources' (2001) 45 *European Economic Review* 827.

Sanders, F. 'Case C-112/05, European Commission v. Federal Rebublic of Germany: The Volkswagen Case and Art. 56 EC – A Proper Result, Yet Also a Missed Opportunity?' (2007–2008) 14 *Columbia Journal of European Law* 359.

Sapir, A. 'European Integration at the Crossroads: A Review Essay on the 50th Anniversary of Bela Balassa's Theory of Economic Integration' (2011) 49 *Journal of Economic Literature* 1200.

Sappington, D. and Stiglitz, J. 'Privatization, Information and Incentives' (1987) 6 *Journal of Policy Analysis and Management* 567.

Sauter, W. 'The Economic Constitution of the European Union' (1998) 4 *Columbia Journal of European Law* 27.

Scharpf, FW. 'Legitimacy in the Multilevel European Polity' (2009) 1 *European Political Science Review* 173.

Scharpf, FW. 'The Double Asymmetry of European Integration Or: Why the EU Cannot Be a Social Market Economy' (2010) 8 *Socio-Economic Review* 211.

Scheinin, M. 'Is the ECJ Ruling in Kadi Incompatible with International Law?' (2009) 28 *Yearbook of European Law* 637.

Schepel, H. 'The Enforcement of EC Law in Contractual Relations: Case Studies in How Not to 'Constitutionalize' Private Law' (2004) 12 *European Review of Private Law* 661.

Schepel, H. 'Constitutionalising the Market, Marketising the Constitution, and to Tell the Difference: On the Horizontal Application of the Free Movement Provisions in EU Law' (2012) 18 *European Law Journal* 177.

Schön, W. 'Free Movement of Capital and Freedom of Establishment' (2016) 17 *European Business Organization Law Review* 229.

Sciarra, S. 'Viking and Laval: Collective Labour Rights and Market Freedoms in the Enlarged EU' (2007–2008) 10 *Cambridge Yearbook of European Legal Studies* 563.

Seifert, S. 'L'effet horizontal des droits fondamentaux' (2012) 48 *Revue Trimestrielle de Droit Européen* 801.

Sever, Sa. 'Horizontal Effect and the Charter' (2014) 10 *Croatian Yearbook of European Law and Policy* 39.

Shapiro, M. 'Comparative Law and Comparative Politics' (1980) 53 *California Law Review* 537.

Sinn, H-W. 'The Dilemma of Globalisation: A German Perspective' (2004) 4 *Economie Internationale* p. 111.

Skog, R. 'The Takeover Directive, the "Breakthrough" Rule and the Swedish System of Dual CLass Common Stock' (2004) 15 *European Business Law Review* 1439.

Skouris, V. 'Effet Utile Versus Legal Certainty: The Case-law of the Court of Justice on the Direct Effect of Directives' (2006) 17 *European Business Law Review* 241.

Slattery, B. 'Charter of Rights and Freedoms – Does it Bind Private Persons' (1985) 63 *Canadian Bar Review* 148.

Smit, D. 'The relationship between the free movement of capital and the other EC Treaty freedoms in third country relationships in the field of direct taxation: a question of exclusivity, parallelism or causality?' (2007) 16 *EC Tax Review* 252.

Snell, J. 'Non-Discriminatory Tax Obstacles in Community Law' (2007) 56 *International and Comparative Law Quarterly* 339.

Snell, J. 'The Notion of Market Access: A Concept or a Slogan?' (2010) 47 *Common Market Law Review* 437.

Snell, J. 'Varieties of Capitalism and the Limits of European Economic Integration' (2012) 13 *Cambridge Yearbook of European Legal Studies* 415.

Snodgrass, E. 'Protecting Investors' Legitimate Expectations – Recognizing and Delimiting a General Principle' (2006) 21 *ICSID Review – Foreign Investment Law Journal* 1.

Sørensen, KE. 'Company Law as a Restriction to Free Movement – Examination of the Notion of 'Restriction' Using Company Law as the Frame of Reference' (2014) 11 *European Company Law* 178.

Spano, A. 'Free Movement of Capital and Golden Shares: A New Perspective on Corporate Control? (Joined Cases C-463/04 and C-464/04 Federconsumatori and Others v Comune di Milano)' (2010) 13 *International Trade and Business Law Review* 291.

Spaventa, E. 'From Gebhard to Carpenter: Towards a (non-)economic European constitution' (2004) 41 *Common Market Law Review* 743.

Steiner, J. 'Drawing the line: Uses and abuses of Article 30 EEC' (1992) 29 *Common Market Law Review* 749.

Stiglitz, J. 'Capital Market Liberalization, Economic Growth and Instability' (2000) 28 *World Development* 1075.

Stiglitz, J. 'Financial Market Stability and Monetary Policy' (2002) 7 *Pacific Economic Review* 13.

Stiglitz, J. 'Capital-market Liberalization, Globalization, and the IMF' (2004) 20 *Oxford Review of Economic Policy* 57.

Stiglitz, J. 'Whither Reform? Towards a New Agenda for Latin America' (2003) 80 *Revista de la CEPAL* 7.

Streit, M. 'Economic Order, Private Law and Public Policy: The Freiburg School of Law and Economics in Perspective' (1992) 148 *Journal of International and Theoretical Economics* 675.

Syrpis, P. and Novitz, T. 'Economic and social rights in conflict: Political and judicial approaches to their reconciliation' (2008) 33 *European Law Review* 411.

Syrpis, P. and Novitz, T. 'Economic and social rights in conflict: political and judicial approaches to their reconciliation' (2008) 33 *European Law Review* 411.

Szydło, M. Continuing the judicial gambling saga in Berlington' (2016) 53 *Common Market Law Review* 1089.

Szyszczak, E. 'Golden Shares and Market Governance' (2002) 29 *Legal Issues of Economic Integration* 255.

Taylor, G. 'The Horizontal Effect of Human Rights Provisions, the German Model and Its Applicability to Common-Law Jurisdictions' (2002) 13 *King's College Law Journal* 187.

Thirion, 'Existe-t-il des limites juridiques à la privatisation des entreprises publiques?' (2002) XVI *Revue internationale de droit économique* 627.

Tobin, J. 'Financial Globalization' (2000) 28 *World Development* 1101.

Toner, H. 'Non-discriminatory obstacles to the exercise of Treaty Rights – Articles 39, 43, 49, and 18 EC' (2004) 23 *Yearbook of European Law* 275.

Tridimas, T. 'Economic Sanctions, Procedural Rights and Judicial Scrutiny: Post-Kadi Developments' (2009–2010) 12 *Cambridge Yearbook of European Legal Studies* 455.

Tryfonidou, A. 'Was Keck a Half-baked Solution After All?' (2007) 34 *Legal Issues of Economic Integration* 167.

Tushnet, M. 'The issue of state action/horizontal effect in comparative constitutional law' (2003) 1 *International Journal of Constitutional Law* 79.

Usher, J. 'The Evolution of the Free Movement of Capital' (2007) 31 *Fordhman International Law Journal* 1533.

Vamvakidis, A. 'Regional Trade Agreements or Broad Liberalization: Which Path Leads to Faster Growth?' (1999) 46 *International Monetary Fund Staff Papers* 42.

Van Bekkum, J. 'Golden Shares: A New Approach' (2010) 7 *European Company Law* 13.

Van Cleynenbreugel, P. 'No privatisation in the service of fair competition? Article 345 TFEU and the EU market-state balance after Essent' (2014) 39 *European Law Review* 264.

Van den Bogaert, S. and Cuyvers, A. ' "Money for nothing": The case law of the EU Court of Justice on the regulation of gambling' (2011) 48 *Common Market Law Review* 1175.

Van den Herik, L. 'The Security Council's Targeted Sanctions Regimes: In Need of Better Protection of the Individual' (2007) 20 *Leiden Journal of International Law* 797.

Vasciannie, S. 'The Fair and Equitable Treatment Standard in International Investment Law and Practice' (1999) 70 *British Yearbook of International Law* 99.

Verbruggen, P. 'The Impact of Primary EU Law on Private Law Relationships: Horizontal Direct Effect under the Free Movement of Goods and Services' (2014) 22 *European Review of Private Law* 201.

Vigneron, P. 'L'effet erga omnes de la libre circulation des capitaux dans la Constitution européenne: un retour en arrière?' (2004) 23 *Euredia* 369.

Vossestein, G-J. 'Volkswagen: the State of Affairs of Golden Shares, General Company Law and European Free Movement of Capital – A discussion of Case C-112/05 Commission v Germany of 23.10.2007' (2008) 5 *European Company and Financial Law Review* 115.

Wacziarg, R. 'Measuring the dynamic gains from trade' (2011) 15 *The World Bank Economic Review* 393.

Wade, HWR. 'Horizons of horizontality' (2000) 116 *Law Quarterly Review* 217.

Waele, Hd. and Meulman, J. 'A Retreat from Säger? Servicing or Fine-Tuning the Application of Article 49 EC' (2006) 33 *Legal Issues of Economic Integration* 207.

Weatherill, S. 'The Road to Ruin: 'Restrictions on Use' and the Circular Lifecycle of Article 34 TFEU' (2012) 2 *European Journal of Consumer Law* 359.

Weatherill, S. 'After *Keck*: Some Thoughts on How to Clarify the Clarification' (1996) 33 *Common Market Law Review* 885.

Weiler, J. 'The Transformation of Europe' (1991) 100 *The Yale Law Journal* 2403.

Wenneras, P. and Boe Moen, K. 'Selling Arrangements, Keeping Keck' (2010) 35 *European Law Review* 387.

Werner, B. 'National responses to the European Court of Justice case law on Golden Shares: the role of protective equivalents' (2016) 24 *Journal of European Public Policy* 989.

White, EL. 'In Search Of The Limits To Article 30 Of The EEC Treaty' (1989) 26 *Common Market Law Review* 235.

Wooldridge, F. 'The Recent Directive on Takeover Bids' (2004) 15 *European Business Law Review* 147.

Zamora, S. 'Sir Joseph Gold and the Development of International Monetary Law' (1989) 23 *The International Lawyer* 1009.

Zumbansen, P and Saam, D. 'The ECJ, Volkswagen and European Corporate Law: Reshaping the European Varieties of Capitalism' (2007) 8 *German Law Journal.*

Reports

Aizenman, J. and Glick, R. *Sterilization, monetary policy, and global financial integration* (National Bureau of Economic Research, Working Paper No 13902, 2008).

Aizenman, J. and Sushko, V. *Capital Flows: Catalyst or Hindrance to Economic Takeoffs?* (National Bureau of Economic Research Working Paper No 17258, 2011).

Akandji-Kombe, J-Fo. *Positive obligations under the European Convention on Human Rights – A guide to the implementation of the European Convention on Human Rights* (Human rights handbooks, No 7, Council of Europe, 2007).

Chen, H., Jonung, L. and Unteroberdoerster, O. *Lessons for China from financial liberalization in Scandinavia* (European Commission, Economic and Financial Affairs, Economic Papers 383, 2009).

Chowla, P. *Time for a New Consensus: Regulating Financial Flows for Stability and Development* (London: Bretton Woods Project, 2011).

Christiansen, H. *The Size and Composition of the SOE Sector in OECD Countries* (OECD Corporate Governance Working Papers, No 5, 2011).

Cobham, A. *Capital Account Liberalisation and Poverty in Go with the flow? Capital account liberalisation and poverty* (Bretton Woods Project and Oxfam, 2001).

E Commission, *Bulletin of the European Commission* (No 7/8, Vol 24, 1991).

E Commission, *Services of General Interest in Europe* (OJ C281/3, 1996).

E Commission, *Communication of the Commission on Certain Legal Aspects concerning Intra-EU Investment* (Official Journal C 220, 1997).

E Commission, *Modernising Company Law and Enhancing Corporate Governance in the European Union – A Plan to Move Forward* (Communication from the Commission to the Council and the European Parliament, 2003).

E Commission, *Impact Assessment on the Proportionality between Capital and Control in Listed Companies* (Commission Staff Working Document, 2007).

E Commission, *Commission notice on the enforcement of State aid law by national courts* (OJ C 85, p 1–22, 2009).

E Commission, *Action Plan: European company law and corporate governance – a modern legal framework for more engaged shareholders and sustainable companies* (Communication from the Commission to the European Parliament, the Council, the European Economic and Social Committee and the Committee of the Regions, 2012).

BIBLIOGRAPHY 213

E Commission, *Commission Staff Working Document, Guidance Paper on state-aid-compliant financing, restructuring and privatisation of State-owned enterprises* (Brussels, swd(2012) 14 final, 2012).

E Commission, *Commission Staff Working Document: Online gambling in the Internal Market* (SWD(2012) 345 final, 2012).

E Commission, *Case Law Guide of the European Court of Justice on articles 63 et seq. TFEU, Free Movement of Capital* (DG FISMA, 2015).

E Commission, *Communication: Action Plan on Building a Capital Markets Union* (COM(2015) 468 final, 2015).

E Commission, *Green Paper: Building a Capital Markets Union* (COM(2015) 63 final, 2015).

E Commission, *Proposal for a Directive of the European Parliament and of the Council relating to certain aspects of company law (codification)* (COM(2015) 616 final, 2015/0283 (COD), 2015).

E Commission, *Communication of 26 April 2017 establishing a European Pillar of Social Rights* (COM(2017) 250 final, 2017).

E Commission, *Press release – Commission closes infringement procedures and complaints in the gambling sector, Brussels, 7 December 2017* (IP/17/5109, 2017).

E Commission, *Press Release – Commission refers Croatia to the Court for failing to amend the law on the privatisation of the energy company INA-Industrija Nafte, d.d. (INA), Brussels, 13 July 2017* (IP/17/1949, 2017).

E Commission, *Proposal for a Regulation of the European Parliament and the Council establishing a framework for screening of foreign direct investments into the European Union* ({SWD(2017) 297 final}, 2017).

E Commission, *Recommendation on the European Pillar of Social Rights* (C(2017) 2600 final, 2017).

E Commission, *Completing the Capital Markets Union by 2019 – time to accelerate delivery, Communication from the Commission* (COM(2018) 114 final, 2018).

E Commission, *Press release – Commission suspends referral of CROATIA to the Court for failing to amend the law on the privatisation of the energy company INA-Industrija Nafte, d.d. (INA), Brussels, 19 July 2018* (IP/18/4489, 2018).

E Commission, *European Economy* (Directorate-General for Economic and Financial Affairs, No 6/2003).

E Commission, *Special rights in privatized companies in the enlarged Union – a decade full of developments* (Commission Staff Working Document, 2005).

Dell'Ariccia, G., Giovanni, Jd., Faria, A., Kose, A., Schindler, M. and Terrones, M. *Reaping the Benefits of Financial Globalization* (IMF Occasional Paper No 264, 2008).

Edison, H., Klein, M., Ricci. L and Sløk, T. *Capital Account Liberalization and Economic Performance: A Review of the Literature* (IMF Working Paper 02/120, 2002).

Edwards, S. *Capital Mobility and Economic Performance: Are Emerging Economies Different?* (National Bureau of Economic Research, Working Paper No 8076, 2001).

Edwards, S. *Capital Controls, Sudden Stops and Current Account Reversals* (National Bureau of Economic Research, Working Paper No 11170, 2005).

Eichengreen, B., Mussa, M., Dell'Ariccia, G., Detragiache, E., Milesi-Ferretti, GM. and Tweedie, A. *Liberalizing Capital Movements: Some Analytical Issues* (IMF Economic Issues No 17, 1999).

Epstein, G., Grabel, I. and Jomo, KS. *Capital Management Techniques in Developing Countries: An Assessment of Experiences from the 1990s and Lessons for the Future* (UN G-24 Discussion Paper Series, 2004).

Eurosummit, *Euro Summit Statement, Brussels, 12 July 2015* (SN 4070/15, 2015).

Furceri, D. and Loungani, P. *Capital Account Liberalization and Inequality'* (IMF Working Paper WP/15/243, 2015).

Gallagher, KP. Griffith-Jones, S. and Ocampo, JA. *Capital Account Regulations for Stability and Development: A New Approach* (The Frederick S Pardee Center for the Study of the Longer-Range Future, No 22, 2011).

Gallagher, KP. Jones, SG. and Ocampo, JA. *Regulating Global Capital Flows for Long-Run Development* (Boston, Pardee Center for the Study of the Longer Range Future, 2012).

Hemming, R. and Mansoor, AM. *Privatization and Public Enterprises* (IMF, Occasional Paper No 56, 1988).

Höpner, M. and Schäfer, A. *A New Phase of European Integration: Organized Capitalisms in Post-Ricardian Europe* (Max Planck Institute for the Study of Societies, MPIfG Discussion Paper 07/04, 2007).

Höpner, M. and Schäfer, A. *Integration among unequals: How the heterogeneity of European varieties of capitalism shapes the social and democratic potential of the EU* (MPIfG Discussion Paper, No 12/5 Cologne, Max Planck Institute for the Study of Societies, 2012).

IMF, *Article IV of the Fund's Articles of Agreement: An Overview of the Legal Framework* (Prepared by the Legal Department, 2006).

IMF, *The IMF's Approach to Capital Account Liberalization* (Independent Evaluation Office of the International Monetary Fund, 2015).

IMF, *Communiqué of the Interim Committee of the Board of Governors of the International Monetary Fund* (Press Release Number 97/44, 1997).

IMF, *The Liberalization and Management of Capital Flows – An Institutional View* (Staff Paper of the IMF Executive Board, 2012).

Ishii, S. and Habermeier, K. *Capital Account Liberalization and Financial Sector Stability* (IMF Occasional Paper No 211, 2002).

Katsoulakos, Y. and Likoyanni, E. *Fiscal and Other Macroeconomic Effects of Privatization* (FEEM Working Paper No 1132002, 2002).

Kinderman, D. *Challenging Varieties of Capitalism's Account of Business Interests – The New Social Market Initiative and German Employers' Quest for Liberalization, 2000–2014* (Max Planck Institute for the Studies of Societies, Cologne, MPIfG Discussion Paper 14/16, 2014).

Kokott, J. and Sobotta, C. *The Charter of Fundamental Rights of the European Union after Lisbon* (EUI Working Papers, Academy of European Law (2010) No 2010/06, 2010).

Kose, MA., Prasad, E., Rogoff, K. and Wei, S-J. *Financial Globalization: A Reappraisal* (IMF Staff Papers, Vol 56, No 1 2009).

Kose, MA., Prasad, ES. and Terrones, ME. *How Do Trade and Financial Integration Affect the Relationship between Growth and Volatility?* (IMF Working Paper WP/05/19, 2005).

Kose, MA., Prasad, ES. and Terrones, ME. *Does Openness to International Financial Flows Contribute to Productivity Growth?* (National Bureau of Economic Research, Working Paper No 14558, 2008).

Kowalski, P., Büge, M., Sztajerowska, M. and Egeland, M. *State-Owned Enterprises, Trade Effects and Policy Implications* (OECD Trade Policy Papers No 147, 2013).

Nellis, J. *The World Bank, privatization, and enterprise reform in transition economies: a retrospective analysis* (The World Bank Operations Evaluation Department, 2002).

OECD, *Lack of Proportionality Between Ownership and Control: Overview and Issues for Discussion* (OECD Steering Group on Corporate Governance, 2007).

OECD, *Privatisation in the 21st Century: Recent Experiences of OECD Countries* (Report on Good Practices, 2009).

OECD, *The OECD's Approach to Capital Flow Management Measures Used with a Macro-Prudential Intent* (Report to G20 Finance Ministers, 2015).

OECD, *Getting the most out of International Capital Flows* (OECD Economic Outlook, 2011).

OECD, *International capital flows: Structural reforms and experience with the OECD Code of Liberalisation of Capital Movements* (Report from the OECD to the G20 Sub-Group on Capital Flow Management, 2011).

Ostry, J., Prati, A., and Spilimbergo, A. *Structural Reforms and Economic Performance in Advanced and Developing Countries* (IMF Occasional Paper 268, 2009).

Ostry, JD., Ghosh, AR., and Korinek, A. *Multilateral Aspects of Managing the Capital Account* (IMF Staff Discussion Note, 2012).

Oxera, *Special rights of public authorities in privatised EU companies: the microeconomic impact* (Report prepared for the European Commission, 2005).

Prasad, E., Rogoff, K., Wei, S-J. and Kose, MA. *Effects of Financial Globalization on Developing Countries: Some Empirical Evidence* (IMF, Occasional Paper 220, 2003).

Prasad, ES. and Rajan, R. *A Pragmatic Approach to Capital Account Liberalization* (National Bureau of Economic Research Working Paper No 14051, 2008).

Ruffert, M. *Free Flow of Capital* (Max Planck Encyclopedia of Public International law, 2013).

Singh, A. *Capital Account Liberalization, Free Long-term Capital Flows, Financial Crises and Economic Development* (University of Cambridge, ESRC Centre for Business Research – Working Papers, No 245, 2002).

Spaak, P-H. *The Brussels Report on the General Common Market* (The European Community for Coal and Steel, 1956).

Sushil, B. and Sunil, S. *Herd Behavior in Financial Markets* (IMF Staff Papers Vol 47, No 3, 2001).

Wei, SJ. and Wu, Y. *The Life-and-Death Implications of Globalization* (National Bureau of Economic Research, Inter-American Seminar in Economics, 2002).

Yellen, JL. *Improving the International Monetary and Financial System* (Speech at the Banque de France International Symposium, Paris, 4 March 2011).

Blog

Frantziou, E. *Mangold Recast? The ECJ's Flirtation with Drittwirkung in Egenberger* (European Law Blog 2018).

Ringe, W-G. *Kornhaas and the Limits of Corporate Establishment* (Oxfrod Business Law Blog 2016).

Newspaper and Magazine Articles

Briefing, 'State-owned assets – Setting out the store' *The Economist* (11 January 2014).

Editorial, 'The Guardian view on rail privatisation: going off the tracks' *The Guardian* (05-12-2017) <https://www.theguardian.com/commentisfree/2017/dec/05/the-guardian-view-on-rail-privatisation-going-off-the-tracks> accessed 31-12-2019.

Leaders, 'Privatisation – The $9 trillion sale' *The Economist* (11 January 2014).

Thornhill, J. and Jones, A. 'De Villepin stands by calls for 'economic patriotism'' *Financial Times* (22 September 2005) <https://www.ft.com/content/028bacac-2b94-11da-995a-00000e2511c8> accessed 01-09-2018.

Web Pages

E Commission, 'Company Law and Corporate Governance' (<https://ec.europa.eu/info/business-economy-euro/doing-business-eu/company-law-and-corporate-governance_en> accessed 31-01-2019.

E Commission, 'Legal framework of the free movement of capital in the EU' (<https://ec.europa.eu/info/files/document-legal-framework-free-movement-capital-eu_en> accessed 31-01-2019.
ISS Inc., 'Analysis: Differentiated Voting Rights in Europe' (<https://www.issgovernance.com/analysis-differentiated-voting-rights-in-europe/ > accessed 31-01-2019.
Lagarde, C. 'Fix the Roof While the Window of Opportunity is Open: Three Priorities for the Global Economy, Speech at University of Hong Kong' (*IMF*, 2018) <https://www.imf.org/en/News/Articles/2018/04/09/spring-meetings-curtain-raiser-speech> accessed 31-01-2019.
OECD, 'Investment Policy' (<http://www.oecd.org/daf/inv/investment-policy/codes.htm> accessed 31-01-2019.

Dictionaries and Encyclopedias

Angelet, N. *Fair and Equitable Treatment*, (Max Planck Encyclopedia of Public International Law, 2011).
Black, J., Hashimzade, N. and Myles, G. *A Dictionary of Economics*, (Oxford University Press 2009).
Moles, P. and Terry, N. *The Handbook of International Financial Terms*, (Oxford University Press 2005).
Schlemmer-Schulte, S. *International Monetary Fund (IMF)*, (Max Planck Encyclopedia of Public international Law, Oxford University Press 2013).
Scott, J. and Marshall, G. *Dictionary of Sociology*, (Oxford University Press 2009).

Index

anti-trust   47, 83
articles of association   45, 76, 112, 113, 157
asymmetric information   14
austerity   2, 8

Banking Union   18, 18n36, 188, 200, 204
Bilateral Investment Treaties   17
board neutrality   88, 88n76, 89, 90, 117
break-through rule   88, 89, 90
Bretton Woods   11n2, 14n18, 18, 186, 188, 190, 200, 205, 212
burden of proof   127

capital controls   13, 16, 17, 19
capital flows
    volatility of   2, 15
Capital Markets Union   18, 18n36, 213
capital restrictions   2, 3, 4, 10, 19, 23, 33, 34, 35, 39, 67, 72, 91, 92, 111, 115, 119, 120, 121, 122, 137, 138, 149, 151, 154, 160, 161, 162, 164, 165
capitalism   14, 43, 49, 58, 75, 75n6, 81, 156, 214
    comparative   81, 82
cash flow   77, 154
Charter of Fundamental Rights   8n17, 92, 93n91, 93n93, 101n136, 106, 106n164, 106n164, 106n165, 106n165, 107, 107n166, 108, 108n172, 108n172, 109, 110, 121, 169, 199, 203, 205, 207, 209, 215
Charter of Shareholder Rights   156
coherence   128, 131, 132
cohesion   22, 33, 38, 38n143, 71
collective action   103
Common Commercial Policy   53
competition   6n13, 14, 40, 46, 46n20, 47n25, 47n26, 47n28, 47n31, 48, 48n38, 50n48, 51, 53, 57n103, 58n105, 62, 64n129, 68n150, 83, 84, 101, 104, 105, 127, 156, 162, 187, 191, 200, 211
consistency   120, 128, 130, 131, 132
control enhancing mechanisms   10, 75, 76, 77, 80, 119, 154
convergence criteria   49
corporate control   10, 49, 79, 87, 89, 90, 136, 161

corporate governance   4, 5, 10, 50, 74, 75, 76, 78, 80, 83, 84, 84n51, 84n52, 86n65, 90, 91, 111, 119, 120, 121, 132, 133, 134, 136, 137, 149, 151, 154, 156, 157, 160, 161, 162, 164, 165, 212
corporate law   78, 83, 84
corporation   78, 96, 136, 155
corruption   13, 44, 48, 50
credits   17, 21, 23, 27, 32
cross-subsidisation   40, 62, 68n150

de minimis   143, 143n337, 143n338
declaration   41
definite influence   28
democratic   2, 15, 75n6, 94, 136, 214
deregulation   3, 44, 48n36, 66, 82, 204
derogations   17, 33, 35, 36, 37, 70, 71
deterrent   10, 119, 137, 153, 155
developping countries   15
direct effect   5, 18, 20, 30, 53, 97n115, 198, 202
    horizontal   10, 31, 92, 98, 113, 115, 119
    indirect   107
    vertical   30
direct investment   21, 23, 27, 28, 39, 169, 213
Directive 88/361   18, 22, 22n54, 22n56, 22n60, 23, 27, 167
discrimination   31, 33, 34, 60, 64, 65, 95, 99, 101, 103, 107, 108, 109, 117, 118, 119, 156, 162
dowries   21, 23

Economic and Monetary Union   3, 4, 8n17, 18, 22, 24, 37, 49, 49n41, 53, 183, 184, 185, 189, 201, 202
economic considerations   34, 69, 70, 71, 126
economic efficiency   1, 3, 11, 12, 15, 43, 47, 48, 50, 57, 84, 91, 163
economic growth   1, 3, 7, 9, 11, 13, 44, 163, 166
economic protectionism   3, 9, 73, 163
economic rule   69, 71, 126
effective judicial protection   37, 109
electricity   39, 40, 51, 52, 61, 62, 62n122, 62n123, 67, 68n150, 73, 114, 135n302, 152, 166, 167, 168, 169
endowments   17, 21, 23, 27

INDEX

equal pay between men and women 98
equality
　income 2, 4, 11, 15, 163, 164
　social 1, 2, 3, 166
erga omnes 24, 24n64, 25, 29, 211
eurocrisis 8, 45
European Central Bank 37
European Economic Constitution 9, 53, 53n68, 66, 190
European Monetary System 22
European Pillar of Social Rights 8, 8n18, 199, 213
exchange controls 19
extra-EU 24, 81

financial crisis 2, 3, 15, 18
financial sanctions 37
financial services 25, 29, 36, 144n341, 152
fiscal sovereignty 33
foreign direct investment 2, 11
foreign investment 1, 3, 4, 7, 7n15, 10, 17, 58n107, 76, 119, 126, 133, 134, 153, 155, 160, 163, 165, 183
free movement of capital 1n.*, 2, 3, 4, 5, 9, 10, 13, 16, 18, 19, 19n37, 20, 21, 22, 23, 24, 25, 25n64, 26, 28, 29, 29n93, 30, 31, 34, 35, 39, 41, 61, 62, 63, 66, 67, 68, 68n150, 71, 72, 73, 74, 80, 90, 91, 98, 110, 111, 112, 114, 115, 116, 117, 118, 119, 120, 121, 122, 123, 125, 126n259, 127, 128, 137, 138, 149, 150, 151, 152, 153, 154, 157, 159, 160, 161, 162, 163, 164, 165, 201, 207, 208, 209, 217
free movement of goods 20, 36n131, 65, 92, 97n115, 104, 105, 123, 138, 141, 144n343, 145n352, 146, 150, 160, 165, 197, 198, 202
free movement of workers 99, 100, 103, 146
freedom of establishment 20, 26, 28, 71, 90n87, 103, 104, 147, 148, 149
freedom of expression 96, 96n111, 204
freedom to provide services 26, 29, 103, 125n257, 146
fundamental rights 8n17, 65, 92, 94, 96, 101, 102n140, 108, 121, 131, 133n294, 197, 205, 207

gambling 128, 129n274, 130n277, 130n278, 131, 131n282, 132, 202, 203, 210, 211, 213
gas distribution 39, 51, 61, 67

GATS 16
gifts 17, 21, 23, 27, 139n317
globalisation convergence 81
golden shares 1n.*, 3, 4, 6, 8, 9, 27n77, 28n87, 29n88, 29n89, 31, 31n98, 32, 32n105, 35n130, 37n138, 38n139, 39n150, 39n151, 39n154, 45, 57n102, 58, 58n106, 59, 60, 61n118, 63, 64, 64n130, 67, 67n147, 68, 73, 74, 74n4, 74n5, 75, 76, 77n13, 80, 89, 90, 91, 92, 110, 112, 112n188, 112n189, 113, 113n191, 113n192, 114, 114n199, 116n207, 117, 117n214, 118, 121, 122, 123, 123n239, 123n241, 123n243, 123n244, 123n245, 124, 124n247, 124n250, 125, 125n251, 125n253, 125n257, 126, 126n261, 127n263, 127n265, 127n266, 128, 132, 132n291, 133, 133n296, 134, 134n301, 134n302, 135, 135n303, 135n304, 136, 137, 137n309, 138, 138n312, 149, 150n373, 150n374, 150n375, 150n376, 152n387, 152n389, 153, 153n391, 153n393, 153n397, 153n399, 154, 154n401, 155, 156, 157, 157n413, 158n415, 158n416, 158n420, 158n421, 159n428, 160n430, 161, 163, 164, 165, 173, 174, 175, 176, 177, 178, 179, 181, 203
good governance 131, 132, 133, 137
grandfather clause 36

harmonisation 6n13, 33, 85, 87, 90, 122, 200
hostile takeovers 73, 83, 87, 88, 90, 91, 163
human rights 8n17, 93, 93n90, 94, 96, 207

IMF 2, 11n1, 11n3, 12n6, 12n8, 13n10, 13n11, 13n9, 14n18, 15, 16, 16n23, 44n4, 45, 47, 163, 163n1, 169, 188, 191, 199, 200, 201, 202, 204, 206, 213, 214, 215, 216, 217
immovable property 31, 34n116, 34n120, 178, 180
industrial policies 10, 74, 85, 118
inheritances 17, 21, 23, 27, 36
insolvency 147, 148, 149
integration
　economic 3, 4, 24, 24n63, 139, 189
　European 3, 8, 54, 166
　financial 3, 12, 13n10, 14, 15, 18, 24, 156, 163, 194, 212
　market 5, 54, 136, 149, 156, 157, 162
　monetary 49

Internal Market 3, 4, 5, 5n12, 6n14, 7n15, 9, 18, 19, 22, 23, 25, 26, 29, 52n66, 53n68, 54n78, 55n82, 55n86, 63, 68, 69, 73n3, 74, 80, 84, 87n74, 91, 98n115, 116n204, 116n206, 117, 126n258, 128, 131n287, 132n290, 132n292, 137, 137n309, 139, 142n331, 155n404, 164, 187, 189, 190, 192, 203, 205, 213
International Investment law 17
investment arrangements 4, 138, 160, 165

Keck 4, 137n309, 138, 138n311, 139, 140, 141n324, 142, 142n331, 142n332, 142n333, 143n338, 144, 144n343, 145n352, 146, 147, 147n362, 148, 148n368, 150, 151, 152, 153, 165, 171, 194, 195, 200, 204, 207, 208, 210, 211

laissez-faire 3, 43
legal certainty 41, 74, 74n5, 122, 128, 132, 133, 134, 137, 161
legislative procedure 36, 37
liberalisation 1, 3, 11, 12, 14n18, 17, 18, 19, 19n37, 20, 21, 22, 24, 36, 44, 46, 48, 50, 53, 57, 90, 128, 131, 163, 212
  capital 1, 2, 3, 4, 9, 11, 12, 13, 14, 15, 16, 17, 17n30, 18, 19, 22, 23, 24, 156, 163, 164, 165
  capital account 2, 12, 15
  financial 12, 14, 82
  market 12, 46
  trade 1, 14, 66
loans 17, 21, 23, 27

macroeconomic discipline 12
market access 75, 114, 140, 143, 143n338, 144n343, 145, 145n349, 146, 149, 151, 152, 153, 157, 158, 162, 198
market economy 4, 46, 52, 61, 75, 81, 84, 92, 102n140, 132, 154, 157, 164, 189, 195, 197
  coordinated 3, 75, 81, 82, 83, 164
  liberal 3, 54, 75, 81, 82, 83, 164
  social 9, 54
measure having equivalent effect to a quantitative restriction 139, 143
mergers and acquisitions 83
minority 76, 78, 113, 114, 126, 135, 158, 159, 160
moral hazard 13
mutual recognition 105, 140, 145

nationalisation 45, 57
necessity 40, 41, 74, 130, 131
neoclassical economics 11, 14
neoliberalism 2, 44, 44n7, 196, 201
network industries 43

OECD 2, 12n6, 15, 16n23, 16n29, 17, 17n30, 17n32, 17n33, 17n34, 43, 43n1, 45, 45n14, 46n20, 47, 47n28, 47n29, 47n31, 48n33, 48n38, 50n48, 50n50, 51n55, 51n59, 52, 52n64, 52n65, 77n19, 79n31, 84n49, 84n53, 163, 166n3, 169, 183, 186, 191, 206, 212, 215, 217
opposition procedure 58n107, 134
ordoliberalism 9, 53, 53n71, 53n72, 53n73, 185
overriding reasons 33, 37, 39, 68n150, 122, 126, 161

postal service 39, 124, 135n302
poverty 14n18, 15, 212
predominant consideration 29
primacy 136, 156
principle of neutrality 4, 9, 57, 61, 62, 66, 153, 165
principle of sincere cooperation 116
prior authorisation 19, 29, 41, 76, 153
private autonomy 53, 54, 92, 95, 99, 111, 119, 121, 161
privatisation 9, 43, 44n9, 45, 45n12, 46, 47, 48, 49, 50, 51, 51n58, 52, 56, 56n94, 57, 57n103, 57n98, 58n105, 61, 62, 63, 64, 64n129, 66, 67, 68, 71, 72, 76, 82, 89, 95, 113, 127, 150, 152, 153, 164, 165, 166, 186, 210, 211, 213, 216
privatisations 3, 4, 8, 57, 57n99, 58n103, 67, 137n309, 163, 165, 191
property ownership 4, 5, 9, 40, 57, 58, 59, 60, 61, 63, 64, 65, 68, 71, 72, 134, 153, 164, 165
proportionality 10, 38, 40, 40n159, 41, 41n160, 72, 74, 74n5, 75, 77, 78, 79, 80, 90, 92, 95, 121, 122, 127, 127n267, 128, 131, 132, 133, 135, 136, 137, 154, 156, 161, 164, 191, 193
protection of consumers 130
protection of the environment 39
protection of workers 70, 126, 135, 166

INDEX

prudential supervision   1, 3, 15, 35, 163
public debt   2, 43, 44, 48
public interest objectives   1, 4, 8, 10, 71, 73, 75, 130, 133, 136, 137, 154, 162, 163, 164, 165, 166
public ownership   3, 4, 44, 50, 51, 52, 63, 64, 66, 69, 71, 72, 154n401, 163, 165, 166
public policy   35, 42, 100, 118
public procurement   117, 120, 162
public security   35, 70, 73, 100, 123, 124

ratione loci   25
ratione materiae   28
ratione temporis   62
real estate   17, 21, 23, 27, 32, 36, 38, 45
reciprocity   89
Regional Free Trade Agreements   17
regulatory autonomy   15, 134, 137, 140, 142n331, 195
regulatory powers   96, 99, 101, 104, 111, 112, 116, 120, 162
research and development   38, 51
residence   31, 32, 33, 34
risk management   15, 92n89, 200

securities   17, 21, 23, 27, 36, 87, 89, 111
selling arrangements   138, 140, 141, 142, 144, 146, 150, 152, 153, 160, 165
service of general interest   39, 124
service public   9, 54, 54n81, 56, 183, 187, 202, 207
share value   154, 155
shareholder democracy   78
shareholders   45, 48, 75, 77n13, 78, 79, 80, 83, 84, 84n51, 84n52, 86n65, 88, 91, 110, 112, 114, 117, 120, 121, 126, 132, 135, 135n302, 136, 151, 154, 155, 156, 157, 158, 159, 163, 164, 212
shareholders' primacy   75, 120, 121, 132, 136, 154, 156, 164
shield interpretation   58
social deficit   8
social justice   2, 7
social objectives   3, 4, 9, 50, 52, 71, 126, 137n309
societal values   4, 164
special rights   10, 58, 59, 73, 74, 74n5, 76, 89, 112, 113, 114, 119, 123, 124, 125, 126, 128, 133, 134, 135n302, 137, 151, 154, 155n406, 157, 157n414
special shareholding   3, 9, 73, 74, 89, 122, 137, 150, 151, 153, 157, 158
stability
   economic   2, 14, 15, 18
   financial   1, 2, 4, 5, 15, 84, 163, 166
stakeholders   43, 84, 132, 136, 156
State aid   118, 212
State intervention   3, 43, 54, 64, 66
State sovereignty   16
State-owned enterprise   43, 46
strategic assets   59n107, 134
suitability   40, 41, 74, 127, 130
supervisory board   113, 159, 160
supremacy   97n115, 198
sword interpretation   58, 66

Takeover Directive   87, 87n74, 88n80, 90, 191, 201, 202, 209
tax avoidance   22
tax evasion   22, 38, 111
taxation   5, 6, 22, 30, 30n93, 32, 33, 34, 35, 38, 110, 167, 209
taxpayers   33, 34
telecommunications   9, 48, 57, 73, 124, 152, 158
territorial scope   26, 29
territoriality   33, 34
terrorism   36, 37, 124
third countries   3, 24, 25, 25n64, 26, 32, 33, 36, 37, 206, 207
trade unions   103, 113, 118
transparency   3, 15, 40, 62, 68n150, 80, 117, 128, 132, 162, 163

unavoidable consequence   29
unbundling   61, 62
universality clause   34
usufruct   31

veto   73, 76, 114, 125
voting   76, 77, 79, 88, 91, 92n89, 113, 114, 117, 150, 154, 155n402, 158, 159, 160, 163, 164, 217

WTO   16